THE CONTINENTAL RATIONALISTS

This complimentary book
is sent to you with the
best wishes of

ROBERT E. SWEENEY

THE BRUCE PUBLISHING COMPANY
400 North Broadway
Milwaukee, Wisconsin 53201

THE CONTINENTAL RATIONALISTS

List Price:
Net Price: $2.50
F.O.B., Milwaukee, Wis. 2.00

THE CONTINENTAL RATIONALISTS:

Descartes, Spinoza, Leibniz

By JAMES COLLINS

PROFESSOR OF PHILOSOPHY
ST. LOUIS UNIVERSITY

THE BRUCE PUBLISHING COMPANY
MILWAUKEE

Library of Congress Catalog Card Number: 67-26507

© 1967 The Bruce Publishing Company

MADE IN THE UNITED STATES OF AMERICA

PREFACE

MODERN philosophy begins to achieve a distinctive shape and spirit of its own during the seventeenth century. By this time, the older school philosophies are definitely on the wane, having cut themselves off from direct engagement with the new tendencies in the mathematical and physical sciences, the arts, and the sociopolitical reorganization of life. On the European continent, this entire period is dominated by the philosophical work of three great thinkers: Descartes, Spinoza, and Leibniz. Descartes the Frenchman stirs men's minds, during the first half of the century, with his vision of a new method for obtaining strictly demonstrated truths in all the branches of philosophy. His whole enterprise is nourished and guided by a new metaphysics, founded in the life of the self and its ordination to God. The middle years of this era are filled with the rigorous speculations of the Dutch thinker, Spinoza. His aim is to establish an intimate and embracing synthesis of method and metaphysics with ethics itself, or man's enduring quest for virtue, happiness, and life with God. Finally, the closing decades witness the amazingly fertile efforts of Leibniz to bring about an intellectual, cultural, and religious unification, not only in his native Germany but throughout modern Europe.

People sometimes predispose themselves unfavorably toward these three philosophers by approaching a study of them with the dictionary definition of "rationalism." As commonly understood, this term designates a style of thought that is excessively abstract and formalistic, cut off from the groundwork in human experience, and more concerned with system-building than with attending to actual scientific reports about our universe. But here, as elsewhere in the history of philosophy, the safest rule is to liberate one's mind from such artificial prejudgments, in order to make a direct and more authentic acquaintance with the philosophies in question. Whatever the later vagaries of this tradition, the foundational work of the classical rationalists is marked by a truly fresh and open spirit.

There is an admirable sensitivity here to all the new currents of thought in the early modern age. In part, the great rationalists are

moved by their awareness of the radical breakdown of the older
syntheses in thought and life underscored for them by the arguments of the skeptics, but they seek to give a more creative response
than is possible within the framework of skepticism. Their recon-
structive aims are encouraged by the accomplishments in the new
science, which offers solid testimony about the power of human
intelligence to attain some certain knowledge of the universe.
Descartes and Leibniz make notable personal contributions in the
fields of mathematics and scientific methodology, while Spinoza
displays a keen appreciation of both the mathematical and the
experimental sides of the scientific revolution. Another stimulating
source for the philosophizing of the rationalists lies in the practical
order of morality and religion. In an age that is pockmarked by
political upheavals and religious wars, these philosophers try to
meet the challenge of laying some foundations for the moral,
political, and religious ordering of life that can be accepted by men
of very diverse backgrounds.

What makes philosophers out of Descartes, Spinoza, and Leibniz,
however, is not just their awareness of these stresses but their intellectual manner of responding to them. They insist upon matching
an experiential fullness of data and problems with a vigorous development of the rational principles required for interpreting the experience
and ordering our actions. They are philosophical rationalists, not
because of any disdain for the living world, but because of a positive
working conviction that the human mind can uncover the unifying
principles of this world. The aim of the following chapters is to
determine the methods and leading concepts and arguments whereby
the continental rationalists seek to understand and bring more closely
together the reality of man, nature, and God. In this separate publishing of chapters 5, 6, and 7 of my *History of Modern European Philosophy,* I use the opportunity to make a few corrections in the main
text and to continue updating the Bibliographical Notes.

JAMES COLLINS

St. Louis University
June, 1967

CONTENTS

THE CONTINENTAL RATIONALISTS

Chapter I. RENÉ DESCARTES

I. LIFE AND WRITINGS

THE son of a provincial gentleman, René Descartes was born at La Haye in Touraine, in 1596. He received his basic education at the newly founded Jesuit college of Henry IV at La Flèche, where he studied from 1606 until about 1614. There, he took the regular curriculum in the humanities (grammar, history, poetry, and rhetoric) and then in philosophy (logic, philosophy of nature, metaphysics, and ethics) and mathematics. The philosophy professors based their lectures mainly upon Aristotelian manuals. He continued his studies at the University of Poitiers, where he received the degrees of bachelor and licentiate in law (1616) and also took instruction in medicine. There followed a period in which he turned from the academic life to the great book of the world, joined the army of Maurice of Nassau in the Netherlands, and broadened his knowledge of men and customs. His friendship with Isaac Beeckman led him to investigate several problems in mechanics, mathematics, and music. In 1619, he went to Denmark and the Germanies, joined the army of the Duke of Bavaria for a while, and witnessed the coronation of the Emperor Ferdinand at Frankfort. He spent that winter near the town of Ulm, meditating upon the project of solving all geometrical problems by a single method. Gradually, he conceived the plan of dealing with all philosophical problems by means of a single, mathematically orientated method and thus of achieving a perfect unity among the sciences. Descartes' famous dreams occurred on the night of November 10-11, 1619. They confirmed his resolve to bring all the sciences into a single body of wisdom and led him to regard this task as a heaven-sent mission. The "private thoughts" which he jotted down in notebooks during the next few years have been lost, except for some fragments copied out by his first biographer, Abbé Baillet, and by Leibniz.

By 1627-1628, the main features of his system were fairly well established in Descartes' mind. He had sufficient confidence to enter into a public discussion at Paris, in the presence of the papal nuncio, Cardinal Bérulle, and Father Marin Mersenne. Descartes so impressed Bérulle with his claims for a clearer and surer method of thinking that the cardinal urged it, as his duty, to publish his doctrine against the skeptics and atheists. Descartes' thoughts on methodology were set down in the *Rules for the Direction of the Mind* (written about 1628; circulated in manuscript, posthumously, among philosophers; published in 1701). At the same time, he made a rough draft of his metaphysical position in a set of notes, later expanded into the *Meditations on First Philosophy*. He settled permanently in the Netherlands in 1628, a move dictated mainly by reasons of health and the desire for greater privacy in study. But throughout the years, Descartes kept up a vast correspondence, which provides precious biographical and doctrinal information about him.

He was working on his conception of the physical universe, *The World* or *Treatise on Light,* which advocated the motion of the earth, when he received news of Galileo's condemnation by the Holy Office (1633). Descartes refused to take the risk of publication of this book during his lifetime; editions of the surviving first part were issued posthumously in 1664 and 1667. In order to prepare a more favorable reception for his physical doctrines, he issued in 1637 three specimens of his scientific work (*Optics, Meteorology,* and *Geometry*), along with an introductory essay on the spirit of his method and philosophy, the *Discourse on Method.* This was followed by the *Meditations on First Philosophy* (1641), his metaphysical masterpiece, to which were appended the criticisms offered by several eminent philosophers and Descartes' detailed replies. In the vain hope of having his system adopted as a Jesuit textbook, he next cast his thoughts into Scholastic form in *Principles of Philosophy* (1644). During his closing years, Descartes' interests turned more definitely toward moral philosophy, although he continued his dissections of bodies and other scientific activities. His letters to the exiled Princess Elizabeth of Bohemia and his treatise on *The Passions of the Soul* (1649), which he first submitted to the Princess for criticism, contained a sketch of his psychologico-moral views. In 1649, he went to Sweden to give philosophical instructions to Queen Christina. Her custom of discussing philosophy with him at five o'clock in the morning undermined Descartes' congenitally weak constitution and he died in February, 1650.

2. THE NATURE AND DIVISIONS OF PHILOSOPHY

Despite his dissatisfaction with the theories taught him by teachers and books, Descartes was not discouraged about the prospects for philosophy. He felt that it was his mission to achieve a singlehanded reconstruction of philosophy, with the aid of new principles. The revolution was to begin with the very notion of philosophy itself. Starting in the traditional way with the meaning of the word itself, he defined philosophy as the study of wisdom. But he pointed out, at once, certain traits of wisdom which had been overlooked or obscured by his predecessors of the Middle Ages and Renaissance.

In opposition to Renaissance humanists like Montaigne, Descartes sought to close the gap between *science* and *wisdom*.[1] Instead of retaining the contrast between the two, he affirmed that wisdom is an affair of scientific reason rather than of erudition. Its resources are drawn not from memory, history, and literature (as the humanists believed), but from the same rational power that operates in mathematics. Yet even the mathematicians had failed to recognize this truth, since they were reluctant to apply their procedures to the most lofty questions of metaphysics and morals. For his part, Descartes affirmed that nothing was more sorely needed than precisely this extension of mathematical reason into wider fields. At the same time, he wished to preserve two characteristics of the humanistic view of wisdom: its purely *natural* basis and its concern for *practical moral* issues. He told his interlocutor, Burman, that he wrote his philosophy so that it could be accepted everywhere, even among the Turks. Philosophical wisdom is grounded in the natural use of reason, without seeking reliance upon, or guidance from, revelation and theology. It is the work of man as man, and studies man himself *prout in naturalibus,* rather than as the recipient of supernatural revelation. Philosophical wisdom is also orientated toward man's welfare and permanent happiness. The ancient Stoic regard for human conduct joins company, in Descartes' mind, with the modern scientific concern for the control of nature and the betterment of human living conditions.

---

[1] On the wisdom, principles, and divisions proper to philosophy, see both Descartes' "Letter to the Translator" of the French edition of *The Principles of Philosophy,* and his "Dedication" of the same work (in *The Philosophical Works of Descartes* [translated by Haldane and Ross], I, 203–218). On Cartesian wisdom, see James Collins, *The Lure of Wisdom* (Milwaukee, Marquette University Press, 1962), 40–122.

Descartes was not unmindful of the Scholastic distinction between speculative and practical wisdom, nor of the Scholastic teaching that the latter should build upon the former. For this reason, he observed that the practical wisdom in which philosophy comes to full flower is something more than shrewdness in managing one's affairs. It springs from *a perfect knowledge of all that is needful* for human life. In this plenary sense of a complete knowledge of the truth, only God is truly wise; but men can share more or less in wisdom, to the extent that they acquire an understanding of at least the major truths. Philosophy's task is to supply the principles of knowledge and thus bring the mind to the highest peak of humanly attainable wisdom.

Although this conception recalls the Aristotelian definition of philosophy as a study of all things in their highest principles and causes, Descartes interprets "principles" in a distinctive way. They mean principles of knowledge, even more than of being. The two requirements for *philosophical principles* are that they be absolutely *indubitable* in themselves, due to their clarity and evidence, and completely *independent* of other truths in such a way that the latter can be known only through these principles, without involving any reciprocal dependence of the principles upon the subsequent truths. Both these criteria bear the mark of Descartes' distinctive approach. He explains that his principles alone achieve perfect clarity and evidence, since they are established only *after* an attempt is made to reject everything that is in the least way doubtful. Thus the theory of first principles has a solidarity with the method of universal doubt. The absolutely first principle of philosophy is the indubitable knowledge of the existence of the thinking self. The traditional principle of contradiction and other general principles are themselves true, only by reason of their implication in this unconditionally first concrete truth and principle.

Moreover, Cartesian principles have the independence belonging to the very first steps in a deductive process. They must be such that from them all other truths can be derived by necessary inference. Once Descartes has deduced God and extended matter from the thinking self, he is equipped with the basic principles for demonstrating the truth of all other things in a systematic fashion. This claim is only possible in virtue of his conception of the *unity of all the sciences*. They are so connected and interdependent that they constitute a single body of truth. Explicitly repudiating the Scholastic differentiation of sciences on the basis of formal differences in their objects,

Descartes stresses the *subjective unity of the mind,* in which the sciences reside, and of the *act of scientific knowing,* whereby they are apprehended. Human knowledge remains one and the same process: the methodic combining of self-evident truths. In place of the older doctrine of an interconnection among the moral virtues, Descartes substitutes an interconnection and mutual dependence of the speculative sciences. Philosophical first principles are generative of a chain of truths, each link of which is arrived at by the same sort of scientific act and attains the same scientific certitude. This homogeneity of scientific knowledge assures the unity of philosophy, the fruitfulness of its principles, and the rigor of its demonstrations.

Distinctions within the body of philosophy arise only in terms of the mind's manner of application to the study of principles and their consequences. Descartes employs the metaphor of the tree of wisdom, in order to convey the organic unity and order existing among the *parts of philosophy.* Metaphysics comprises the roots of the tree; physics its trunk; medicine, mechanics, and ethics its branches. *Metaphysics* or first philosophy treats of the first principles of all knowledge: the finite thinking self, the infinitely powerful and veracious God, the criterion of truth, the common notions of the mind, the existence of an external world. To this extent, Descartes agrees with St. Augustine that God and the soul are the most proper objects of philosophical contemplation. But at the same time, metaphysics provides the basis for a philosophical account of the physical universe. Only insofar as it is founded upon metaphysical principles, does *physics* acquire a strictly scientific standing. There may be many discoveries in physics previous to its incorporation into philosophical wisdom, but as a rigorous body of indubitable truths, it awaits the principles of deduction and other guarantees of knowledge supplied only by metaphysics.

The *practical parts* of philosophy, in their turn, depend upon the completion of philosophical physics and its prolongation in philosophical anthropology. Although the practical disciplines occupy a subsequent position in the movement of philosophical thought, they also provide the *goal* of all philosophy. For, they enable man to become the master of nature, the possessor of bodily health, and the subject of moral perfections and blessings. *Wisdom* in the unqualified sense embraces all these sciences, speculative and practical, as a totality. Only in the sense that all branches of philosophy serve to nourish and develop the single tree of wisdom, is it true that metaphysics is for the sake of physics, and physics for the sake of the practical sciences. The ultimate aim of the philosopher is to attain the happiness which ensues upon a synoptic understanding and controlled use of the entire order and concatenation of scientifically established truths. The happy life is the life of wisdom, as it enlightens the mind and fortifies the practical judgment in the face of life's contingencies. Here lies man's sovereign good in the natural order.

Descartes does not regard this ideal as impossible of attainment. Although it belongs only to the gifted few to *discover* the proper method and philosophical truths, yet all men are natively equipped with the rational power of discerning the true from the false, and hence all men can *recognize* these truths, once discovered. It is because all men have *reason* or *good sense* in at least a minimal way, that there is solid assurance of their attaining the fullness of good sense, which is nothing other than philosophical wisdom. Descartes regards his principles as sufficiently clear to be grasped by all men, and his conclusions as sufficiently evident in their demonstration to be accepted by all men. But, like Bacon, he warns that the mind can apprehend philosophical truths only after it frees itself from prejudice and accepts some reliable guide. The guide is furnished by the new method, which is nothing else than the way in which the mind must proceed in order to acquire wisdom.

3. THE METHOD FOR THE DISCOVERY AND DEMONSTRATION OF TRUTH

Three fountainheads contributed to Descartes' theory of method: his own natural habits of thinking, the precepts of Scholastic logic, and the procedures of mathematics. The first two sources gave him some general guidance, whereas the more specific techniques were supplied by his study of Greek analysis and modern algebra. The synthesis of these three sources was achieved in function of his notion of a universal mathematics, which provided the organizing principle of his entire methodology.

Through reflection upon his own common-sense habits of mind and the testimony of ordinary men, Descartes found that unspoiled *natural intelligence* has an active tendency to grasp certain great, simple truths and to reason in the right way concerning more complex problems. He referred to this native ability of the mind as the seedbed of our knowledge, as a sort of divine principle containing the germs of true science, somewhat as a flint stone contains its sparks.[2] Although basic truths are not present in any ready-made fashion, they are innate in the understanding, insofar as this power is stirred from within to come to an explicit apprehension of them, with the aid of experience and reasoning. No one has to wait for learned definitions, before finding out what it means to exist, to feel, to think, or to doubt. Through his natural inclination and perspicacity, even the untutored individual seizes, at once, upon the meaning of these terms. Moreover, he learns to deal with more complicated issues by meditating upon the simple, primary truths, to which his own mind impels him, in order to discover some connection between these starting points and the more remote and subtle problems. As Descartes viewed it, the gradual approach of common sense to theoretical difficulties displays the same sort of orderliness found in the operations of a weaver. Starting from a few simple but basic movements of the mind, the ordinary man can gradually develop a grand pattern of thought, embracing the most universal truths about his life. Surely, there is something here for the philosopher to attend to and imitate.

Furthermore, Descartes found that the maxims of informal thinking agreed, in large measure, with the practical directions about correct thinking provided in his logic course at La Flèche. *Scholastic logic* teaches the student to proceed from simple to complex cognitions, from the easier to the more difficult, and from what one understands better to what is more intelligible in itself. This logic advises one to remove nonessentials in the statement of a problem or definition and to reduce complicated questions to their basic parts. In the case of induction, it also recommends as complete a survey of the parts of the problem and the classes of instances as is feasible. Comparing these precepts with those of his own informal studies, Descartes became convinced of their soundness and practical value. They were to be incorporated into the definitive method as permanent acquisitions of mankind, reflecting upon its own mental operations.

But there was one teaching in Scholastic logic that troubled Descartes, because it set a high goal without also supplying the

---

[2] *Rules for the Direction of the Mind*, IV, VIII (Haldane-Ross, I, 10, 12, 25–26). This work presents the Cartesian methodology in a highly technical way, whereas the *Discourse on Method* offers a more popular and personal presentation. The *Discourse* begins with the programmatic statement that "good sense [*le bon sens*] is mankind's most equitably divided endowment." *Discourse on Method*, I (Lafleur translation, 1). Everyone's mind has a native impulsion toward truth to which Descartes constantly appeals, over the heads of academic thinkers.

means of its attainment. Knowledge in the strict sense of *scientific knowledge* was traditionally defined as true, certain, and evident cognition, based on the proper causes of the thing. Yet it did not require the diatribes of Galileo and Bacon to convince Descartes that a major part of the actual curriculum in philosophy was being devoted to speculations that never attained more than a high degree of probability and that failed to remove the original obscurity of the question. The widespread use of dialectical arguments supplied no adequate answer to the skeptical contention that strict knowledge is beyond our ability to attain. In searching for an answer to this charge of the skeptics, Descartes turned to mathematics for assurance and guidance concerning our possession of scientific knowledge.

Even the mathematics books used at La Flèche regarded *mathematics* as the key and primary science, since it not only excludes the false and merely probable but also proves its own conclusions by the most certain and universally accepted demonstrations.[8] These sources did not add, however, that all knowledge constitutes a single body of science, based solely on the mathematical type of reasoning. This radical step was reserved for Descartes to take. He resolved to accept as scientific truth only those propositions which contain the same sort of evidence and certitude as is found in mathematics. He did not mean that philosophical reasoning must embody all the features of mathematical inference but that it must employ the *same kind* of method and cognition as in mathematics. The basic Cartesian assumption here is that the *ingenium mathematicum* is nothing other than the reasoning power and method proper to "man as thinking." This led him to take a univocal view of the common instrument of speculation and of the standards for philosophical knowledge.

Descartes' own discoveries in analytic geometry convinced him of the possibility of generalizing mathematical procedures. He found that the heretofore unyielding distinction between continuous and discontinuous quantity could be overcome through his *analytic geometry,* in which geometrical figures, laid out upon co-ordinates, are expressed by algebraic equations. Conversely, he was able to express numerical quantities and algebraic functions in terms of lines and figures. The mind's intrinsic power was also strengthened, when it learned to take advantage of both the brevity of algebraic nota-

---

[8] The opinion of the Jesuit mathematician Clavius (whose writings were probably known to Descartes at La Flèche) is quoted at length by E. Gilson, *René Descartes: Discours de la méthode, texte et commentaire,* 128.

tion and the pictorial clarity of geometrical figures. Thus two broad regions of mathematics were brought together, through the discovery of an underlying unity. This unification on a relatively small scale suggested to Descartes that a new science might be founded, which would resolve all problems concerning every sort of quantity, continuous as well as discrete. It was only a step from this ambitious scheme to an even more daring and comprehensive project: the foundation of a *completely universal science* or *mathesis universalis,* which could resolve all philosophical problems, even those lying entirely beyond the realm of quantity, with the aid of the mathematical method.[4]

THE CARTESIAN METHOD OF PROOF

1. Formal object of universal mathematics: order and measure.
2. Instruments of proof.
   a) Resolutive analysis, the logic of discovery and intuition.
      1) Objects of intuition: simple natures (material, spiritual, and their links and axioms).
      2) Necessary condition for the systematic employment of the findings of intuition: universal methodic doubt, leading to indubitable knowledge of an existential basis for ideas and a point of departure for the philosophical system.
   b) Compositive synthesis, the logic of demonstrative deduction.
      1) Immediate deduction.
      2) Mediate deduction (aided by induction, analogy, and experience).
3. Criterion of truth: clarity and distinctness of ideas.
4. Order of proof: from the first indubitably known existent thing, as the first principle in the order of knowing, to its noetic consequences in the chain of existential truths.
   a) The finite, thinking self.
   b) The infinitely powerful and veracious God.
   c) The extended, material world.

In determining the *formal object* of his new universal mathematics, Descartes followed a clue provided by ordinary mathematics. All the branches of mathematics, both pure and applied, are concerned with a study of quantitative order and measure. Descartes saw no intrinsic reason why these relations should be confined to the quantitative sphere. Hence he proposed as the formal object of

[4] *Rules for the Direction of the Mind,* IV (Haldane-Ross, I, 11–13); *Discourse on Method,* II (Lafleur, 12–13).

universal science: *the general study of order and measure,* insofar as they are implicated in our knowledge of all sorts of beings, regardless of particular subject matter. This would enable all the sciences to share in a common pattern of inquiry: a comparison among objects in virtue of some shared trait, which establishes an order among them and a certain proportion that can be measured. The Cartesian claim for the unity of the sciences and the homogeneity of philosophical wisdom rested upon this determination of a common formal procedure in scientific investigation. But, in fact, the issue cannot be resolved solely in methodological terms, apart from all reference to subject matter or the actual modes of being in which order and measure are realized. Where the method in question is that of *philosophical knowledge of real existents,* there can be no purely formal methodological study, in which the relation of objects to our understanding is divorced from the manner in which they exercise their own act of being. As far as the philosophical sciences are concerned, a general study of our way of ascertaining order and measure among objects can be carried through, only within the context of a metaphysical doctrine on the ways of real order and measure. Descartes himself eventually recognized the inadequacy of a purely formal methodology. But he failed to see that, in providing an existential foundation, one must either revise drastically the theory of the homogeneity of the sciences or else adopt a pantheistic metaphysical basis of method, as Spinoza suggested.

In specifying the *instruments of proof* for his universal science, Descartes was guided by the examples of both the pure mathematicians and Galileo. *Analysis* or *the method of resolution* and *synthesis* or *the method of composition* are the main tools of scientific reasoning.[5] In Euclidean geometry, for instance, one starts with certain definitions,

---

[5] The contrast between analysis and synthesis is brought out in *Replies to Objections,* II (Haldane-Ross, II, 48–50). This should be compared with the Thomistic doctrine on *resolutio* and *compositio,* as explained by L. M. Régis, O.P., "Analyze et synthèse dans l'oeuvre de saint Thomas," *Studia Mediaevalia in honorem . . . Raymundi Josephi Martin, O.P.* (Bruges, De Tempel, c. 1948), 303–330. St. Thomas emphasizes the nonmathematical, properly metaphysical analysis or resolution of knowledge to the senses, to being and its first principles, and to the judgment of separation. This type of resolution includes both the *experiential* and the *intellectual* principles of knowledge, and hence transcends the modern controversy between the empiricist and the rationalist types of resolution or analysis. The intermediate developments are discussed by R. I. Markus, "Method and Metaphysics: Origins of Some Cartesian Presuppositions in the Philosophy of the Renaissance," *Dominican Studies,* 2 (1949), 356–384, and N. W. Gilbert, *Renaissance Concepts of Method* (1960).

postulates, and axioms. With their aid, the synthetic approach demonstrates the conclusions of the science so rigorously, that a denial of any particular step also entails a denial of all the previous ones. Yet however coercive this synthetic method may be, it has the serious drawback of failing to justify its foundations by showing how the original set of definitions, postulates, and axioms was reached. Hence the priority must be given to the analytic method, which does show the *how* and the *why* of the premises themselves. Analysis is preeminently a *logic of discovery,* a justification of the basic truths upon which all subsequent inferences depend. It works back from given complex wholes to their constituent elements, from given problems to the underlying principles of solution. Hence the analytic method must be used, in order to discover the first principles of philosophical knowledge, the metaphysical truths upon which the entire edifice of wisdom rests. Only after these principles have been ascertained in analytic or resolutive fashion, can the work of synthetic demonstration or deduction begin. Unlike Hobbes (who held that the synthetic method alone should be used in exposition of one's system), Descartes felt that the philosopher had the prime obligation of showing the genesis of his first principles and definitions. Hence he wrote the *Meditations on First Philosophy* in the analytic manner, showing precisely how he arrived at his basic truths; subsequently, he presented his system synthetically in the *Principles of Philosophy.*

Descartes' main contribution here is to establish a firm correlation between analysis and synthesis, on the one hand, and intuition and deduction, on the other. Analysis is the mental operation that clears a path for intellectual intuition, whereas the synthetic composition of principles is a scientific process, only if it results in a demonstrative deduction. Hence there are only two methodic ways of arriving at the truth of things: *intuition* and *deduction.*

> By a method I mean certain and simple rules, such that, if a man observe them accurately, he shall never assume what is false as true, and will never spend his mental efforts to no purpose, but will always gradually increase his knowledge and so arrive at a true understanding of all that does not surpass his powers. . . . But if our method rightly explains how our mental vision [*mentis intuitu*] should be used, so as not to fall into the contrary error, and how deduction should be discovered in order that we may arrive at the knowledge of all things, I do not see what else is needed to make it complete.[6]

---

[6] *Rules for the Direction of the Mind,* IV (Haldane-Ross, I, 9).

Descartes is sure that his method is not only useful but definitive, because his rules rest upon the requirements of the only two operations whereby the systematic body of truths can be discovered and organized.

He affirms that *intuition* (*intuitus:* inspection, insight, or view) is "the undoubting conception of an unclouded [pure] and attentive mind, and springs from the light of reason alone."[7] It is the proper operation of the natural light of the understanding and hence is the primary means for bringing the truth in evidence before our minds. The fact that this act springs from reason or the pure intellectual power alone is important to note, since this means that the intuitional view is possible only when the mind has been freed from dependence on the senses. It is a *purely intellectual* operation and is not integrated with sense perception. Furthermore, the mind must learn to *discipline its attention* upon the object of intuition in its intelligible structure, so that the mind will not be distracted by opinions derived from some sensory source. Because insight or intuition is conditioned upon this purgation and disciplining of the mind, it is by no means a facilely acquired perfection. The painful work of analytic resolution of complex data into their simple elements is always required, before the mind can gain a vision of the simple truths.

Reflection upon the undoubting quality of intuition provides Descartes with his *criterion* of philosophical truth: *clarity and distinctness* of our intellectual perception. "I term that *clear* which is present and apparent to an attentive mind . . . but *the distinct* is that which is so precise and different from all other objects that it contains within itself nothing but what is clear."[8] The object is inspected or seen in its evident truth, when it is given to the mind in an act of intuition. This involves an immediate self-presence of the object, in the idea, under conditions of clarity and distinctness. The clarity of the idea means the actual presentation of an intelligible structure to a mind that is undividedly attentive. Clarity supposes not only that what belongs to the nature of the object is present but also that the mind itself is attentive and responsive, in a purely intellectual way, to this

---

[7] *Ibid.*, III (Haldane-Ross, I, 7).

[8] *The Principles of Philosophy*, I, 45 (Haldane-Ross, I, 237). Since the *Principles* was written in textbook fashion, it contains concise definitions of many terms which Descartes elsewhere left undefined. A. Gewirth, in "Clearness and Distinctness in Descartes," *Philosophy*, 18 (1943), 17–36, shows that this criterion has a logical and objective import for Descartes, not merely a psychological and subjective one, since it is integrated with his metaphysics.

presented structure. Hence it rests on the same conditions as does the act of intuitional insight, which is the mind's proper response to the object thus furnished. An idea is distinct when *only* that which clearly belongs to the nature of the object is placed before the mind, and all else is excluded. A distinct idea is clear to the point of excluding all obscurity, even though it may not be comprehensive of the entire reality of the object. When the mind acquires a direct mental vision of the object in this clear and distinct perception, it is in possession of the evident truth in an undoubting way. Intuition eliminates both doubt and falsity about the object known.

The objects about which the mind is directly concerned are its own ideas. These ideal objects are either simple or composite natures. Composite natures are capable of being analyzed into simpler and more distinctly known parts. Analysis terminates in the *simple natures,* which are analytically irreducible elements of intelligibility.[9] Intuition is directed primarily toward these simple natures, which can be known immediately and *per se,* without engaging any judgment about their significance for the order of existent things. Descartes distinguishes between three classes of simple natures: purely *spiritual* natures or those which the mind knows through reflection upon its own intellectual light (knowing, doubting, willing); purely *material* ones or those grasped only insofar as the mind turns its attention to bodies (extension, figure, motion); those that are *common to both* spiritual and corporeal things (existence, unity, duration). In the latter class are also included the common notions and axioms (such as the principle of causality), which are links connecting the other simple natures together and thus permitting deductions to be made.

Although these simple natures loom large in Descartes' *Rules for the Direction of the Mind,* they do not hold as important a place in his later systematic work as might be expected. They raise a number of difficult questions, which Descartes never satisfactorily answered. If the simple natures are to fulfill any systematic function, they must be able to serve the purposes of deductive demonstration. To do so, they must satisfy the three following conditions: (1) the number of unconditionally absolute, simple natures must be finite;

9 Cf. *Rules for the Direction of the Mind,* VI, VIII, XII (Haldane-Ross, I, 15–17, 27, 41–47). Cartesian scholars are divided over whether the simple natures are ontological principles, as well as logical ultimates in the order of mental analysis. For this debate, consult S. V. Keeling, "Le réalisme de Descartes et le rôle des natures simples," *Revue de Métaphysique et de Morale,* 44 (1937), 63–99, and J. Hartland-Swann, "Descartes' 'Simple Natures,' " *Philosophy,* 22 (1947), 139–152.

(2) the simple natures must have intrinsic relations with each other; (3) they must be connected in a serial arrangement, according to a natural order. Although the Cartesian conception of the unity of scientific knowledge hinged upon these conditions, Descartes was unable to show that they are satisfied by the simple natures. The Baconian and Cartesian assumption of a finite number of simple natures was eventually abandoned by Leibniz, who saw that, on purely methodological grounds, there is no way of setting a limit to the points at which analysis may terminate in some irreducible intelligibility. The second difficulty revealed one of the dangerous tensions in Cartesian methodology. The emphasis placed upon clear and distinct objects of intuition offered a threat to deductive inference, since the *distinctness* was apt to *isolate* one idea completely from another. As a remedy, Descartes suggested that the meaning of any one simple nature includes its reference to other natures, as well as its own intrinsic constitution. He posited that the simple natures are bound up with each other by various links in a natural order, establishing both contingent and necessary relations among the ideas. Once more, however, the criticism of Spinoza has to be faced: either these connections are an *ad hoc* device to counteract the atomizing effect of analytic intuition and the standard of distinctness or else they rest upon an implicit metaphysical foundation in a doctrine on the monism of being. When Descartes invoked a "natural order" of truths in serial arrangement, he was overpassing the boundaries of methodology and supposing some special metaphysical conception. Spinoza's monism and Leibniz' calculus of essences were historical efforts to provide a more adequate metaphysical basis for scientific demonstration of a rationalistic sort.

Toward the resolution of a fourth difficulty connected with the doctrine on intuition and simple natures, Descartes marshaled all the resources of his philosophy. Even granted the connections and order among simple natures, they remain in the *ideal* order. A deductive system built upon them would have no guarantee that its connections have any bearing upon the relations among real things, or that its conclusions demonstrate anything about the structure of actual beings. This consideration led Descartes to seek for some *existential foundation,* in which the basic simple natures could be seen to be implicated. Such an existential basis would both show the ontological relevance of the simple natures and provide a real point of departure for the philosophical system. But even here, the general condition of intuition

—that it be an undoubting conception of the pure understanding—would have to be fulfilled. There was no other way open for Descartes to show that his existential foundation was indeed indubitable than by subjecting all his beliefs about existing beings and our ways of knowing them to a *methodic doubt*. The primary existential certitude was found to be the thinking self, in which the simple natures were given metaphysical significance for the system of philosophy. Thus the problem of methodic doubt and the thinking self (examined more at length in the following section) had its roots in the relationship between the theory of method and metaphysics.

Deduction or *compositive synthesis* supposes that the intuitive basis of the elements and principles of knowledge has already been secured. Descartes defines deduction, briefly, as "all necessary inference from other facts that are known with certainty."[10] Deduction can be either *immediate* or *mediate,* depending upon whether the link among objects can be established through a simple comparison or whether a complicated process of reasoning is required. When a direct comparison can be made between A and B, and again between B and C, the deduction concerning A and C is an immediate one. Where the issues are complex, however, a long series of inferences may be required, before another link in the chain of indubitable truths can be forged. Under the heading of "mediate deduction," Descartes includes such auxiliary processes as enumeration and induction, conjecture and hypothesis, analogy and the appeal to experience. Their aid is needed to gather together all the relevant evidence. The question is to be divided into its basic parts, and no more truth may be sought than can be drawn from these component data, considered in relation with the general chain of inferences already established. Further simplification of the issue can be achieved by distinguishing between the known and the unknown factors and by determining the precise points of contact between the two groups. A mediate deduction can then be made from what is already demonstrated to a newly discovered truth.

But deduction is always less simple and, therefore, less certain than intuition. Each stage in the deductive process must itself be grasped by an intuitive act. And the ultimate purpose of science is to reduce the entire series of deductions as closely as possible to

---

[10] *Rules for the Direction of the Mind,* III (Haldane-Ross, I, 8). See Gerd Buchdahl, "Descartes's Anticipation of a 'Logic of Scientific Discovery,'" in A. C. Crombie, ed., *Scientific Change* (New York: Basic Books, 1963), 399–417.

a single intuitive comprehension of the whole body of truth. For this purpose, constant reviews and enumerations are helpful. They assure us that no necessary step has been overlooked, and they dispose the mind to seize the concatenation of inferences in a quasi-intuitive vision, in which philosophical wisdom consists.

The *order of Cartesian proof* rests upon a fundamental distinction between the order of knowing and the order of being. Whereas Spinoza held that these two orders should be made to coincide, Descartes insisted upon their distinction. In this respect, he remained in contact with the tradition of theistic realism, which denies that the human mind can begin its inferential activity with God. But while St. Thomas recognized sense apprehension of the material world as constituting a true principle of philosophical knowledge, Descartes subjected the senses to doubt and looked rather for a starting point that would be appropriate to the act of a purely intellectual intuition or mental vision. This he found in the *finite thinking self*. Its finite character set his point of departure off from Spinoza's, whereas its purely immaterial nature distinguished it from the Thomistic beginning of knowledge. Since he had called the senses into question, Descartes was unable to proceed directly from the existence of the finite thinking self to that of the material world. His second step was to prove the existence of an *infinitely powerful and yet veracious God*. Since this demonstration was made through an analysis of certain implications in the finite thinking self, the latter manifested itself as the first noetic principle or principle in the order of knowing. But Descartes could prove the existence of the *extended, material world,* only with the aid of God, who is the first principle in the order of being and the guarantor of the trust-worthiness of our cognitive power. After this third existential truth was established, Descartes was in possession of all the principles needed for a methodic reconstruction of the physical world and the world of human power and conduct.

In the *Discourse on Method,* Descartes summed up his general views on methodic doubt in four well-known rules:

> The first rule was never to accept anything as true unless I recognized it to be evidently such: that is, carefully to avoid precipitation and pre-judgment, and to include nothing in my conclusions unless it presented itself so clearly and distinctly to my mind that I had no occasion to doubt it.
> The second was to divide each of the difficulties which I encountered

into as many parts as possible, and as might be required for an easier solution.

The third was to think in an orderly fashion, beginning with the things which were simplest and easiest to understand, and gradually and by degrees reaching toward more complex knowledge, even treating as though ordered materials which were not necessarily so.

The last was always to make enumerations so complete and reviews so general, that I was certain that nothing was omitted.[11]

This text is a masterpiece of philosophical diplomacy. It could be read with some understanding and profit by readers trained in the traditional logic manuals. Each of these four precepts had its counterpart in the ordinary directions given for definition and reasoning by the Scholastic logicians. These authors suggested that we avoid prejudice, strive after clear and distinct knowledge, divide a problem into its parts, proceed from the better known to the more difficult, and assure the completeness of a complex inference through a review of the subordinate steps. But on each of these points, Descartes offered a distinctive interpretation, in conformity with his own methodology. His safeguard against prejudgment and haste was universal, methodic doubt; his standard of clarity and distinctness was correlated with the technique of doubt and with an attempt to argue from the ideal to the real order; division into parts became, in his hands, a definite method of resolutive analysis; Cartesian simple things are simple natures, intuitively grasped; the gradual order of inferences must respect the requirements of a chain of truths and the necessity of proceeding existentially from self to God and the world; the reviews are made with a view toward securing the homogeneous body of wisdom, through a single intuitive habit of mind. And throughout these four rules can be noticed the unobtrusive but dominating presence of the first personal pronoun — an indication that all methodic thinking is referred ultimately to the Cogito, the thinking self, which alone has withstood the initial test of doubt. In this respect, these four precepts bear the indelible mark of Descartes' unique venture in philosophizing.

4. UNIVERSAL DOUBT AND THE COGITO

Descartes came to realize that his methodology was not self-validating but required a metaphysical foundation. Not only the problem of the simple natures but also certain features about

---

[11] *Discourse on Method*, II (Lafleur, 12).

mathematical thinking itself convinced him of this need. Mathematics has two shortcomings, as far as philosophical knowledge is concerned: it is a *nonexistential* discipline and it is *not resistant to the ultimate doubt* that the human mind may be intrinsically framed so as to deceive itself about even the clearest and simplest mathematical propositions. Now, without an existential content, known to be proof against any extreme of doubt, philosophy can only build upon shifting sands, which are incapable of supporting the edifice of the sciences. Hence Descartes was led to seek a sound basis for his thought in the *existing,* thinking self or Cogito ("I am thinking"), which withstands and triumphantly survives the test of a *universal doubt.* Cartesian metaphysics is more than an application of method: it is the ultimate validation and existential grounding of method.

The first rule of method, requesting us to avoid precipitation and prejudgment, entails the condition that a properly conducted metaphysical inquiry must begin with a methodic doubt. For at any given moment, the mind is laden down with many uncritically accepted opinions and prejudices. The only way to make sure that none of these unfounded convictions remain to infect our philosophical system is to subject all our presently held beliefs to a radical doubt. Obviously, each individual conviction cannot be treated separately, for then the process of doubting would go on indefinitely, without ever leading to the reconstruction of philosophy. Hence Descartes proposes to concentrate his doubt upon the *foundations* of accepted knowledge, with the consequence that everything based upon these foundations will topple along with them, leading to a general over-throw — *eversio generalis* — of all previous opinions.[12] To carry out this project of sapping the foundations of customary belief, Descartes must cast doubt upon the *principles* of these opinions, i.e., upon the several knowing powers and areas of objects supposedly known. He questions our external senses, our powers of imagination and memory, and even our purely intellectual power. Judgments about the external world, one's own body, the constructions of the physical and mathematical sciences, and the existence of God, are all submitted to doubt and found to be wanting, in the present condition of philosophy. Finally, Descartes arrives at the finite thinking self

---

[12] In *The Meditations concerning First Philosophy,* I (Lafleur translation, 15–20), Descartes shows us the methodic doubt in actual operation; in *The Principles of Philosophy,* I, 1–7 (Haldane-Ross, I, 219–221), he gives a systematic analysis of the entire process.

as an indubitable existent and, by a careful analysis of its implications, proceeds to give a scientific basis to our convictions about God, the material world, and the various sciences.

In executing this ambitious plan, Descartes relies upon two maxims that are explicitly directed against any variety of moderate realism. The first is that one should treat *the probable* as though it were entirely *false;* the second is that one should make the *senses* the special target of doubt and should therefore detach the understanding from reliance upon the senses and belief in the material world.

> Since reason already convinces me that I should abstain from the belief in things which are not entirely certain and indubitable no less carefully than from the belief in those which appear to me to be manifestly false, it will be enough to make me reject them all if I can find in each some ground for doubt. . . . Everything which I have thus far accepted as entirely true [and assured] has been acquired from the senses or by means of the senses. But I have learned by experience that these senses sometimes mislead me, and it is prudent never to trust wholly those things which have once deceived us.[13]

It is fortunate that Descartes himself has high-lighted these two points, since they do express the basic grounds of his quarrel with realism. The issue does not simply concern the use of a universal doubt but also the use of precisely this sort of doubt, in which the probable is methodically merged with the false and in which the existential judgment based upon sense perception of the material world is revoked, as a genuine principle of knowledge.

Descartes regards the first maxim as the natural teaching of reason, because he is disposed to erect a psychological experience into a methodological principle. The experience is the fact that sometimes we give to mere opinions or probabilities the unqualified assent due only to evidently certain truths. As a curative against this excessive practice, he proposes that we refrain entirely (at the outset of metaphysics) from giving assent to the probable. In effect, this counterbalancing policy places the probable on an equal footing with the false, since we seek to withhold assent entirely from both. Cartesian doubt is a sort of secular, ascetic technique for detachment from the probable. Now, in some instances, this may be a *psychologically* helpful rule; but no justification is given for transforming it into a *universal, methodological* principle. Even Descartes admits a place (further on in philosophical inquiry) for hypothesis, conjecture,

---

[13] *The Meditations concerning First Philosophy,* I (Lafleur, 15–16).

and probable reasoning, functioning in the service of mediate deduction. The aim of methodic thinking is to give to a proposition the sort of assent that its evidence warrants. Even at the outset of metaphysical investigations, one can proceed cautiously on the rule of giving to a proposition only the kind of assent *proportioned* to the evidence at hand. Here, the systematic aim is to treat the probable as probable, without either mistaking it for apodictically certain truth or classifying it strategically with the false.

Furthermore, some definite indications must be provided concerning the "entirely certain and indubitable" standard, in respect to which some particular proposition is to be adjudged merely probable. Descartes cannot yet define it as that which passes the test of universal doubt, since this would be a circular argument. Nor can he appeal here to the mathematical kind of evidence, since he has not established precisely what sort of modifications are needed before this sort of evidence can be accepted as prototypal for existential matters, from which mathematics as such prescinds. Hence, in dealing with the senses, he merely appeals to the advice of prudence that we should not place complete confidence in anything that has once deceived us. Two critical comments can be made upon this advice.

1. A distinction is required between a morally malicious counteragent, such as a deceiving human being, and an occasion for speculative deception on the part of one's own knowing powers, as in the present instance. Since the senses are not malicious counteragents, the same sort of avoidance need not be demanded in both cases. We need not shun the senses entirely, in order to avoid cognitive deception, but should maintain a cautious watch over the conditions of sense perception. Furthermore, the probable state of a body of evidence is not deceptive by itself. It becomes the occasion of deception, when the investigator follows the policy of accepting the probable as demonstrated or when the polemist presents dialectical arguments as though they were strict demonstrations. But these are *intellectual decisions about how to use the probable:* they are not generated by the probable character of the evidence itself, and they are not decisions made by the senses. Hence we can effectively oppose such unwarranted uses of probable evidence, without going to the opposite extreme of regarding the probable as false and the senses as untrustworthy. Methodic, universal doubt is not a necessary and indispensable means to the attainment of certain and indubitable knowledge.

2. If the deception concerns the senses as a supposed source of truth, then the principle of deception must be traced to the *judging power,* rather than to the senses. Descartes agrees that the senses can be only "materially false," insofar as they may dispose the mind toward false judgments. But it does not follow that intellect and will must be methodically severed from reliance upon sense data. Such a severance would remove the human way of access to existential reality. In this instance, ordinary good sense or prudence distinguishes between not trusting a source *in every instance* and not trusting it *at all as a basic principle* of knowledge. Sensory occasions of deception oblige us to be watchful over the senses in particular instances but not to reject their constant testimony to sensible existence. Descartes wanted to meet Montaigne and other skeptics on their own grounds. He accepted their arguments against the senses, as sources of speculative truth. But he sought to undercut the entire skeptical conclusion by showing that the basic metaphysical truths are founded in no way upon the senses and hence are in no way affected by the unreliability of the senses. To carry out this strategy against skepticism, however, he also had to deny the realistic grounding of all existential demonstration in sense perception. Were it not for his polemical intent, Descartes could have understood the advice of prudence to mean that one should exercise vigilance in every instance where sense perception makes a report that can become philosophically significant. This program of dealing *distributively* or one-by-one with cases of sense perception cannot be incorporated within a rationalistic method, that seeks to doubt *collectively* about an entire cognitive source, on the basis of particular occasions of deception. But it does have the merit of drawing no more from the particular instances than is warranted, and hence of permitting each deliverance of the senses to be appraised on its own weight and in view of its own set of attendant circumstances.

Descartes observes that not only the external senses but also *imagination* and *memory* often deceive us. In line with his general principles of doubt, then, they must also be regarded as being infected with falsity. This application of doubt is intended to tell heavily against mathematics and mathematical physics, which rely upon imaginative constructions and upon complicated reasonings, in which memory must be used. Yet even in the case of an immediate mathematical proposition, such as that 2 plus 2 equal 4, there is no absolute certainty. God might have so constructed our minds that we could not but assent to such propositions, even though they were untrue. In this event, even the atheist would be subject to an ironical delusion by the very Being whom he so confidently denies. As for our awareness of *our own existence,* it may well be, as Calderón puts it, that "life is a dream." There seems to be no definite criterion for distinguishing between a waking and a sleeping state. No conviction, personal or scientific, is left untouched by this general overthrow of human knowledge.

The full power of this doubt is concentrated and personified in the hypothesis of a *spiritus malignus, a demon as powerful as it is evil,* one whose will it is to deceive man even in his clearest and most distinct ideas. This extreme supposition is intended to fulfill the final condition of testing the bases of knowledge to the utmost. If any conviction can withstand the assault of this supposed demonic mind, then certainty comes automatically within our grasp and the fear of intrinsic self-deception is removed. Descartes' doubt culminates in the appeal to an evil genius, precisely because of his high standard for philosophical truth.[14] The only route to an unassailable first truth and a real criterion of knowledge lies through the purgatory of entertaining such a suspicion.

This positive purpose of doubt distinguishes the Cartesian position from the skeptical one. The skeptics regard doubt as a permanent state of soul, whereas for Descartes it is a means or method of attaining reliable knowledge. Descartes is not the *victim* of doubt but the *technician* of the method of doubt. His doubt is theoretical, hyperbolical, and metaphysical.[15] It is *theoretical,* in that it concerns the

---

14 Read H. G. Wolz, "The Universal Doubt in the Light of Descartes's Conception of Truth," *The Modern Schoolman,* 27 (1949–1950), 253–279. Descartes' own three reasons for employing the doubt are the following: "Although it is not immediately apparent that so general a doubt can be useful, it is in fact very much so, since it delivers us from all sorts of *prejudices* and makes available to us an easy method of accustoming our minds to become independent of the *senses.* Finally, it is useful in making it subsequently *impossible to doubt* those things which we discover to be true after we have taken doubt into consideration." *The Meditations concerning First Philosophy,* Synopsis (Lafleur, 11; italics added).

15 *Replies to Objections,* VII (Haldane-Ross, II, 266, 277). Descartes recommends his methodic doubt to Mersenne, on the ground that, "although many have already maintained that, in order to understand the facts of metaphysics, the mind must be abstracted from the senses, no one hitherto, so far as I know, has shown how this is to be done." *Ibid.,* II (Haldane-Ross, II, 31–32). The Thomistic judgment of separation and the Cartesian methodic doubt are conflicting ways of making a metaphysical removal from sense experience and sensible modes of being. The former affirms at once the existential trustworthiness and the limited character of the sense report; the

order of speculative truths rather than the practical conduct of life; hence it fails to paralyze one's activities, customs, and beliefs. It is *hyperbolical,* in the sense of advancing the extreme possibility of a deceiving demon and of rejecting as false whatever has the least suspicion of doubt attached to it. This strategy is Descartes' special way of counteracting our proneness to accept mere opinion as truth. Its outcome is to be a critical balance of mind that is neither credulous nor unreasonably skeptical. Cartesian doubt is also hyperbolical (but not fictitious) insofar as it arises from an act of will, that must be deliberately and methodically elicited, rather than from a natural attitude or a facile pose of mind. Methodical doubt is an instrument of human freedom in its cautious search after truth. This illuminates the *metaphysical* aspect of doubt, since it is a device for inquiring "once in a lifetime" whether there is any bedrock, existential truth. Since he lacks the separative judgment grounding metaphysics in both sense and intellect, Descartes must use the purely rationalist means of a universal doubt to achieve some metaphysical abstraction and certainty.

Under the impact of the hypothesis of an evil and very powerful spirit, the self is led to suspect its various cognitive powers, its scientific accomplishments and, at last, its very existence.

> I have just convinced myself that nothing whatsoever existed in the world, that there was no sky, no earth, no minds, and no bodies; have I not thereby convinced myself that I did not exist? Not at all; without doubt I existed if I was convinced [or even if I thought anything]. Even though there may be a deceiver of some sort, very powerful and very tricky, who bends all his efforts to keep me perpetually deceived, there can be no slightest doubt that I exist, since he deceives me; and let him deceive me as much as he will, he can never make me be nothing as long as I think that I am something. Thus, after having thought well on this matter, and after examining all things with care, I must finally conclude and maintain that this proposition: *I am, I exist,* is necessarily true every time that I pronounce it or conceive it in my mind.[16]

---

latter regards the senses as initially untrustworthy for purposes of existential knowledge, and requires a subsequent deductive validation of sensation, as a practical tool and index of sensible existents.

[16] *The Meditations concerning First Philosophy,* II (Lafleur, 21–22); cf. *Discourse on Method,* IV (Lafleur, 20–21). H. G. Frankfurt, "Descartes's Discussion of His Existence in the Second Meditation," *The Philosophical Review,* 75 (1966), 329–356, makes an analytic study of this text, showing that the affirmation of existence is inseparable here from its evidence.

The formula *Cogito ergo sum* (I am thinking, therefore I am) expresses the one existential judgment that can never fall victim to radical doubt, since its evidence is brought home irresistibly in the very act of calling it into question through the extreme supposition of an evil genius. The existing, thinking thing, which is the human self, is the unconditionally first noetic principle of Descartes' philosophy, because it is the first indubitable, existential truth.

Despite its incontrovertible appeal to Descartes' own mind, this first step in his metaphysics became at once a storm center among his contemporaries. The three recurrent objections were: (1) that the Cogito supposes some unproved premises; (2) that it smuggles in the substantial self, without proof; (3) that it leads to a vicious circle, since its full certitude depends upon the demonstration of God's existence — a demonstration that depends, in turn, upon the criterion of truth and the causal principle established along with the Cogito. Since these criticisms are still the outstanding ones, it is worth listening to Descartes' defense of his own position.[17]

1. The use of the word "therefore" contributes to the impression that *Cogito ergo sum* is the conclusion of a syllogism, whose major premise states that "whatever thinks, must exist." But Descartes maintains that the formula is not based on a syllogistic inference but expresses the *most simple intuition* of the human mind, one wherein it sees at a single glance the mutual implication between the simple natures of "actual thinking" and "actual existing." His opponents proceed on the assumption that general, abstract principles must first be posited, in order that concrete, particular truths can be derived. But Cartesian logic takes the concrete, particular, and immaterial existent as a starting point. General principles are discovered to be latent in the particular object and hence are *concomitant* with, rather than *antecedent* to, the judgment about the individual instance. Along with perceiving the truth of the Cogito, the mind also formulates a general proposition about the relation between thought and

[17] *Replies to Objections*, II, IV (Haldane-Ross, II, 38–43, 114–115). The alleged circularity of the Cogito, in regard to both the existence and the thinking nature of the self, is discussed respectively from the historical, analytic, and phenomenological standpoints by: E. G. Salmon, "The Cartesian Circle," *The New Scholasticism*, 12 (1938), 378–391; L. E. Rose, "The Cartesian Circle," *Philosophy and Phenomenological Research*, 26 (1965–1966), 80–89 (and discussion, 90–93); H. G. Frankfurt, "Descartes' Validation of Reason," *American Philosophical Quarterly*, 2 (1965), 149–156; Norman Malcolm, "Descartes's Proof that His Essence is Thinking," *The Philosophical Review*, 74 (1965), 315–338; Robert Champigny, "The Theatrical Aspect of the Cogito," *The Review of Metaphysics*, 12 (1958–1959), 370–377.

existence. The emphatic necessity of the connection between the thinking and the existing is conveyed by the use of the word "therefore," but it implies no inference from anything prior. In addition, the mind discovers, by implication, the truth of three common axioms, which serve as bonds among simple natures and things. The principles of *contradiction, substantiality,* and *causality* are seen to be immediate general implications of the Cogito-situation. Descartes is all too ready to concede their validity and to shelter them under the wing of the first truth. Whereas he assigns these three principles among the common truths to which the natural light of the mind bears immediate witness, they become moot points of discussion among his successors. The latter regard his systematic use of substance and cause as only an uncriticized survival of an earlier dogmatism.

2. Coming to the second objection, Descartes does not challenge the observation that, in order to understand the import of *Cogito ergo sum,* one must already possess some notion of the meaning of thinking and existing and doubting. He classifies these objects among the simple natures, which can be known by intuition. Insofar as they are merely apprehended natures or ideal objects, entailing no existential judgment, they do not fall within the scope of methodic doubt and hence are present throughout the inquiry. Doubt attacks none of these notions in their purely *ideal* and *essential* character. The metaphysical orientation of methodic doubt means precisely that it applies to judgments about *really existing* things. Although in some respects this is an effective reply, it has two drawbacks that Descartes does not consider. First, it makes of existence an essential notion or simple nature, that is first grasped in a nonexistential, nonjudgmental act of apprehension. The problem then arises whether existence, as so understood, is the same as what is expressed in a judgment of existence. Second, Descartes assumes that we all have a fairly clear and distinct notion of what it means to think, to doubt, and to exist. Here, the difficulty is to find any definite content remaining for these facts, after the vagueness and obscurity have been removed — and methodic doubt must remove these obstructing factors.

In any case, once these simple natures are found to be present in an indubitable existential situation, the mind attends at once to the fact that they are being conceived by it precisely *as modifications of some subject.* Instead of covertly interpolating a substantial self, Descartes maintains that this latter affirmation is a necessary implication of the inhering function of thinking and doubting. These operations are ascertained along with a reference to their subject. What reveals itself to my introspection is nothing other than myself thinking, myself existing. To expand the basic formula a bit: it is the *I who am thinking* that is also known as the *I who am existing*. Descartes remains close to the Scholastics, in the degree that it is natural for him to think of being primarily in terms of substantial things and their affections. Whether the naturalness of positing a subject for acts of thinking is due to the natural light of the understanding or only to the inclination of training and habitual association, is the question raised by Malebranche and carried to its skeptical conclusion by Hume.

3. At least at this point in the study, the truth of the Cogito is known only as often as I actually pronounce the proposition. It is true *here and now,* since the perception is borne in upon me with utmost clarity and distinctness. The *criterion of truth* is itself implicated in the Cogito, because the conditions of this perception irresistibly draw the will to assent to its truth. What is more reasonable than to suppose that every clearly and distinctly perceived idea is true and informative about reality? This question may be answered by a universal affirmative, Descartes replies, on condition that there is no ground for suspecting that, in the future, clear and distinct ideas may turn out to be false. The truth of the Cogito is not sufficient to remove this suspicion *about the future,* and hence its truth is limited to present perception in pronouncing the judgment. But unless the suspicion can be removed somehow, the suggested universal criterion can never function at all times and hence can never aid in the construction of a philosophical system. This exigency led Descartes, next, to prove the existence of God.

Contemporary readers urged that Descartes was guilty of circular reasoning, when he accepted the Cogito as indubitable and later on declared that no truth is absolutely certain, until the existence of a veracious God is established. His reply to this criticism was based on a distinction between present, actual perception and remembrance of a former perception. A divine guarantee is needed for *memory* and *reasoning* about past apprehensions of truth but not for *present perception* of clear and distinct ideas. Once having ascertained the existence of a nondeceiving God, Descartes gains retroactive assurance that the situation of the Cogito can be extended to other instances of clear and distinct perception of the connections among ideas. The temporal proviso attached to the criterion of evidence may then be confidently removed. A good God would not permit us to take the false for the true, whether in immediate perception or in memory and reasoning, for otherwise we would be irresistibly drawn to make the judgment and yet would have no means of rectifying the error. Viewed in conjunction with what we come to know about God's nature, the criterion of truth cannot reasonably be doubted and hence can be made a universal rule of reasoning.

5. THE EXISTENCE AND NATURE OF GOD

In reply to a satirical comment that the actual results of his philosophy are surprisingly meager, in comparison with the great energy expended in developing it, Descartes made a distinction between two sorts of innovators. Some thinkers strive at all costs to be original in respect to the *conclusions* of their philosophy, whereas others bestow their care mainly upon the *reasoning* which supports the conclusions. Descartes ridiculed Bruno and Campanella for advancing farfetched innovations for their own sakes. He himself regarded the existence of an immaterial soul, a transcendent God, and an extended universe as the sum of philosophical principles, and did not consider himself original in this respect. His personal contribution lay rather in suggesting new ways of proving these traditional truths. Yet in offering new proofs, he was obliged to change the content of the conclusions much more than he cared to admit. This is clearly seen in his treatment of natural theology, especially his three proofs of God's existence.

1. True to his method, Descartes seeks to prove God's existence solely from truths already established. Hence his point of departure can only be the ideas present in himself as a thinking thing. These he classifies, first of all, according to their descriptive origin. Ideas seem to fall into three classes: *adventitious* (coming from without), *factitious* (coming from the mind's constructive power), and *innate* (coming from the inborn dynamism of the mind). Our idea of God can be tested by this threefold classification. Although the imagination is undoubtedly capable of fashioning its images freely, the *idea of God* does not have a factitious origin. Whenever Descartes thinks of God, he is constrained to think of "an infinite substance, eternal, immutable, independent, omniscient, omnipotent."[18] He cannot think

---

[18] *The Meditations concerning First Philosophy*, III (Lafleur, 40). For the various statements of the proofs for God's existence, compare *ibid.*, III, V (Lafleur, 32–47, 58–61); *Discourse on Method*, IV (Lafleur, 22–23); *The Principles of Philosophy*,

of God otherwise than in these terms, and hence this idea does not have a factitious origin. Nor does it come to him suddenly from without. Indeed, the external origin of *any* idea is doubtful, at this stage of his meditations. Material things, including the self's own body, are not yet known to exist. Our spontaneous impulse to believe that some ideas are adventitious may well be erroneous, since it may be due to some unknown power unconsciously at work in the mind. By elimination, it follows that the idea of God is innate or native to the mind.

Yet the bare fact that the idea of God has an innate origin is not decisive for the problem of God's existence. For, as Suarez taught, any idea can be regarded in two ways: either *formally* (in its own mental mode of being) or *objectively* (as representing various objects). From the formal standpoint, all ideas are on the same level and are adequately accounted for by the human mind, in which they reside. Representatively or objectively, however, they differ vastly and can be arranged in an ascending order, insofar as they refer to different grades of being. Now, Descartes is sure that, even from the standpoint of their representative reality, all ideas (except that of the infinite being) might be accounted for by himself as a thinking being. The crucial question is whether he is also the adequate source of the representative reality of the idea of a purely infinite being.

To answer this question, Descartes appeals to the *principle of efficient causality,* the certainty of which has already been guaranteed in the Cogito. This principle states, in its Cartesian formulation, that there must be at least as much reality in the efficient and total cause as in the effect. Descartes also takes as immediately evident the following propositions: that a thing cannot give what it does not have; that something cannot come from nothing; that the more perfect cannot come from the less perfect. He regards them as inborn truths, taught us by the natural light of the mind. And, following another hint from Suarez, he adds that a sufficient cause is required to explain the *objective* or *representative reality* of the idea, as well as for the formal reality of the idea, taken as a mental mode. From the above principles, it is clear that a finite, thinking self is insufficient to account for the objective reality of the idea of a purely infinite being. This reality comes neither from nothing nor from a being

---

I, 14–21 (Haldane-Ross, I, 224–28); *Replies to Objections,* II (Haldane-Ross, II, 57–58; these demonstrations are in geometrical form).

that is of less reality than the infinite being. Hence it must have been implanted in the human mind by a being which possesses as much reality in a formal, actual way as the idea possesses in a representative way. The conclusion is that the infinitely perfect being, God, must exist as the adequate efficient cause of my idea of God.

2. As a second proof, Descartes shifts his perspective slightly, so as to consider the implications of *the self which possesses this idea* of a being, infinite in perfection. There is no complete distinction between the two proofs, since the self is inspected precisely insofar as it is the subject of the idea of God. But the second one is advanced by Descartes as being more accommodated to a Scholastic audience, which might see in it a proof cognate to the familiar ones from contingency and efficiency. The thinking self is *not independent* or the author of its own being, since in that case it would confer upon itself, in the formal order, whatever reality it can conceive representatively through its ideas. Were it self-caused, the human self would confer infinite perfection upon itself, in correspondence with its idea of God. That I am *not infinite,* however, is evident from my being subject to change of thought, from my capacity both for error-and-doubt and for increase of knowledge, and from my desire for an infinite good existing beyond my own nature. The Cogito participates in the perfection of the simple natures of existence and thought, but it is not their unconditioned actualization. Similarly, the successive moments of my duration are discrete and externally related, so that even if I always existed, I would be everlastingly dependent upon the same cause that produced my first moment of existence. God is the creating and conserving cause of the very being of the thinking self, not merely of its first act of coming-to-be. He provides the only principle of unity among the discrete, atomic moments of the self's duration. The limited and dependent thing which contains the idea of an infinitely perfect being could neither exist nor endure, except as being caused and conserved in being by the infinite being. The idea of God is innate in the thinking self, in the sense that it is, as it were, the seal placed upon His product by the divine artisan. In creating a human self, God also communicates to it the ability to conceive or cause an idea having the infinitely perfect actuality as its object.

3. In order to clear the way for his final proof of God's existence, Descartes has to attack the *problem of error.*[19] In principle, it follows

---

[19] Descartes devotes the fourth section of *The Meditations concerning First Philosophy*

from the infinite perfection of God that He is veracious and cannot be a deceiver, i.e., cannot have the malicious intent of deceiving us. Hence God may not be charged with being the cause of error, and man may not be described as the innocent and impotent victim of error. Descartes' approach to error is quite similar to the approach of St. Thomas to *evil*, an analogy that is not surprising, in view of the fact that Descartes considers the *act of assent or judgment to be an act of the will*. Error is not a positive reality but a privation, a lack of knowledge which ought to be present. The possibility of having this privation rests on the self's condition as a finite being, a creature drawn from nothing. The senses give a confused and indistinct report and hence can be a material source of error, in that the state of sense evidence may lead to a false judgment. But it is in the judgment itself that error formally resides. The judgment is an act of the will rather than of the understanding, since it requires an assent, over and above the cognitive perception of objects. Understanding and will, taken by themselves as faculties given by God, are veracious powers. But in point of fact, they act conjointly in the knowing act, which is a synthesis of *intellectual perception* and *voluntary assent*. By nature, understanding has only a finite range of operation, whereas the range of will is unlimited. Descartes agrees with Mersenne and St. Bernard that man most closely resembles God in respect to will. The uncircumscribed quality of will is both man's glory and his Achilles' heel. For the will often outraces the evidence presented by the understanding and gives a firm assent in matters that are not clearly and distinctly presented. To take the false for the true is thus a misuse of the will's freedom of indifference, and is traceable to a refusal to keep modestly within the bounds set by our cognitive power. Whatever is positive and sound in the act of judgment comes from God, but man himself is the principal cause of the privation or misuse of the will's assent, in which error formally consists.

From this exposition, it follows both that God is not responsible for error and that He has not left us without *remedy* against it. At least, we have the minimal power of recognizing the source of error within us and of refraining from judgment on occasions when the conditions of clarity and distinctness are absent from our ideas.

(Lafleur, 47–66) to this subject; other passages are collated and criticized by L. W. Keeler, S.J., *The Problem of Error from Plato to Kant* (Rome, Gregorian University Press, 1934), 141–177.

Training in method is nothing more than cultivation of the habitual attention required for observance of this rule of refrainment. Both the avoidance of error and the attainment of truth require the mind's disciplined attention to the canons of evidence. The methodically directed mind need have no fear of deceit, when it is in the presence of clear and distinct perceptions. It can reason with confidence from the order of knowing to that of being: *a nosse ad esse valet consequentia.*[20] The mind's *clear* and *distinct ideas,* which alone are direct objects of perception, are nevertheless adequate grounds for drawing conclusions about *existent things.*

Descartes immediately exploits this fully guaranteed criterion in the interests of a third proof of God's existence: that drawn from the perceived connection between *essence and existence in the idea of God.* Just as the first two proofs tend to merge together, so the third proof tends to assimilate the two prior ones. Descartes sometimes confesses that God's existence can *only* be proved from the idea of God, with God taken as efficient rather than final cause.[21] Such proof is either a posteriori (from the representative reality of the idea of God, and from the self which has this idea) or a priori (from the content itself of this idea). Although the a priori or so-called ontological argument cannot be advanced before the objective validity of our ideas has been established, it represents the deepest point of penetration of Cartesian analysis into the significance of human thought. The ultimate meaning of the Cogito is that the finite thinking self shares to some degree in the *divine dynamism* itself, in the *self-affirmation* that is God's distinctive way of being. One becomes aware of this affinity in reflecting upon the import of the clearest and most distinct idea in the mind: the idea of an infinitely perfect being. This essence contains existence as a property, just as necessarily as the notion of triangle contains the properties demonstrable of it. The notion of actual and eternal existence is a positive perfection, clearly and distinctly known as belonging to the infinitely perfect essence, and hence it can be affirmed as true of this essence

---

[20] "The argument from knowledge to existence is quite valid, because it is impossible to know anything, unless it really is as we know it." *Replies to Objections,* VII (Haldane-Ross, II, 313).

[21] That the contrast between St. Thomas and Descartes in natural theology is fundamentally that between a point of departure taken in the sensible existent and one taken in the idea of God, is established by P. Mesnard, "Les preuves cartésiennes de l'existence de Dieu dans les *Méditations métaphysiques,*" in *Cartesio nel terzo centenario del 'Discorso del Metodo'* (Milan, Vita e Pensiero, 1937), 599–614.

in the actual order. Once existence is seen to be a perfection, I cannot truly think of God or the perfect being otherwise than as actually existing. For the necessity and self-affirmation of His real existence are imposed upon (or rather, determine from within) the structure of my idea of God. I am constrained by necessity of thought, i.e., by the perfect, self-imposing evidence of the connection between a perfect essence and existence, to conceive of the object of that idea as necessarily existing. Since the constraint comes from the most clearly and distinctly perceived connection, the truth of God's own actual and necessary existence follows from the truth of the necessity of including existence in one's idea of God's essence.

Descartes' arguments were placed under fire at once. His atheistic opponents objected against the sudden appeal to the principle of efficient causality, whose validity was not established by a distinct, formal argument. Indirectly, however, Descartes had provided the materials for a defense of this principle. The various modes of the thinking thing not only inhere in it but are also causally determined by it. That is why Descartes held that the finite thinking self could adequately account for the formal being of all ideas and for the representative reality of all ideas, save that of the infinite being. The Cogito is presented immediately to consciousness as an agent, *as the efficient cause* of its own states of thought. Moreover, training in method is a process of learning to use the mind's power of attention, in maintaining its free control over the act of judgment. The ability to give assent or refrain from giving it was, in Descartes' eyes, a supreme instance of human freedom and of finite, efficient causality. Hence he regarded the reality of causation as being adequately founded in such inward facts. But unfortunately, he did not work out any detailed explanation of the principle of causality and left sufficient loopholes for Malebranche to deny created causality, while still speculating *en bon cartésien.*

The argument from the idea of the infinite was attacked by contemporary theologians on the ground that the *idea of an infinite being* need not be an *infinite idea.* They held that the so-called objective or representative reality of ideas does not demand any special causal explanation.[22] Meaning can be adequately accounted for by the mind's

---

[22] The theologians, Caterus and Arnauld, presented some serious objections to the Cartesian proofs for God's existence: *Objections,* I, IV (Haldane-Ross, II, 1–8, 86–93); cf. Descartes' *Replies to Objections,* I, IV (Haldane-Ross, II, 9–22, 104–115), for his rejoinders. Source readings on the ontological argument are edited by A. Plantinga: *The Ontological Argument from St. Anselm to Contemporary Philosophers* (New York: Doubleday Anchor, 1965).

ability to abstract intentional likenesses, and by the contribution of experienced things to our notions. Must an exception be made in the case of the idea of God? Descartes maintained that this idea is a *positive* one, even though it is not *comprehensive* of God's infinite perfection. It is a clear and distinct idea, and hence can be used somewhat like the distinct ideas in mathematics which are applied to the infinite limit. Just as geometry deals with the properties of the circle by superposition of a rectilinear polyhedron, having an indefinite number of sides, so our idea of infinite perfection can be used to know, but never to comprehend, the infinite God. This answer did not really meet the Scholastic objection, since the point at issue would then be whether our mind has the power to frame this idea, with the aid of its knowledge of finite things and its ability to negate imperfections. Furthermore, the comparison was not a happy one, since the mathematical type of analogy is reducible to univocal predication. Both terms of the mathematical relation (the circle and the polyhedron) belong to the class of geometrical figures, whereas Descartes' own theism would prevent him from placing God and any finite entity in the same class. His predicament was that he had to use the mathematical example, if he wanted to evade the alternative of either discarding innatism in favor of an *abstraction-theory* of the origin of the idea of God or else claiming to have a fully *comprehensive* idea of infinite perfection.

It was pointed out to Descartes, moreover, that the traditional view of the idea of God's infinite perfection is not that of a mere negation of finitude but also an eminent affirmation of all pure perfections. The human mind is able to conceive these perfections and to affirm them of God, apart from the finite modes in which they are embodied in our experience and thought. This activity of *predication by way of eminence and analogical affirmation,* along with a denial of limitation, would account for the idea of God, without having recourse to innatism. In the face of this explanation, Descartes was obliged to make an important concession. He allowed that, in the order of our *explicit* notions, the idea of finite perfections comes first. But he still awarded an *implicit* priority to the notion of the infinite, on the ground that otherwise we could never have a standard of comparison in the light of which finite things are seen to be finite. To this distinction, his Thomistic critics replied that the transcendental notions of being and actual perfection are sufficient to account for our recognition of the finite character of the objects of experience.

Descartes' final remark was in the form of a question about the source of the mind's power of *amplifying* perfections somehow, so that they may signify the infinite. This reference to the mind's power of amplification marks Descartes' failure to release himself from a purely mathematical approach to the infinite and his substitution of a question about the causal origin of a mental power for the more pertinent one about the range of that power's knowledge.

When the theologian Caterus remarked that the second proof resembles the Thomistic proof from efficient causality, Descartes approved of the general comparison but added a list of four significant differences. (1) Descartes never argued from an order of efficient causes operating in the sensible world. He had to start from immaterial entities, since the existence of sensible things was still under doubt. (2) Moreover, he thought (incorrectly) that the Thomistic proof from efficient cause was based on the impossibility of an infinite series of accidentally subordinated agents. He did not appreciate the import of the Thomistic conception of divine efficient, *per se* causality of the entire *esse* of presently existing things. Descartes pointed out two further points of difference. (3) His starting point was the self only as a thinking thing and, indeed, only as a thing having the idea of the infinite. (4) Finally, he disagreed with the remark of Thomas that nothing can be its own efficient cause. Descartes juggled a good deal with the terms "efficient cause" and "cause of itself." At times, he reduced God's self-causation to the fact that the divine essence is its own positive principle of intelligibility, comparable to the formal cause of His nature. Yet at other times, he called God a *causa sui* in the sense of having a positive self-origination of His being, in virtue of the affirmation of His infinite efficient power. This obscure notion of the divine being, as standing somehow in relation to itself as an efficient cause to its effect, stems from Descartes' metaphysical view that the divine essence is basically infinite power, and that existence (divine or otherwise) is a terminal perfection in the line of essence itself.

When reminded about St. Thomas' criticism of the argument of St. Anselm, Descartes granted that the Thomistic strictures told against a proof based on the meaning of the *word* "God." But he regarded his own third proof as dealing with the true and immutable *nature* of God, as objectively contained in a clear and distinct idea. Descartes did not join issue with Aquinas over whether the divine essence can be known directly in this way by our minds, so as to permit an a priori proof. For him, it was enough to have a distinct and certain idea, in order to draw an existential conclusion. One reason why Descartes characterized God as *causa sui* was to lend force to the a priori truth of the proposition "God exists," as it follows from our idea of God.[23] The immensity and infinite power of God are such that, needing no cause outside itself, the divine essence nevertheless bestows being upon itself after the manner of an efficient cause. Because God cannot be prior to, or distinct from, His own being, the creaturely meaning of efficient causality is not fully realized in Him, and to this extent God produces His being more after the manner of a formal cause. Still, the active power of the infinite principle is exercised in supplying its own being, as well as in the creation of finite things. The divine existence flows somehow as a property of God's infinite essence. In this sense, Descartes wants to reduce all proofs of God's existence to one grand proof, taken from the idea of God as an efficient cause. His self-causality is mirrored in the necessity with which our mind is led to affirm His existence, on the basis of our clear and distinct idea of His essence. To this idea, the divine workman imparts all its representative vigor of affirming existence. It is not merely the idea of existence that is seen to be entailed by that of the divine essence, but the *true* or *existentially relevant idea* of necessary existence.

Descartes follows the voluntaristic strain in later Scholasticism in his explanation of the *divine attributes:* infinity, incomprehensibility, omnipotence, independence, and immutability. Each of these attributes is made to perform a distinctive function in the Cartesian synthesis. The divine *infinity* and *incomprehensibility* are used to eliminate *final cause* as an explanatory principle of the visible universe. It is true that God Himself does set an end for the universe and hence does exercise final causality in its respect. But the infinite depths of the divine purpose are inscrutable and incomprehensible to us, preventing any appeal to this purpose in our physical investigations.

---

[23] Another reason was that the principle of causality is metaphysically useful, only if it applies in some manner to God, as well as to finite things. The Cogito assures the existential relevance of this principle, only because it reveals that this principle expresses an ontological exigency of *every* being to have a cause. Unless God is *esse a se tanquam a causa,* the ultimate existential and systematic ground for regarding everything else as *esse a causa* is lacking, in accord with the Cartesian method of tracing the dependence of eternal truths upon the divine will and its self-affirmation of existence. Cf. H. Gouhier, "Les exigences de l'existence dans la métaphysique de Descartes," *La Pensée métaphysique de Descartes,* 265–291.

A mechanistic explanation of the world can be given, without recourse to the ends for which God intends the various motions. Descartes limits the meaning of the term "finality," however, to this universal extrinsic purpose. He readily admits that the human mind can discover the intrinsic adaptation of parts to the whole, in particular things, but he assigns such adaptation to the efficient cause alone. One of Leibniz' points of dispute with Descartes concerned whether the purely mechanistic interpretation of living things is adequate and, indeed, is a truly philosophical approach. Leibniz held that a thorough metaphysical interpretation of living things requires an appeal to final cause, and that the philosopher can make use of final causality, without pretending to have sounded the depths of the divine infinity or to be privy to God's secret designs.

Descartes uses the divine *omnipotence* and *independence* to resolve the question of the *eternal truths,* including immutable mathematical propositions.[24] He wants to steer a middle course between what he regards as the ordinary Scholastic position and that of the atheistic freethinkers. He interprets Suarez as holding that the eternal truths have an independent, objective presence in the divine understanding, in such a way that the divine will must conform with an independent set of essential necessities. And it is the atheistic contention that eternal truths can be adequately understood and founded, apart from any reference to God, with the consequence that God is superfluous for a true system of philosophy. The Cartesian doctrine on the eternal truths is completely determined by a resolve to avoid these extremes. There is no indication that Descartes ever weighed the Thomistic position that the eternal truths are founded in the divine creative essence, considered as identical with the divine act of existing and as being the primary object of the divine intellect. He cannot allow the atheistic view that our knowledge of the eternal truths may dispense with a divine foundation, for then it would be exempt from his universal doubt and hence could not be shown to have any existential reference. And he cannot grant that these truths constitute a quasi-autonomous region in the divine mind, for then God would

---

[24] Descartes' most forthright declarations about the dependence of eternal truths on the divine will and about the divine power to make these truths untrue, are contained in a series of letters to Mersenne, written during April and May, 1630 (*Correspondance,* edited by Adam and Milhaud, I, 135–136, 139–142), and in *Replies to Objections,* V, VI (Haldane-Ross, II, 226, 248, 250–251). Cf. T. J. Cronin, "Eternal Truths in the Thought of Suarez and Descartes," *The Modern Schoolman,* 38 (1960–1961), 269–288, and *ibid.,* 39 (1961–1962), 23–38.

be subjected to a mythological sort of Fate. Consequently, the eternal truths must have their foundation in the divine will, without compromising the infinite power and independence of God's action.

Descartes asks us to consider that a truth is a form of being, and that a being is either independent or dependent on the divine will. Now since the eternal truths can be *comprehended* by us, they are finite and hence utterly *dependent* upon God. In God, to know and to will are the same. Hence divine knowledge of the eternal truths is also a free, divine determination of them, through an act of will. God's will produces them, just as completely as it creates individual, contingent things: but in producing the eternal truths, He specifically determines them to an immutable mode of being. God could have decreed that it should be untrue that twice four equals eight, even though we cannot comprehend how He could have done so. No limits can be set upon the divine power by our understanding. Even though God *can* do everything which we can comprehend, we have no right to conclude that He *cannot* do that which we cannot comprehend, such as a counterdecree concerning the eternal truths. Divine power is bounded only by its spontaneous ordination to the infinite, divine perfection. Thus the structure of the eternal truths depends upon God's eternal will and affirmation of His own existence.

By using this method of safeguarding the divine omnipotence and independence, however, Descartes imperils the *rational foundations of science*. If the basic truths are contingent upon an exercise of God's power, then they are wholly arbitrary and subject to imminent change. This outcome would also be self-defeating for Descartes' own project of establishing a universal body of certain and reliable truths. Hence he is obliged, finally, to enlist the special aid of the divine attribute of *immutability*. Although God is autonomous and indifferently free in respect to the eternal truths, He does not leave the essential natures and laws of things in utter chaos. Within the context of his unlimited power over all essences, He institutes *a stable order of nature* and gives continuity of duration to the atomic moments of things having temporal existence. Scientific knowledge is based upon this order of nature, which shares in the immutability of the divine essence itself. Philosophical truths are measured ultimately by the divinely established, immutable order of ideas and things. This solution rests upon the qualifying phrase: "within the context of God's unlimited power." The question of the eternal truths remained a lively one for post-Cartesian rationalists, precisely because they suspected that this qualification nullified the effectiveness of Descartes' appeal to the divine immutability. Hence Spinoza suggested that the power and immutability of God should be merged, with the consequence that God cannot but produce precisely this determined world and its laws. Since this solution endangered the divine freedom in creation, Leibniz turned to the view that the world of ideal essences has its own inviolable structure, but that the actual world of existents is freely chosen by God, in accordance with His decree to produce the maximum of perfection. Between fate and chaos, it is difficult to find a middle ground for either the eternal truths or the act of creation, when the problem is formulated in such a way that the relation between the divine ideas and the divine existing essence is given no controlling role.

6. METAPHYSICAL PRINCIPLES OF THE MATERIAL WORLD

Descartes once informed Mersenne that he would never have discovered the principles of his physics, had he not first meditated upon the metaphysical themes of God and self. This does not mean that Cartesian metaphysics is merely a prelude to a philosophy of nature. But it does underline the fact that, despite his early successes in mathematical physics, Descartes was unable to organize his views on the material world in a systematic and demonstrative way, until he settled the main lines of his metaphysics. Only then did he possess the principles which would permit *an a priori explanation of material phenomena through their distinctly perceived causes.* Descartes had tried to reduce physics directly to mechanics and thus to mathematicize the entire study of nature, without having recourse to metaphysical truths. This project had not met with success. Even in pure mathematics, he had encountered types of curves which he despaired of expressing in mathematical equations (yet which, as the later history of mathematics shows, he was overhasty in declaring to be irreducible to equational form). As for the physical phenomena, he found them to be even more multifarious and intractable before exact mathematical analysis and deduction from general notions.

These obstacles forced him to refine his conception of geometrical demonstration and to seek out the metaphysical principles that could confer scientific status upon his physical views. He remarked on the great difference between *abstract* and *concrete geometry,* a distinction which his followers tended to ignore and which Newton had to bring again to the fore. Abstract geometry limits itself to problems that exercise the mind in the realm of pure constructive imagination, which operates without disturbance from actual sense experience. But in *applying* mathematical findings to the actual, concrete universe, grave difficulties are encountered. Even after they agree to regard only the quantitative aspects of things, mathematical physicists are exposed to the insecurities and obscurities of the sensible world and hence must remain satisfied with something less than absolute mathematical certainty. Physical investigations must begin with commonly known facts, together with suppositions or hypotheses about these facts. If the hypotheses lead to further deductions of a predictive sort, which are borne out by the actual phenomena, then there is a *mutual confirmation* between hypothesis and fact.[25] The hypothesis renders intelligible a wider range of phenomena, whereas the facts furnish experimental proof of the predictions. Once verified in this way, the tested hypotheses can be regarded as reliable physical theories.

But even such reliable theories do not satisfy the strict standards of an a priori development of scientific knowledge. Hence Descartes argued for the need to supply *metaphysical principles* for physical science. Metaphysics is at least as certain as geometry, and enjoys the additional advantage of not being confined by the limits of imagination. Pure understanding is the proper metaphysical instrument in dealing with the natural world, since only this power enables one to grasp the true nature of material substance and differentiate it properly from the mind or immaterial substance.

The first contribution of metaphysics to physical theory is its *critique of the senses* and its consequent elimination of the *Scholastic philosophy of nature*. Descartes' famous *analysis of a piece of wax* serves quite vividly to illustrate this contribution. Fresh from the hive, the wax has a definite white color, a lingering odor and taste of honey, a certain figure and size. It is hard and cold; it emits a sound, when struck with the finger. But upon being brought close to the fire, some of these qualities disappear and others are modified. It loses its qualities of taste and smell; its hue is altered, as are its figure and size. The wax becomes a liquid, hot to the touch, soundless; yet it is still recognized as being this piece of wax. The wax has no necessary connection with the forms of its previous appearance, and hence its real nature is to be sought elsewhere. Having stripped

---

[25] *Discourse on Method*, VI (Lafleur, 49). Cf. R. M. Blake, "The Role of Experience in Descartes' Theory of Method," in *Theories of Scientific Method: The Renaissance through the Nineteenth Century*, by R. M. Blake, C. J. Ducasse, and E. H. Madden (Seattle: University of Washington Press, 1960), 75–103.

off the various modes that are not essential to it, "certainly nothing is left but something extended, flexible, and movable."[26] This perception is not an act of the senses, since it provides a correction of the sense conviction that all the appearances constitute the wax's nature. Neither is it an act of imagination, since I can clearly conceive that the wax may assume an infinite variety of shapes and modifications in extension, even beyond those that I can imagine. The true nature of this wax or of any other material thing is accessible only to a *purely intellectual* insight. Only pure understanding can judge that a *material substance* or *body* is nothing else than an *extended thing, having figure and motion*. Only the understanding, operating at its own level, can discern the subjective character of the remaining qualities. This correlation of the doctrine of primary and secondary qualities with a theory of pure understanding is the distinctive mark of Descartes' approach to this question.

The senses have only a *utilitarian* value in ministering to our bodily needs. They are not instruments of reliable cognition: those who rely upon them are bound to mistake subjective need for objective fact. Descartes accuses the Scholastics of systematizing the everyday illusion that the material thing resembles, in every respect, the perceptions we have of it. He takes no account of the persistent criticism of precisely this thesis by St. Thomas, in his discussion of universals.

In his polemic against *hylemorphism,* Descartes avoids the metaphysical issue entirely, by outlawing the theory of actual and potential coprinciples and by concentrating upon a psychological critique. In the Cartesian vision of the real order, there is room only for actual, substantial *things* and their *affections*. Substantial principles of being that are not the same as substantial things are inconceivable to him, since their status in being evades precise mathematical determination. Matter is an extended, actual thing, since potency is only a confused notion of sense. And there is no cogent metaphysical reason why substantial form should be admitted. If the form is substantial, then it must be capable of subsisting by itself and hence must be a thing or complete substance. Now, in addition to the matter, which is a

[26] *The Meditations concerning First Philosophy,* II (Lafleur, 27). For the psychological criticism of the senses, secondary qualities, and hylemorphism, see *ibid.,* VI (Lafleur, 73–74); *The Principles of Philosophy,* I, 66, 71, and II, 3 (Haldane-Ross, I, 247, 249–250, 255); *Replies to Objections,* VI (Haldane-Ross, II, 254–255); also, the *Letter to Regius,* cited below in note 31. Read R. J. Blackwell's two articles: "Matter as Extension," in *The Concept of Matter,* vol. 2, ed. by E. McMullin (Notre Dame: University of Notre Dame Press, 1967); "Descartes' Laws of Motion," *Isis,* 57 (1966), 220–234.

complete, actual thing or substance, there is no need to suppose another substantial thing, the form. It is superfluous and can be eliminated. Since the full force of the Thomistic distinction between a *thing* and a *principle of being* eludes him, Descartes is obliged to invoke a purely subjective reason why the Thomists defend substantial form. They do so, only because they expect to find in material things the same generic sort of independent substance as the human mind, in respect to its body. Similarly, he explains real secondary qualities and powers of bodies as entities that have been read into material things by analogy with the human soul and its powers. This psychological line of criticism never comes to grips, however, with the metaphysical doctrine on the principles of act and potency, as applied to moving, material things of various kinds.

In Descartes' own metaphysical outlook, a radical distinction is drawn between *mind* or thinking thing (*res cogitans*) and *body* or extended thing (*res extensa*). Each is regarded as a complete thing or finite substance, derived from the infinite substance, God. Minds are immaterial substances, having *thought* (*cogitatio*) as their principal or special attribute, and the various acts of thought (knowing, opining, willing, perceiving, feeling, doubting) as their modes. Bodies are reducible to one corporeal substance, having *extension* as its principal or special attribute, and the varieties of figure and motion as its modes. This explanation rests upon a doctrine on the nature of substance and its affections, along with a special theory of distinctions.

DESCARTES' METAPHYSICAL SCHEMA
(The Order of Being)

1. Absolute substance.	God	
2. Relative substances.	Minds	Body
3. Attributes.	Thought	Extension
4. Modes.	Knowing, Willing	Figure, Movement

A substance is an existing thing or being. Descartes defines *substance* as "a thing which so exists that it needs no other thing in order to exist."[27] This meaning departs from the traditional minimal

---

[27] *The Principles of Philosophy*, I, 51 (Haldane-Ross, I, 239); the second definition, given at the end of the paragraph, is from *Replies to Objections*, II (Haldane-Ross, II, 53).

requirement of "that by which the being exists in itself," and hence Descartes admits that it applies in the strict sense only to God. He is the only *absolute* substance, in that He alone has a completely independent manner of existing. All other things stand in need of God's creative and conserving power. Finite minds and body are substances only in a *relative* sense, and Descartes even speaks of them as being quasi-modes of God. Without explaining the meaning of nonunivocal predication in his system, he nevertheless denies that "substance" applies univocally to the one absolute substance and to the relative substances. Yet he advances two reasons why created things may be regarded as substances. Although extended thing and thinking thing depend on God, they do not depend on, or inhere in, *each other* for existence. Furthermore, created things do serve as the *support* of their various affections, and thus satisfy one meaning for "substance." As far as finite things are concerned, then, substance may also be defined as "everything in which there resides immediately, as in a subject, or by means of which there exists anything we perceive, i.e., any property, quality, or attribute, of which we have a real idea."

This second definition casts some retrospective light upon why Descartes affirms unhesitatingly that the thinking self is a *substantial* self. Since I have a real idea of the property of thought, I am assured of the real presence of a mental substance or subject of this property. Similarly, my idea of extension and its modes is sufficient ground for affirming the presence of a material substance or subject of these properties. Substance cannot be apprehended in a completely bare condition, however, but must be grasped along with at least one privileged affection, the *attribute*. Descartes refers, in a loose way, to all the qualities and perfections of a thing as its attributes. But in a more special sense, this term is reserved for "one principal property of substance which constitutes its nature and essence, and on which all the others depend."[28] Thought is the *special* attribute of mind, and extension the *special* attribute of bodily substance. There are also certain *general* attributes (e.g., existence *per se,* unity, duration) which are found commonly among all kinds of substances. The remaining properties and qualities are classified as *modes* of substance, since the substance may be regarded as being "modified" in these different ways.

Although Descartes follows some Scholastics in holding that sub-

---

[28] *The Principles of Philosophy,* I, 53 (Haldane-Ross, I, 240).

stance is known only through its properties, still he goes much farther in maintaining that the special attribute gives an *adequate, essential knowledge* of the substance which surpasses our knowledge of its various affections. In apprehending the attribute, I thereby directly apprehend the substantial essence itself, since there is only a logical distinction between the two. The attribute is nothing other than the substance itself, insofar as it stands open to our direct vision. The philosopher of nature need not worry about hidden forms and qualities since, in grasping the attribute of extension, he gains sufficient insight into the substantial nature of bodily things to dispense with any occult powers.

The Cartesian theory of distinctions confirms this view of substance and its affections. Descartes uses for his own purpose the terms that were common among his Scholastic contemporaries. Distinctions are of three sorts: real, modal, and logical.[29] A *real distinction* obtains between two substances, whether they belong to the same class or to different classes. Two things are known to be really distinct when the one can be clearly and distinctly conceived without the other, not by reason of an act of abstraction but because of a positive understanding of its nature. This means that the one can be seen in its own essence to be at least capable of separate existence. *Modal distinctions* hold either between a mode and the substance of which it is properly a mode or between two modes of the same substance. In the former case, the substance can be conceived distinctly without the mode, but conversely, the mode cannot be conceived distinctly apart from reference to its subject of inherence. Where two modes of the same substance are concerned, one can be understood without the other, but neither can be properly understood without reference to the common substance supporting them. As for the distinction between modes belonging to *different* substances or between a mode and the substance to which it does not *properly* belong, Descartes assigns this to the class of real distinctions, in view of the real distinction between the different substances that are ultimately implicated. Finally, the *logical distinction* or distinction actively drawn by reason is made between a substance and its attributes (both special and general) or between two attributes of a substance. Without the

---

29 *Ibid.*, I, 60–62 (Haldane-Ross, I, 243–245); for the Scholastic background, cf. E. Gilson, *Index scolastico-cartésien*, 86–90 (quotations from Suarez and Eustace of St. Paul). Consult N. J. Wells, "Descartes and the Modal Distinction," *The Modern Schoolman*, 43 (1965–1966), 1–22.

attribute, the substance cannot be known clearly and distinctly; if there be two attributes, the one cannot be known clearly without reference to the other.

This discussion of distinctions is tailored to achieve two ends: to guarantee an adequate, essential understanding of the nature of mind and matter through their respective attributes, and to secure a real distinction between these widest classes of created substance. Descartes is careful to describe each type of distinction in terms of the mind's manner of knowing its objects. Thus the classification is a thorough-going application of the criterion of clear and distinct knowledge. This is manifest in the test case of the *real distinction between mind and body* in man. Introspection reveals a sharp contrast between the clear and distinct idea of self as a *thinking* and *unextended* thing, and the clear and distinct idea of body as an *extended* and *unthinking* thing. It can be safely concluded that the thinking thing is really distinct from the body and can exist without it. Because the thinking self can be conceived clearly and distinctly apart from the body, it is not only really distinct from the latter but can be made by God to exist apart from bodily substance. Hence mind and body are really distinct substances. In knowing the attributes of thought and extension in an adequate way, we know mind and body "completely," i.e., we know each as a complete substance, capable of separate existence. No confusion is possible between the two substances; their respective properties should therefore be kept strictly apart.

This real distinction between thinking and extended things can be established, even before the real existence of a material world and our own body has been proved. The mind is known to exist as a complete substance, even before any material things are known to exist. Even the Cartesian proof of the *existence of material objects* outside the mind is based on an analysis of the contents and acts of the mind.[30] I recognize in myself a *passive* power of perception which is capable of entertaining the images of sensible things. This power could not function, unless there were a corresponding *active* power, whether in myself or in some other being, for arousing these images in me. Such an active power is not resident in myself as a pure thinking thing, since some impressions come about without my deliberate intention or even (as in the case of a painful experience

---

[30] See the sixth section of *The Meditations concerning First Philosophy* (Lafleur, 64–80) and, more schematically, *The Principles of Philosophy*, II, 1 (Haldane-Ross, I, 255).

of heat) against my own desire. Hence the excitation or active arousal of sense perceptions in me is due to *some other substance,* which contains either formally or eminently all the reality found objectively in the sense ideas themselves. The sense arousal of my mind may come either from God or from another immaterial agent or from a material body. Descartes eliminates the possibility that sense perceptions are excited in us by God alone or by some other immaterial agent alone, and that existing sensible things contribute in no way to the arousal of such ideas. Were this so, a conflict would arise between God's *veracity* and the incorrigible, *natural belief* that these ideas somehow come directly from existing corporeal things. We cannot help but think that our mind has sense perceptions because it is somehow aroused by sensibly existent things, i.e., by beings that possess the objective reality of sensible ideas in a formal but noneminent way, and hence at the material level of existence. God is the author of this natural belief. Hence if He is not to violate His own truthfulness, a world of material substance, having concrete geometrical attributes of extension, must really exist. My own body and the world of extended nature enjoy an extramental reality of their own. Thus Descartes bridges the gap between real mind and real matter, not directly, but by an appeal to the divine veracity and to an incorrigible fact of natural belief. He does not anticipate the attempt of Berkeley to show that this belief in the reality of matter is indeed corrigible and that, therefore, the *non*existence of matter is perfectly reconcilable with God's truthfulness.

A final service rendered by metaphysics to philosophical physics is to supply the most general principles of physical deduction, along with the guarantee of *memory* as a God-given and, therefore, trustworthy power needed in all reasoning. Demonstration in physical matters rests upon the assurance of God's *immutability* (His fixed resolve to act in the same way in the production of the same sort of effect) and His constant *conserving* action from moment to moment of temporal duration. On this metaphysical foundation, Descartes formulates the three laws of motion which govern all change, specification, and duration of extended bodies. These explanatory laws of mechanics are so universal that they express the basic way in which *any* world would be framed by an efficient cause of local motion, acting without regard for substantial forms or qualitative change. The very infinity of the divine power and the generality of the primary physical laws prevent, however, any rigorous a priori derivation of *this* particular world of ours. Only by appeal to the deliverances of sense can one settle the question about which of several equally possible worlds has been *actually* produced by the cosmic maker. There is need of the empirical touchstone of *sensible experience,* as an indispensable principle of verification of the actual structure of material things. Descartes feels that he can appeal to the senses as a test of hypotheses about the real world, now that he has proved God's existence, His veracity, and hence the trustworthiness of the God-given senses in cases where reason is constrained to appeal to them, in order to anchor its deduction about our world. Cartesian rationalism admits this saving grace of an empirical residue of nondeducible experience, which provides a certain measure for deductive reasoning, whenever the latter claims to draw conclusions about the actual constitution of this world. But the senses hold a posterior and auxiliary position and are never permitted by Descartes to contribute toward the principles of knowledge.

7. MIND AND THE HUMAN COMPOSITE

There is a double gain for Descartes in the theory of mind and body as radically different substances, based upon mutually exclusive attributes of thought and extension. This dualism justifies at once a *mechanistic* philosophy of nature and a *spiritualistic* philosophy of mind. The *immateriality* of the mind is an immediate corollary from its nonextended character. It is sufficient to know that thinking is an attribute of mind, in order to conclude that extension and materiality have no foothold in the self. Does the *immortality* of the human mind flow from its immateriality? After some hesitation, Descartes declined to furnish a demonstration of immortality, a refusal shared in common with the nominalistic Scholastic thinkers. He contended that his critique of the senses and his proof of a substantial and immaterial (or spiritual) self supply the requisite principles for at least a strong belief in the mind's survival. Since it is nonmaterial and substantial, it *can* continue to exist after the body's dissolution. But in order to transform this possibility into an incontrovertible fact, the disposition of divine providence must be consulted, and this consultation lies beyond our power. Descartes refrained from making any final pronouncement about the issue, lest he be accused by freethinkers of pretending to have special access to the actual designs of God's providence.

The steep price Descartes had to pay for achieving this sharp
dualism between the mechanism of matter and the spiritualism of
mind was to place in jeopardy the *composite nature of man.* This is
a capital instance where his methodic approach compelled him to
become an innovator not only in regard to the mode of proof but
also the content itself. His problem was to explain how two complete,
substantial things, each essentially unordained to the other, could
nevertheless form a composite whole of a substantial sort. When
his onetime disciple Regius declared that the doctrine of two complete substances leads merely to a *per accidens* unity in man, Descartes
replied with acerbity that, according to his intention, the unity is a
per se one, a true substantial union or "commingling" of mind and
body.[31] From the standpoint of an act-potency theory of the nature
of a *per se,* substantial union, Regius was right in drawing such an
inference. What Descartes had to do, then, was to redefine the
meaning of a "per se unity," in order to bring it in line with his
dualism. This task he carried out in two steps: first, by explaining
a composite entity in terms of his theory of distinctions, and, second,
by explaining a substantial union in terms of his doctrine on nature.

1. A *composite entity* is a subject in which are found two or
more special attributes, each of which can be understood distinctly
without reference to the rest.[32] If two special attributes are present
in the same subject, and yet each can be understood distinctly without reference to the other, in that subject there are two really distinct
substances, which are not united together by any necessary bond.
The only kind of union possible between these two substances is a
contingent one, that is, one which is not required essentially by the
natures in question and hence not capable of an a priori, scientific
deduction. Only a sheer fact of *experience* can assure us of the actual
presence of a composite entity. Now this is precisely the case with
man. He is subject to such states of confused awareness as sensations
and feelings of pain and hunger, which seem to invade the thinking
thing from without and yet which belong intimately to it. We could
describe the pure thinking thing, apart from such disturbing states,
but we could never describe the actual man of our experience, without
pointing out that these confused states — where thinking and being

---

[31] *Letter to Regius,* January, 1642 (*Correspondance,* Adam-Milhaud, V, 112–114,
134–135).
[32] *Notes Directed against a Certain Programme* (Haldane-Ross, I, 437); for the
application to man, cf. *The Meditations concerning First Philosophy,* VI (Lafleur, 72).

extended are intermingled — belong to his make-up. The actual fact
of the union of thought and extension in a common subject cannot
be deduced from the essence of either a thinking thing or an extended
thing: it can be grasped only in an empirical way. The composite
nature of man is an unexpected melange, a disconcerting datum that
remains irremediably obscure and confused within the Cartesian
perspective of mental and bodily substances.

2. Given the undeniable fact of the human composite entity,
however, can it at least be explained in such a way that the union
of the two substances is more than an accidental one and yet not
modeled after the Thomistic account of a matter-form union?
Descartes attempts to satisfy these conditions with the aid of his
doctrine on *nature*. The term "nature" has four distinct, real meanings.[33] It signifies: (*a*) God Himself, insofar as He is the author of
the system of the world and its all-powerful conserver; (*b*) the total
order and system of finite things themselves, as dependent upon God;
(*c*) the arrangement or assemblage of all that God has disposed for
the thinking self alone or for the bodily world alone; (*d*) the
arrangement of things bearing reference to the human composite
entity, taken precisely as a union of mind and body.

The significance of the third and fourth senses of "nature" is that
there is a difference in nature between the self and the man.[34] *The
self* is the mind alone, the thinking substance, completely independent
from, and unreferred to, matter. *The man,* however, is the human
composite entity, a contingent whole, made up of the two substances:
thinking thing and extended thing. The self and the man agree,
insofar as each is a substantial unity in itself. But they are different
kinds of substantial unity, since they are different kinds of natures.
Descartes usually reserves the term *substantial unity of essence or
nature* to characterize the essential undividedness of the self, with
its single, special attribute of thought. He calls the human composite
entity or the man a *substantial unity of composition,* i.e., of nature in
the fourth sense. The man does not enjoy a strict unity of essence,
since there is no essential and necessary ordination of the thinking
thing and the extended thing to each other, or of their respective

---

[33] *Ibid.* (Lafleur, 72–73); later on (p. 76), Descartes mentions a purely con-
ceptual meaning of "nature," as when we say that something has a faulty nature.
[34] On the problem of the human composite, cf. *Replies to Objections,* IV, VI
(Haldane-Ross, II, 97–99, 102, 242–243, 256). Cf. the comparative study by J. A.
Mourant, "Cartesian Man and Thomistic Man," *The Journal of Philosophy,* 54 (1957),
373–382 (and discussion, 383–390).

attributes to each other. They are present together in the same human subject or unity of composition, but they do not constitute a unity of essence or of nature in the third and stricter sense. The unity of composition between two complete things or substances is a fact, manifested to us by our own experience of sensations and feelings, but its nature remains *incomprehensible* to us. All that we can say is that God produces such composite things for the sake of securing the order and unity of nature as a whole (in the second sense of "nature"). But since this involves God's final purpose for the universe, Descartes restrains philosophical inquiry at this point and rests content with the given but confused fact of the composite human entity, the man.

In working out this theory, Descartes accomplished a philosophical revolution. With respect to previous philosophy, he changed the meaning of the very problem of a substantial union. For the medievals, this problem was primarily one of *how* substantial principles could be joined in a composite whole. Descartes relegated this question entirely to the realm of the incomprehensible, since the previous solutions depended upon the theory of actual and potential coprinciples, which he had rejected. Instead, he restricted the problem of a substantial union to a description of the *fact* or *outcome* of the composition of two complete substances. The fact is known, since the special attributes of thought and extension indicate that the constituents in the composition are not merely logically distinct or related in a modal way: they are complete, substantial things. How the union can occur and what its structure is, are questions deliberately placed beyond human explanation and left for the infinite power and purpose of God. To say that mind and body are joined in a *per se* unity, then, does not specify anything positive about the manner of their union but only adverts to a given fact. The real distinction and independence of each constituent substance remain uncompromised by the union of composition, since the mind is still conceived as being an unextended and thinking thing.

For Descartes, *the self* remains intrinsically and essentially unaffected by its incorporation into *the man*. This is the conclusion he wishes to draw from his doctrine on the unity of the human composite, since it seems to provide an incontrovertible answer to the skeptical arguments against the immateriality and immortality of the soul. There is no intrinsic difficulty against survival of the self, since its contingent union with the body leaves its independence intact. The most that Descartes will concede to the experience of human unity is the following highly qualified admission:

> Nature also teaches me by these feelings of pain, hunger, thirst, and so on that I am not only residing in my body, as a pilot in his ship, but furthermore, that I am intimately connected with it, and that [the mixture is] so blended (as it were) that [something like] a single whole is produced.[35]

The "I" or the self is connected and "blended" with the body, but also retains its sovereign independence and essential lack of reference to the body and to the composite whole, which the soul and body together constitute. The union is a substantial one, only in the sense that the composite as such can exist, but this specifies nothing about the way in which the components are united. In the final analysis, Descartes admits that the union of mind and body can be looked at in two ways: from the standpoint of the self and from the standpoint of the man. In reference to *the man,* the union constitutes an *ens per se,* insofar as the human composite would not be an actual fact of unity of composition, unless the two substances were somehow joined together. But from the standpoint of the parts, especially *the self,* the union is *somehow accidental,* since it disturbs in no way the essential independence and self-subsistence of the substances involved. To counteract the freethinkers, Descartes is ready to sacrifice the substantial unity of the human composite to the immateriality of the thinking self.

This sinuous argument proved unsatisfactory both to Descartes' Thomistic opponents and to his rationalistic successors. The former regarded it as an ignoring of the main issue, which concerns the unity of the essence. Descartes did not establish the unity *of* a composite, substantial essence, actuated by a *single act of existing,* but rather a composition *among* substances, each of which retains its own act of existing. In the Thomistic meaning of the term, then, he did not secure the *per se* unity in the human essence. He transformed the problem from that of a union between proper act and potency to that between two substantial acts. Spinoza regarded this as an impossibility, unless there were a reduction of the supposed extended and thinking substances to the ontological status of modes of the one divine substance. Leibniz recoiled from this pantheistic solution but saw more

---

[35] *The Meditations concerning First Philosophy,* VI (Lafleur, 72).

clearly than did Descartes that (however one may choose to name it) the only possible sort of union between two or more substances, each of which retains its own existential act, is an operational one. But he contended that this operational union between act and act could rest upon essential relations among the united substances, even though each maintains its intrinsic autonomy. Among the empiricists, there developed the tendency simply to bypass any metaphysical explanation of the mind-body problem by declaring the investigation of substances to be out of bounds for the human mind. Whereas Descartes wanted to draw the line of inquiry at an explanation of the fact of a substantial union, the empiricists questioned even whether we can have any knowledge of a fact in the substantial order.

Another obstacle against securing a *per se* unity in man was Descartes' *mechanistic explanation of life.* In eliminating substantial forms in general, he also eliminated the soul, taken in the strict Aristotelian sense of the first informing principle of life. Hence he usually formulated the problem of man as one concerning *mind and body,* rather than *soul and matter.* Life is found only in mind and at the level of mind. Hence Descartes regarded animals as being only more complicated and subtle automata, the movements of which can be explained just as mechanically as the operations of cleverly constructed clocks or the fountains in the royal gardens. The human body is itself a machine, although one that gives ample evidence of being in intimate union with a higher substance. But that union cannot be patterned after the substantial union between a rational soul and its matter. Descartes had to explain it mechanistically, in terms of an *interactionist theory* of mind and body.[36] There is reciprocal influence of mind and body, each acting upon the other through efficient causality. The mind or soul (in a loose, non-hylemorphic sense) is joined to the whole body, but exercises its controlling functions through its special association with the pineal gland. This gland, which is the main seat of the soul, is a small and undivided mass in the brain. When an external object impinges upon the corporeal organs, it arouses an impulse that is carried by the nerves to the animal spirits (minute parts of the blood), bathing the cavity in which the pineal gland is situated. By this mechanism, different objects agitate the pineal in different ways. Since the mind

---

[36] Cf. *The Passions of the Soul,* I, 30–39 (Haldane-Ross, I, 345–349). See S. V. Keeling's expository and critical essay, "Cartesian Mechanism," *Philosophy,* 9 (1934), 51–66.

is naturally attuned to the movements of the pineal, the various agitations in that gland incite the mind to entertain perceptions corresponding to these movements and to their sources in the external world. Conversely, the pineal is so responsive to the commands of the mind, that it communicates the decisions of the human will to the animal spirits and thence to the nerves and muscles. In this way, the mind is affected by the body and can, in its turn, direct the body according to its own will.

Thus Descartes shifted the problem of the human composite from the metaphysical to the physiological plane. But the change of venue did not alleviate his difficulties, as his contemporaries were quick to point out. For one thing, the smallness of the pineal gland and the fact that it is not composed of two halves, do not dematerialize it or endow it with spiritual simplicity. It remains completely on the side of extended substance, leaving the chasm still unbridged between extended thing and thinking thing. Descartes begged the question of the mutual attunement of the mind and the pineal, as well as their ability to act directly upon one another. Having eliminated any intrinsic, act-potency causality between material and formal principles, Descartes was restricted to a mechanistic, efficient causality between mind and body. But his previous analysis of the antithesis between the special attributes of thought and extension militated against the ability of two mutually exclusive and independent kinds of substance to join together and act upon each other. A signal indication of the failure of interactionism to explain the unity of being and operation in man was the strictly *equivocal* way in which Descartes had to treat sensation, the presumed outcome of the interaction. Since he did not have a composite substantial essence, constituted by the substantial union of actual and potential principles, he could not regard sensation and feeling as *distinctive acts of the composite*. He was obliged to posit a *double set of sensations*. The sense powers and operations were viewed now as bodily states, and now as aspects of the mind, insofar as it attends to the body. This did not bridge the gap between corresponding modes belonging to really different and even opposed substances.

A similar stalemate is reached in regard to the *origin of ideas*. Descartes cannot allow the provisional description of their origin (as being adventitious, factitious, and innate) to stand unmodified. The measure of a successful theory of the human composite is its ability to explain ideas that seem to be adventitious or external in origin.

Descartes does not dismiss the note of externality as an illusion; yet his dualism of mind and body does not permit him to grant a genuine derivation of ideas from material existents. His compromise lies within the ambit of the Plotinian-Augustinian *active theory of sensation.*[37] Although mind as such is purely intellectual, it counts sense, imagination, and memory among its modes. These modes signify the mind's attention or reference to corporeal objects in certain of its cognitive acts. Adventitious ideas are said to come from bodies, insofar as the presence of certain bodily states determines the particular time of appearance, the complexity, and the obscure condition of certain ideas. The mind cannot really receive any corporeal likeness, but the presence of such a likeness as a bodily state is required so that the understanding may exercise the functions of sense, imagination, and sense memory. Even under these latter modes, the understanding neither *receives* the corporeal likeness nor *abstracts* from it an intentional or cognitive likeness, after the manner of the Aristotelian agent intellect. Rather, the mind *actively attends* to the bodily image and, in virtue of its own attending action, draws forth the "adventitious" ideas from itself.

Descartes feels himself warranted in calling the bodily motions the *occasion* of such ideas, since they furnish the external, bodily circumstances that stimulate the mind to act at a certain time and to refer its ideas to a certain external object. The mind itself is the principal cause, but, in its imaginative and sensitive functions, it requires an excitation from material things and images. In effect, this reduces *adventitious* to *innate ideas,* since the effect of the occasional cause is only to arouse the mind to produce ideas *by itself* and out of its own capacities. This satisfies the definition of innate ideas and, at the same time, reinforces the doctrine of the self-enclosure of minds, which Descartes describes (in anticipation of Leibniz) as existing with closed windows. The manner in which bodily images can arouse or

---

[37] For the historical background of this theory, consult V. J. Bourke, *Augustine's Quest of Wisdom* (Milwaukee, Bruce, 1945), 111–112, and the unpublished doctoral dissertation of Sister Mary Ann Ida Gannon, B.V.M., *The Active Theory of Sensation in Plotinus and Saint Augustine* (St. Louis University, 1952). Bourke notes that this view of sensation suffers from an essential subjectivity and requires an appeal to God as the guarantor of the veracity of human knowledge. For the Cartesian position on sensation, imagination, and innate ideas, cf. *The Principles of Philosophy,* IV, 189–190 (Haldane-Ross, I, 289–291); *The Passions of the Soul,* I, 20–23 (Haldane-Ross, I, 341–342); *The Meditations concerning First Philosophy,* II, VI (Lafleur, 34–35, 64–66); *Replies to Objections,* V (Haldane-Ross, II, 217, 227–228, 231); *Notes Directed against a Certain Programme* (Haldane-Ross, I, 442–444).

stimulate the mind is rendered no more intelligible, however, than the hypothesis of the pineal gland will permit.

8. TOWARD THE MORAL LIFE

Since Descartes never completed his work in the other parts of philosophy, he was never in the methodologically warranted position of developing a systematic ethics. But there is a moral purposiveness to all his speculations. Just as method begins with an appeal to every man's *bon sens* or good sense, so it culminates in the cultivation of *bona mens* or the capacity for acquiring moral wisdom. It is the same good sense and sound judgment which Descartes counts on, in us all, to develop from the universal doubt, through the various speculative parts of philosophy, to the plenitude of moral perfection, which crowns the search for philosophical wisdom.

The distinction between the *contemplation of truth* and the *conduct of life* means that methodic doubt, whose aim is the contemplation of truth, does not apply immediately to the moral convictions. For, unlike the order of pure thought, practical life consists of situations where a man must make forced options on probable grounds. He must choose some definite line of conduct, and hence he cannot and ought not wait for scientific certitude before making his decisions. Hence Descartes offers a *provisional code of morality,* intended to govern the active sphere during the period of doubt and critical inspection of all speculative truths. There are three basic precepts in this interim morality of temporal happiness, as set forth in the *Discourse on Method.* (1) Obey the prevailing laws and customs, adhere to the traditional religion, and follow the more moderate opinions; (2) be firm in resolutions and act on doubtful decisions just as firmly as on certain ones; (3) conquer oneself rather than fortune, be concerned about controlling one's own ideas, and be indifferent to whatever remains in external matters, after having done one's best.[38] These counsels reflect the popular Stoic moral attitude of the late Renaissance, especially as presented in the Lowlands by Justus Lipsius and in France by Guillaume Du Vair. Lest the program degenerate into sheer conformism and opportunism, Descartes specifically integrates it with his continued search after truth. The views of others are temporarily acceptable, only because

---

[38] *Discourse on Method,* III (Lafleur, 15–18). See R. Cumming, "Descartes' Provisional Morality," *The Review of Metaphysics,* 9 (1955), 207–235.

one is prepared eventually to *follow his own judgment,* when it becomes enlightened, and is presently doing all in his power to sift his convictions and discover better ones, if possible. Practical decisions are made with a view to their eventual revision, in the light of tested knowledge.

In a letter to the Princess Elizabeth, Descartes gave a succinct statement of the *definitive morality* toward which he was aiming.[39] Significantly, its three major precepts parallel those of the *Discourse,* thus giving a sample of the transformation to which moral convictions must submit. The chief difference is that, at the end of its quest, the trained mind is now equipped with a sound conception of reason, its fundamental truths and its central skills, especially the power of critical attention. (1) The well-disposed individual will use his mind as best he can in discovering what should be done; (2) he will have a firm and constant resolution to do all that his reason counsels; (3) doing all that he can, in accord with reason's dictates, he will regard the rest as lying beyond his power and will accustom himself not to desire it. In a word, the moral life depends upon a virtuous will, but the latter is one that is formed according to the truths perceived by right reason.

Man, however, is vulnerable to the exaggerated valuations induced by the passions, which sometimes displace the right estimates of reason. Descartes defines the *passions* as "the perceptions, feelings, or emotions of the soul which we relate specially to it, and which are caused, maintained, and fortified by some movement of the [animal] spirits."[40] He explains their genesis in the soul with the aid of the pineal gland, which is ordained "by nature" to make the mind sensitive to certain states of body and thus to arouse passions within it. The passions dispose us to desire the things that are of use to the maintenance and perfection of the body. They do not absolutely compel the will, and they can be indirectly controlled, by calling to mind images of the things which are usually united with the passions we desire to have. Descartes discards the Scholastic principle of division of the passions into the concupiscible and irascible, on the ground that it involves a distinction of parts in the soul. In its place, he substitutes an enumeration of *six primitive passions:* wonder, love, hatred, desire, pleasurable joy, and painful sadness. They are the

---

[39] *Letter to Princess Elizabeth,* August 4, 1645 (*Oeuvres de Descartes,* edited by Adam and Tannery, IV, 265–266).

[40] *The Passions of the Soul,* I, 27 (Haldane-Ross, I, 240).

components, by the combination of which all our passional states are formed. The discipline of the moral life consists in *mastering the passions,* by training the mind to judge deeds not merely by their immediate satisfaction but according to their real nature. Reason's estimate must then be adhered to, throughout a particular course of action and throughout a lifetime's search after happiness.

Two metaphysical truths are especially helpful in gaining self-control. Once God is known to exist and exercise a *loving providence,* a man can bear the ills of fortune with the assurance that they must eventually work to his true welfare. In the Cartesian blend of Stoicism and Christianity, "to follow nature" means to adhere to God's will and benevolent governance of all events. Similarly, the knowledge of the *soul's immateriality* and the belief in its *immortality* help the mind to overcome bodily dangers, especially the fear of death, and to establish a proper scale of values in which the primacy is given to the goods of the mind. All men aim at pleasure, but not all men are philosophically prepared to distinguish between pleasures of imagination and those of pure intelligence. The highest pleasure is *contentment of mind.* It springs from a stable will and an informed reason, from the inner assurance of making a virtuous use of free will or right judgment in practical affairs. The aim of the virtuous man's actions is the sovereign good, and his beatitude consists in the possession of this good. *God* is the objective sovereign good. If philosophy cannot put us in possession of Him, it can at least endow us with the degree of wisdom and self-control proportionate to our nature.[41]

The philosophical beatitude of a mind that is content within itself, and safe from fortune's slings and darts, is only surpassed on this earth by the certitude of faith. Descartes includes religion among the areas not touched provisionally by doubt, since religion is primarily a matter of salvation rather than of speculation, and stands on the side of the practical goods of life. Although he seeks to divorce

---

[41] In "The Moral Philosophy of Descartes and the Catholic Doctrine of Grace," *Dominican Studies,* 1 (1948), 149–167, M. Versfeld suggests that Cartesian morality finds its true center of gravity not in the objective good, God, but in a Neo-Stoic independence of mind, which comes close to Pelagianism (although Descartes formally denied this consequence). In the chain of the sciences, morality depends upon the progress made in the natural sciences. Since scientific progress is indefinite, we are never definitely sure of our concrete, objective moral good, and hence must rely inwardly upon mental contentment and outwardly upon the commands of civil authority.

philosophy from *theology,* Descartes claims that his philosophy is better able to defend the truths of *faith* than is Scholastic theology. He depreciates the intellectualist tendency in theology and views religion and faith as belonging in the practical domain of the will. Faith has a foundation in reason but is formally an *act of will.* After completing his inspection of the nature of reason, Descartes draws an analogy between the natural light of reason and the light of grace. Both can move the will infallibly and freely in its act of judgment. The supernatural authority of God makes the *light* of grace more evident and certain than that of natural evidence. But the *matter* or *content* of faith remains obscure in this life, whereas the content of philosophy and reason is clear and distinct. The point of contact between faith and philosophy is, as Pascal also surmised, *the idea of the infinite.* For all his tremendous urge to bring the knowable within the range of mathematical lucidity, Descartes allows the presence of the mystery of the infinite, as confronting our natural intelligence, and permits the hope of a further beatitude in eternal life. He avoids theological entanglements whenever he can, but he cannot finally seal off the movement of good sense toward a wisdom that is more than the wisdom of his philosophy.

SUMMARY

Descartes' aim was to give philosophy a rigorous, scientific method that could demonstrate the new world of physics and also some metaphysical truths about God and the soul. He broadened the meaning of the mathematical method to include every precise determination of order and measure, whether in the quantitative or the immaterial sphere. In order to have demonstration, he supposed that the number of simple natures is finite and that these natures are joined by an objective set of connections, observable by the mind. By "mind," moreover, he meant the purely intellectual power, operating apart from the senses in the formation of clear and distinct ideas. He accepted the Renaissance skeptical distrust of the senses, but added triumphantly that pure intelligence does not depend upon the senses for its proper data. His use of methodic doubt was aimed at providing philosophy with a starting point at once existential and independent of the testimony of the senses. Having obtained a purely intellectual grasp of the Cogito, however, he found himself faced with a new set of difficulties. He had to prove God's existence solely from himself, existing as equipped with the idea of God. This provided a wholly spiritual and inward demonstration, leading to an infinitely powerful essence, which brings forth its own existence and an idea of itself in the finite mind. From the twofold premise of self and God, Descartes then had to derive the knowledge of his own bodily existence and that of the physical world. The divine attributes of veracity and immutability were exploited, respectively, in the existential demonstration of the body and the world and in that of the laws of physical motion. Because of the complete distinction between the idea of a thinking thing and that of an extended thing, Descartes concluded that there are two different and complete substances in man. The self or thinking thing is immaterial and hence intrinsically independent of the body. This provides philosophical ground enough for belief in the immortality of man's spiritual principle. But then Descartes was faced with the problem of the human composite or the man, in which these two substances are somehow united in a substantial way. His appeal to the pineal gland extended the mechanistic view of man as far as possible, whereas his affirmation of the mind's ability to influence bodily states fitted in with his theory of the passions and his Stoic conception of moral self-control.

BIBLIOGRAPHICAL NOTE

1. *Sources and Translations.* The critical edition of the *Oeuvres de Descartes* was edited by C. Adam and P. Tannery, 12 Vols. (Paris: Cerf, 1897–1910), with a supplement and general index issued as Vol. 13 in 1913. For the use of students today, this edition is currently being reissued (Paris: Vrin, 1964 ff.), under the general editorship of B. Rochot, and with supplementary volumes intended to convey the Cartesian textual scholarship of the past half-century, especially in regard to the Correspondence. A new edition of the *Oeuvres philosophiques de Descartes* (Paris: Garnier, 1963), is being edited by F. Alquié, with all texts translated, arranged chronologically, and given an informative commentary. Two of the 3 Vols. have appeared. C. Adam and G. Milhaud issued a new edition of the *Correspondance de Descartes,* 8 Vols. (Paris: Presses Universitaires, 1936–1963), adding newly discovered letters, translating the Latin letters, and identifying Descartes' correspondents. A critical edition of the Latin text and a Dutch manuscript of the *Regulae ad directionem ingenii* ('The Hague: Nijhoff, 1966) is edited by G. Crapulli. Four good translations are: *The Philosophical Works of Descartes,* 2 Vols., reprinted with corrections (Cambridge: The University Press, 1931; New York: Dover Publications, 1955), translated by E. S. Haldane and G. R. T. Ross; *Philosophical Essays* (Indianapolis: Bobbs-Merrill, 1964), translated by L. J. Lafleur (includes the *Rules, Discourse on Method,* and *Meditations*); *Philosophical Writings* (New York: Modern Library, 1958), translated by N. K. Smith; *Discourse on Method, Optics, Geometry, and Meteorology* (Indianapolis: Bobbs-Merrill, 1965), translated by P. J. Olscamp.

2. *Studies.* E. S. Haldane's excellent biography, *Descartes, His Life and Times* (London: Murray, 1905), is based on the Adam-Tannery edition of his letters. The twelfth volume of this same edition contains Charles Adam's *Vie et oeuvres de Descartes,* the findings of which are summarized in a shorter book, *Descartes, sa vie et son oeuvre* (Paris: Boivin, 1937). A more recent biographical approach is C. Serrurier's *Descartes, l'homme*

et le penseur (Paris: Presses Universitaires, 1951). A comprehensive doctrinal synthesis is given by M. Guéroult, *Descartes selon l'ordre des raisons,* 2 Vols. (Paris: Aubier, 1953). Two multi-volumed interpretations of the intent and achievement of Descartes are notable. That Descartes seeks a new synthesis between Christianity, science, and humanism is the main theme in R. Lefèvre's four studies (Paris: Presses Universitaires): *La Vocation de Descartes* (1956); *L'Humanisme de Descartes* (1957); *Le Criticisme de Descartes* (1958); *La Bataille du "Cogito"* (1960). A careful historical analysis of major phases in Descartes' development is made in four books by Henri Gouhier (Paris: Vrin): *La Pensée religieuse de Descartes* (1924); *Essais sur Descartes* (1937): *Les Premières pensées de Descartes* (1958); and especially on the metaphysical foundations, *La Pensée métaphysique de Descartes* (1962). Three informative general introductions in English are: A. B. Gibson, *The Philosophy of Descartes* (London: Metheun, 1932); S. V. Keeling, *Descartes* (London: Benn, 1934); N. K. Smith, *New Studies in the Philosophy of Descartes* (London: Macmillan, 1952).

Cartesian methodology is examined from various standpoints by: C. Serrus, *La Méthode de Descartes et son application à la métaphysique* (Paris: Alcan, 1933); L. Roth, *Descartes' Discourse on Method* (Oxford: Clarendon, 1937); H. H. Joachim, *Descartes's Rules for the Direction of the Mind* (London: Allen and Unwin, 1957). An especially close analysis of the *Rules* is made in L. J. Beck's *The Method of Descartes* (Oxford: Clarendon, 1952). Beck makes a similar study of the *Meditations* in *The Metaphysics of Descartes* (New York: Oxford University Press, 1965). The originality of the Cartesian metaphysical meditation is defended by M. Versfeld, *An Essay on the Metaphysics of Descartes* (London: Metheun, 1940), and the presence of a strong empiricist strain in this rationalist thinker is brilliantly argued by J. Laporte, *Le Rationalisme de Descartes,* second ed. (Paris: Presses Universitaires, 1950). The mathematical and scientific sides of Descartes are studied by: J.-L. Allard, *Le Mathématisme de Descartes* (Ottawa: Éditions de l'Université, 1963); J. F. Scott, *The Scientific Work of René Descartes* (London: Taylor and Francis, 1952); J. Vuillemin, *Mathématiques et métaphysique chez Descartes* (Paris: Presses Universitaires, 1960). On the moral and religious thought of Descartes (in addition to the 1924 book by Gouhier, above), see: P. Mesnard, *Essai sur la morale de Descartes* (Paris: Boivin, 1936); J. Russier, *Sagesse cartésienne et religion* (Paris: Presses Universitaires, 1958), with stress on immortality; and J. Combès, *Le Dessein de la sagesse cartésienne* (Paris: Vitte, 1960).

A place apart has been earned by Étienne Gilson's publications in the Cartesian field. His *Index scolastico-cartésien* (Paris: Alcan, 1912) lists key terms in Descartes, provides the references in the Adam-Tannery edition, and then gives apposite quotations, under each term, from Scholastic sources probably known to Descartes; *La Liberté chez Descartes et la théologie* (Paris: Alcan, 1913) still illuminates Descartes' relations with the Oratorians, even though some of its findings are no longer acceptable to Gilson; *Études sur le rôle de la pensée médiévale dans la formation du système cartésien,* which is the second part of *Études de philosophie médiévale,* revised and considerably augmented (Paris: Vrin, 1951), discusses the Scholastic background of many Cartesian arguments; *René Descartes: Discours de la méthode, texte et commentaire,* second ed. (Paris: Vrin, 1947), reprints the Adam-Tannery text of the *Discours* and makes an exhaustive commentary, doctrinal and historical, with ramifications throughout the Cartesian system; the second part of *The Unity of Philosophical Experience* (New York: Scribner, 1937) is on "The Cartesian Experiment"; and there is a chapter on Descartes in E. Gilson and T. Langan, *Modern Philosophy: Descartes to Kant* (New York: Random House, 1963). Comparisons between Descartes and Aquinas are made in: J. Maritain, *Three Reformers: Luther, Descartes, Rousseau* (London: Sheed and Ward, 1928); J. Maritain, *The Dream of Descartes* (New York: Philosophical Library, 1944); E. A. Maziarz, *The Philosophy of Mathematics* (New York: Philosophical Library, 1950); A. G. A. Balz, *Descartes and the Modern Mind* (New Haven: Yale University Press, 1952), on the secularization of the faith-reason theme; P. Garin, *Thèses cartésiennes et thèses thomistes* (Paris: Desclée, 1933), on the eternal truths; J. De Finance, *Cogito cartésien et réflexion thomiste* (Paris: Beauchesne, 1946); F. Olgiati, *La filosofia di Descartes* (Milan: Vita e Pensiero, 1937). An annotated check list of studies on Descartes published between 1800 and 1960 is provided by G. Sebba, *Bibliographia Cartesiana* (The Hague: Nijhoff, 1964).

3. *Cartesians and Other Philosophers.* The complex relations which Descartes and the Cartesians sustained with skepticism are unraveled by: R. H. Popkin, *The History of Scepticism from Erasmus to Descartes* (New York: Humanities Press, 1960); J. S. Spink, *French Free-Thought from Gassendi to Voltaire* (London: Athlone Press, 1960); R. A. Watson, *The Downfall of Cartesianism, 1673–1712* (The Hague: Nijhoff, 1966), on the persistent skeptical counter-critique. The fortunes of the Cartesian school itself are traced by: F. Boullier, *Histoire de la philosophie cartésienne,* third ed., 2 Vols. (Paris: Delagrave, 1868); A. G. A. Balz, *Cartesian Studies* (New York: Columbia University Press, 1951); E. J. Dijksterhuis and others, *Descartes et le cartésianisme hollandais* (Paris: Presses Universitaires, 1960). Descartes is the point of departure for surveys of French philosophy made by L. Lévy-Bruhl, *History of Modern Philosophy in France* (Chicago: Open Court, 1899), and by H. Gouhier, *Les Grandes avenues de la pensée philosophique en france depuis Descartes* (Louvain: Nauwelaerts, 1966), as well as for L. M. Marsak's anthology: *French Philosophers from Descartes to Sartre* (New York: Meridian Books, 1961).

On Descartes' French contemporaries, Gassendi and Mersenne, consult: G. S. Brett, *The Philosophy of Gassendi* (New York, Macmillan, 1908); B. Rochot and others, *Pierre Gassendi: sa vie et son oeuvre* (Paris: Centre International, 1956); R. Lenoble, *Mersenne, ou la naissance du mecanisme* (Paris: Vrin, 1943). Malebranche's thought is examined from different perspectives in these general studies: H. Gouhier, *La Philosophie de Malebranche et son expérience religieuse,* second ed. (Paris: Vrin, 1948); M. Guéroult, *Malebranche,* 3 Vols. (Paris: Aubier, 1955–1959); A. Robinet,

Système et existence dans l'oeuvre de Malebranche (Paris: Vrin, 1965);
R. W. Church, *A Study in the Philosophy of Malebranche* (London: Allen
and Unwin, 1931); B. Rome, *The Philosophy of Malebranche* (Chicago:
Regnery, 1963), on the synthesis of science and faith. The Lafuma text
of Pascal's *Pensées* (Baltimore: Penguin Books, 1966) is translated by A.
J. Kreilsheimer; see also, *Great Shorter Works of Pascal* (Philadelphia:
Westminster, 1948), translated by E. Cailliet and J. C. Blankenagel; *The
Essential Pascal* (New York: New American Library, 1966), ed. by R.
Gleason and G. F. Pullen. F. Strowski, *Pascal et son temps,* 3 vols. (Paris:
Plon, 1907–1913) is a standard reference; J. Mesnard, *Pascal, His Life and
Works* (New York: Philosophical Library, 1952), reports on more recent
studies; J. Russier, *La Foi selon Pascal,* 2 Vols. (Paris: Presses Universi-
taires, 1949) concentrates on the problem of faith. Among accounts of his
life and thought are: M. Bishop, *Pascal, the Life of Genius* (New York:
Reynal and Hitchcock, 1936); E. Cailliet, *Pascal, the Emergence of Genius,*
second ed. (New York: Harper Torchbook, 1961); M. L. Hubert, *Pascal's
Unfinished Apology* (New Haven: Yale University Press, 1952); E. Mor-
timer, *Blaise Pascal: The Life and Work of a Realist* (New York: Harper,
1959). Antoine Arnauld's influential Port-Royal Logic, *The Art of Thinking* (Indianapolis: Bobbs-Merrill, 1964) is available in a translation by J.
Dickoff, and P. James. A. Levi, *French Moralists* (Oxford: Clarendon,
1964), considers the moral tradition.

Giambattista Vico, the major Italian philosopher and critic of Descartes,
can be read in reliable translations: *The Autobiography of Giambattista
Vico* (Ithaca: Cornell University Press, 1944) (Cornell: Great Seal paperback, 1963), translated by M. H. Fisch and T. G. Bergin; *The New Science
of Giambattista Vico* (Ithaca: Cornell University Press, 1948), revised and
abridged paperback ed. (New York: Doubleday-Anchor, 1961), translated
by T. G. Bergin and M. H. Fisch; *On the Study Methods of Our Time*
(Indianapolis: Bobbs-Merrill, 1965), translated by E. Gianturco. Introductions to his unusually concrete thought-world come from: R. Flint, *Vico*
(Edinburgh: Blackwood, 1884); H. P. Adams, *The Life and Writings of
Giambattista Vico* (London: Allen and Unwin, 1935); and A. R.
Caponigri, *Time and Idea: The Theory of History in Giambattista Vico*
(Chicago: Regnery, 1953). F. Amerio's *Introduzione allo studio di G. B.
Vico* (Turin: Società Editrice Internazionale, 1947) corrects the routine
idealistic view of Vico, discusses his attack upon Descartes, and shows his
stress on providence (in opposition to Bayle) and Christian Platonism. On
Italian philosophy from Vico to the mid-nineteenth century rise of Hege-
lianism, see M. F. Sciacca, *La filosofia nell'età del Risorgimento* (Milan:
Vallardi, 1948), with rich bibliographical aids.

Chapter II. BENEDICT SPINOZA

I. LIFE AND WRITINGS

IN 1593, a band of refugee Spanish and Portuguese Jews sought asylum in Amsterdam, thus forming the core of a Jewish community which soon had its own religious, educational, legal, and economic system. Baruch or Benedict Spinoza was born into this community in 1632. He received a thorough training in Hebrew literature, becoming well versed in the Bible, the Talmud, and the Cabala. Nevertheless his dissatisfaction with the anthropomorphic conceptions of God in the Talmud and the phantasmagoria in the Cabala led him to consult Maimonides, Gersonides, Crescas, and other great Jewish medieval thinkers for rational statements about God and the world. From these latter sources (as well as from certain passages in the Cabala), Spinoza obtained suggestions for his own position concerning the power of reason, the oneness of God and infinite nature, the attribution of infinite, indivisible extension to God, panpsychism, and a deterministic emanation of the world from God. Between 1651 and 1654, his interests broadened to include non-Jewish thought. His mastery of Latin was perfected under an ex-Jesuit, Francis van den Enden, who also probably introduced him to Cartesianism. Besides doing work in physics and mathematics, Spinoza read some of the Renaissance versions of Neo-Platonism and Stoicism and even consulted some Dutch Protestant Scholastic manuals. He ceased to observe Jewish regulations and was tricked into disclosing his belief that extension is present in God, that angels are imaginary beings, and that the Bible does not teach the immortality of the soul. He was examined by a board of Jewish theologians and was solemnly excommunicated from the Jewish community (1656).

After his expulsion, Spinoza supported himself by grinding lenses, the income from which was supplemented by a pension reluctantly accepted from the estate of one of his students who had died prematurely. Spinoza gave private philosophical instruction to several students and engaged in wide correspondence with learned men and amateurs alike. His first book, *Parts I and II of René Descartes' Principles of Philosophy* (with an appendix, *Metaphysical Thoughts;* issued, 1663), was the only one published under his own name during his lifetime. It explained the first two parts of Descartes' *Principles* and made some veiled criticisms. Yet it refrained from making an explicit attack on Descartes, in the hope of interesting Cartesian readers in a formal presentation of Spinoza's own philosophy. He began this positive exposition in the *Short Treatise on God, Man, and His Well-Being* (written, 1658–1660; Latin original lost, but two Dutch translations found and published, 1862 and 1869). The main lines of his pantheism were now fixed but he was still searching for the proper order and form of exposition. After 1660, Spinoza began to recast his thought in the *Treatise on the Healing of the Understanding,* where a general introduction to his philosophy and a theory of method may be found. But the work was never completed and was published only posthumously (1677) in fragmentary form. Its interruption was probably due to the fact that Spinoza had already settled upon the geometrical order of reasoning and had started to develop his definitive philosophy in *Ethics Demonstrated According to the Geometrical Order.* By 1665, he completed a first draft of the *Ethics,* in three parts, but interrupted the project in order to help his friend, Jan De Witt, the Grand Pensionary of Holland.

De Witt's efforts to disestablish the Reformed Church in the Netherlands had met with stiff opposition from the Calvinist clergy. In his *Theologico-Political Treatise* (published anonymously, 1670), Spinoza argued that the Church as such has no sovereignty, either within or alongside of the state. He also undermined the authority of the clergy by giving a rationalistic interpretation of revelation and miracles. When the De Witt brothers were murdered in 1672, Spinoza was outraged. In 1673, he politely refused the offer of the chair of philosophy at Heidelberg University, lest his freedom of thought be restricted by the condition that he should say nothing to disturb the established religion. During the years 1670–1675, he revised his *Ethics* and expanded it to its present five parts. But so great was the public furore at the news of its imminent publication that, in 1675, Spinoza was forced to withdraw it from the printer. He died in February, 1677, the victim of tuberculosis, aggravated by the dust breathed in from the lenses he ground. In November of the same year, his *Ethics* appeared, along with the *Treatise on the*

Healing of the Understanding and the unfinished *Political Treatise* (started in 1675).

2. THE METHOD OF HEALING THE UNDERSTANDING

Descartes' influence upon Spinoza was great but not overpowering. Sometimes the Cartesian contribution is exaggerated to the point where Spinoza is regarded merely as drawing out the latent pantheistic consequences of his predecessor's thought. However, this view overlooks two crucial facts: Spinoza's claim to have made radical innovations, and the origin of the principles wherewith he criticized Descartes. A man who could be accused by the Jewish community of holding that God is somehow a body, that there are no pure spirits or angels, and that the soul is one with the body's life, was already in firm possession of a nucleus of views that were at variance with those of Descartes, even before he became acquainted with the latter's works.[1] Spinoza's early speculation on the nature of God, man, and the material world furnished him with a basic *set of standards* for appraising the Cartesian philosophy and appropriating precisely those elements which proved to be congenial.

Nothing is gained, of course, by going to the other extreme of claiming that Descartes' part in the formation of Spinoza's mind was negligible. His contact with Cartesian philosophy was of decisive importance to his development, saving him from being a minor heterodox thinker, like Uriel da Costa, and installing him at the very center of seventeenth-century speculation. Descartes communicated to Spinoza that confidence in the scientific spirit and the mathematical way of reasoning that marks the difference between inarticulate protest against tradition and a powerfully constructed effort in philosophy. Whereas Maimonides encouraged Spinoza to make independent use of his reason, it was Descartes who introduced him to the *specific procedures, terminology,* and *problems* that made Spinoza's arguments relevant to his own age.

Spinoza surpassed Descartes both in recognizing the importance of forging a sound method and in refusing to cultivate methodology for its own sake. Methodological inquiries are to be integrated with those of philosophy as a whole and are to respect the metaphysical and moral ordination of philosophizing. The purpose of method is not only to promote the theoretical explanation of reality

---

[1] Cf. *The Oldest Biography of Spinoza* (A. Wolf edition, 45–46).

but also to advance the soul in its search after lasting happiness. Both the Cartesian and the Spinozistic doctrines on wisdom have a primarily *practical* and *moral import*. Even to inquire in a speculative spirit about whether there is an infinite and eternal good, and whether it is worth striving for, involves a change of pace and a redirection of one's practical life and energies. Spinoza makes the moral context of his methodology unmistakably clear. We must inquire about the kinds of knowledge and the way to attain the highest sort, because such knowledge is necessary *for pursuing the highest good* and for discovering the extent to which other things are good or evil, i.e., lead us toward or away from the supreme source of happiness.

This underlying moral purpose is brought out in the very title of his book on method: *On the Healing of the Understanding (De Intellectus Emendatione)*. The word *emendatio* means something stronger than an "improvement": it connotes a "correction" or, better still, a "healing" of the mind. The implication is that the understanding, in straying away from the truth, has injured itself and deprived itself of due perfection. To apprehend things truly and without fear of error belongs to the birthright of the understanding, considered in its own nature. *Not* to have the truth is a *privation* that affects one's happiness. In restoring the capacity to judge things correctly, philosophy is simultaneously restoring one's moral power and capacity for lasting happiness. Methodology provides the first step in the right direction, since it makes us aware that there are various grades of knowledge and provides a guide for acquiring the highest.

Spinoza distinguishes *four degrees of perception:* (1) that arising from hearsay and conventional signs, (2) that based upon undisciplined experience, (3) that based on scientific inference from effect to cause or from general definition to a property or particular application, and (4) that issuing from a direct sight of the essential nature, either in itself or in its proximate cause. There is no difficulty about evaluating these sources of information, once the *goal of knowledge* is made clear. Spinoza's theory of method is an instrument for leading people to the summit of wisdom: "the knowledge of the union existing between the mind and the whole of nature."[2]

---

[2] *On the Improvement of the Understanding* (Elwes translation, as reprinted in *Spinoza Selections*, edited by J. Wild, 5). The four degrees of perception are described in *ibid.* (Wild, 7); cf. *Ethics*, II, 40, Scholium 2 (White translation, as reprinted in

There is an entire metaphysics packed behind this simple observation, a metaphysics that is also the core of man's moral rehabilitation. One of the difficulties about examining Spinoza's theory of method is that it is regulated throughout by this *basic postulate* about the goal of human knowledge, which postulate in turn is then defended in terms of the new method. From his own standpoint, this circular procedure is justified by the overruling conviction that a way must be found for conveying the truth about the union of mind and nature to intellects that are crippled and led astray by temporal appearances.

Which of the above modes of perception is *best suited* to yield man a knowledge of himself and nature? The first two varieties are obviously inadequate, since they never attain the essence of the thing and hence never give definite, reliable knowledge. The scientific understanding of the essence begins only at the third level, that of the physical and mathematical sciences. They furnish the genuine idea or essence of the thing and therewith a reliable basis for further inference. But they are far from providing the highest sort of knowledge and the perfection that stems from it. The peak is reached only with the fourth type of perception. For, it is not as satisfactory to infer the cause a posteriori, from the effect, as it is to see the cause directly in its own nature; similarly, a thing is not known as precisely and exhaustively through a general definition as through a priori knowledge of its proximate cause. Hence Spinoza concludes that the proper method in philosophy is the one adapted to the *fourth* or *highest conceivable* sort of knowledge.

He chooses to model his method upon the pattern of the fourth mode of perception because, considered in itself, it would yield the most perfect sort of knowledge. He is impatient of the objection that the highest conceivable degree of knowledge might not be *within the reach of man,* in his actual condition, and hence might not provide a suitable pattern for philosophical method. Spinoza's philosophy is a tremendous plea that the highest knowledge does come within our power. The theory of man's nature must be modified so as to substantiate the claim that a human philosophy can lead to an intuition of the whole of reality. This is the ambitious *emendatio* attempted by Spinoza: it is both a *purging* of human limits and

Spinoza Selections, edited by J. Wild, 186–187). For an epitome of Spinoza's methodology, cf. *Letter XXXVII* (*The Correspondence of Spinoza,* translated by A. Wolf, 227–228). Quotations from *Spinoza Selections* are made with the permission of Charles Scribner's Sons.

an *elevation* to the divine standpoint. Yet, in practice, Spinoza cannot leave behind the three inferior modes of perception. Not only in making contact with other minds but also in building up his own position, he must often conform with the residue of limitations, still remaining upon human intelligence.

Through his doctrine on the *true idea,* Spinoza hopes to show the feasibility of his plan of obtaining intuitive insight into the entire order of nature.[3] A true idea differs from its *ideatum* or referent in the real order. Employing Cartesian terminology, Spinoza distinguishes between the *formal essence* or actual nature of the thing known and its *objective* or *representative essence,* which is nothing other than the true idea of the thing in the mind of the knower. The mind can possess the objective essence of things and thus have truth and certainty about the things in their formal essence. In order to show that there is a complete identity between the objective essence, the true idea and objective certainty about the physical thing, Spinoza explains the meaning of *reflection.* Since the true idea is itself an essence or mode of being, the mind can regard this essence in two ways: either in its objective, representative capacity (as *informing about* the essential nature of another real thing) or in its own formal reality (precisely as *having* an essential structure of its own, albeit one in the ideal order only). Viewing the idea from the latter perspective, the mind can then form an idea of this idea, by a reflective act. Now, in order to know, it is not necessary to know *that I know.* Quite the contrary, in order to know *that I know* (i.e., in order to have reflective knowledge), I must first of all directly know something. Knowledge is grounded ultimately in a direct apprehension of the formal essence of the physical thing, through its objective essence. Possession of this objective essence constitutes truth and certainty in the primary sense. Reflection is possible only within the context of a *given* true idea or objective essence of a thing. Otherwise, there would be an infinite regress and no foothold for the least item of actual knowledge.

This discussion of the true idea is relevant for a *criticism of the*

---

[3] *On the Improvement of the Understanding* (Wild, 11–13); that we do, in fact, possess a true idea as the natural equipment or inborn tool of the mind, is the underlying presupposition. On this theory of truth, see L. Terrasse, "La doctrine spinoziste de la verité d'après le *Traité de la Réforme de l'Entendement,*" *Chronicon Spinozanum,* III (1923), 204–231. The *Chronicon Spinozanum* was a specialized journal, devoted to studies on Spinoza's philosophy written by the leading Spinozistic scholars.

Cartesian method. For an idea is *true by its own nature* and not by reason of any added traits. Instead of occupying himself with the signs or criteria of true ideas, Spinoza declares that it is enough to have the ideas themselves. They carry their own guarantee, through the intrinsic weight of their representative function. To be certain about them, there is no need to go outside of them or to subject them to any technique of doubt. Furthermore, Spinoza's rigorous dualism of mind and body will not permit him to compromise, even in language or loose expression, concerning the origin of true ideas. They are brought forth by the native power of the understanding and are in no way derived from things. True ideas do, indeed, *conform with* the order of reality and inform us about it, but they are *not drawn from* the things they represent. Hence the existential status of the finite thing is not decisive for human knowledge, although we must clarify the meaning of existence.

Not only do individual, true ideas conform with individual things: they also display the same order, connection, and *ratio* as the order, connection, and *ratio* of things.[4] This is the extreme *rationalistic principle* which enables Spinoza to assert that the highest conceivable sort of knowledge can come within our human reach. He censures Descartes for stressing the limits and weakness of the human mind, since to this extent Descartes withdraws from the ultimate consequences of rationalism and refuses to grant a perfect, mirrorlike knowledge to the human mind. Spinoza uses his principle of the correspondence between true ideas and things to settle the important question of the *proper starting point* of methodic thinking. In general, method is the same as reflective knowledge: it is an idea of an idea. Everything depends, therefore, upon the character of the original idea, of which the method is a reflective articulation. A true method will be based on a true idea, and the best method on the best or most perfect idea. As Descartes taught, ideas are graded according to their objective reality or what they represent. If the order of our thoughts should correspond in all ways to that of things, then the best methodic reflection should begin with *the idea of the most perfect being, God,* the origin of all things. Spinoza glides from saying that our thought should *recapture* as much as possible of the order of

---

[4] "The *ratio* existing between two ideas is the same as the *ratio* between the formal essences corresponding to those ideas." *On the Improvement of the Understanding* (Wild, 14; translation modified and italics added). *"The order and connection of ideas is the same as the order and connection of things."* *Ethics,* II, 7 (Wild, 149).

things, to saying that, to be true in the highest, attainable way, human thought must *follow* the same path as the order of things. He lays down an identity between the order of being and the best order of human knowing, between the order of discovery and that of exposition. Hence he criticizes Descartes for starting with the human Cogito. In the real order — which our reflective thought should exactly reproduce — it is from God, and not from the human self, that things emerge to comprise an existing, orderly universe. The right method begins with the idea of God, since in the realm of thought, the idea of God has the same creative vigor as the power of God enjoys in respect to real things.

There is another reason why Spinoza had to deny a proper distinction between the order of knowing and the order of being, at the level of the highest kind of knowledge within human reach. For, he felt that Descartes had provided no adequate ground, epistemological or ontological, for the *process of scientific inference*. In Spinoza's estimation, Descartes was so thoroughly committed to the criterion of distinctness among ideas, that he ultimately cut off one idea from another. His system provided no means of justifying the passage of thought from one true idea to another, except by begging the issue and assuming that all ideas, as well as things, have a participated or interconnected nature. A *discrete* logic of distinct ideas could never develop a system, where *continuity* of inference should reign. Both the empiricists and Spinoza pressed home this difficulty. Hume sought a solution in the psychological laws of association, but Spinoza relegated these laws to the side of the individual organism. They could not serve as the foundation of a meaning open to all men. Hence his solution had to be a metaphysical one.

The continuity of philosophical deduction is only the obverse face of the continuity of things. Even in his treatise on method, Spinoza is obliged to postulate that all things are *connected and rendered continuous by and in God*. He establishes a correlation between a monism of modal things and a methodological precept that reflection should begin with the idea of God. Only by starting reflection with the principle from which things proceed in continuous gradation, can one also achieve continuity in thought. Philosophy becomes an interconnected system of true ideas, by reproducing the concatenation and dynamic unity of things or modes in God. Once in reflective possession of the primal, productive idea of God, the human mind will be nourished by its fertile power and will deduce, in proper order and continuity, the entire series of natural things. If Spinoza had not become a pantheistic monist in virtue of his early religious difficulties, his criticism of Descartes' atomistic logic would have led him to his view, as providing the best guarantee of systematic deduction.

All this supposes, however, that in fact we have a true idea, that we can gain a true idea of God, and that we can explain error and widespread ignorance about having the true idea. The last point represents a serious objection, as Spinoza admits. Skeptics may argue that an infinite regress is unavoidable, since method must start with a given true idea and yet must also prove that any given idea is a true one. Spinoza's reply uncovers another facet of the nature of method. He shows no tolerance toward those cautious, skeptical people, who refuse to take the risk of using their minds in one forthright act, which may well be one of real knowledge. They are rendered speculatively dumb and, in practical affairs, are automata, subject to the necessities of life. Above all, they remain unconscious of their own nature, since they are unwilling to observe it in actual operation. Method, as Spinoza conceives it, is *a practice in inward meditation, a growth in self-consciousness, a coming into reflective awareness of what we really are.*[5] The outstanding hindrances to self-understanding are: current misconceptions of the nature of the human mind (especially the philosophies of Descartes and Bacon), the obscurity of mind caused by the changing temporal order (which convinces us that the mind is not governed by eternal laws), and the lack of disciplined attention and discernment.

Spinoza's metaphysics will show that the human mind is a thinking thing, whose nature is precisely *to give birth to a true idea.* There is no need to pass the test of Cartesian doubt, for this procedure is a sign of the mind's weakness, not of its strength. He who grasps the essence of an idea also perceives its truth: he cannot honestly frame fictions about it, regard it as false, or call it into doubt. Method must begin with the recognition of the presence of a true idea within oneself. More precisely still, Spinoza plans to show that the human mind *is* a true idea, *is* a finite modal expression of the divine substance itself, under the attribute of thought. This is the hidden

---

[5] Men who fail to use the proper method "are not conscious of themselves. . . . [Method] will be absolutely perfect when the mind gains a knowledge of the absolutely perfect being or becomes conscious thereof." *On the Improvement of the Understanding* (Wild, 14, 17).

suggestion toward which the treatise *On the Healing of the Understanding* is directed. Spinoza implies that a sufficiently penetrative self-awareness will reveal that the understanding, in its own nature, is nothing other than a true idea, correlated with a mode of extension, both of them expressing an aspect of the divine being. To look for the true idea is to look for the nature of one's own mind. To seek the idea of God is to seek to know oneself in the most radical way, as an expression of the divine thought: the human mind not only *has* but *is* an idea of God.

Nevertheless, the fact of error presents a stumbling block to this entire project of methodic thinking. Under ideal conditions, there would be no need to expend great mental energies in order to attain the grand metaphysical truths about God, mind, and nature. They would be the natural, undisputed points of departure for all speculation. Spinoza maintains that these truths still have the right to this primary position, and yet he must explain why error can and does arise. He rejects Descartes' explanation, based on the infinite freedom and range of the will. Such a conception of the boundless power of will is highly repugnant to a mind that is seeking an order of rational necessities, to which both our intellect and our will must submit. Instead, Spinoza advances *four causes of human error* that will not embarrass his general outlook.[6] (1) The basic condition, making error possible, is the partial nature of our minds: they are only parts of the divine thinking substance and often give only fragmentary expression to its ideas. (2) The imagination is affected by particular physical objects and external causes, thus subjecting the mind to ideas in a complex, confused state. (3) Our reasoning is often carried on in too abstract and general a fashion. (4) We fail to follow the due order of investigation, which should begin with the primary elements of thought.

The remedy for these defects is, in every case, the same: *make a return to the idea of God* immanent within one's nature. (1) The more the mind feeds on the idea of the most perfect being, the more perfect the mind itself becomes and the less subject to the partial, finite condition of our nature. The power of self-affirmation that Descartes claimed for the idea of God, in proving God's existence, is now extended by Spinoza to include its generative power for producing an entire system of philosophical truths. (2) This growth

---

[6] *Ibid.* (Wild, 28–30). For an idealistic criticism of Spinoza's theory of error, see H. H. Joachim, *Spinoza's Tractatus De Intellectus Emendatione,* 151–181.

in the power of the understanding enables it to rely upon its inward resources and thus to distinguish between its own clear and distinct ideas and the inadequate ones of imagination. Especially, the idea of God cannot be confused with ideas representing mutable things in an indistinct way. (3) Moreover, this idea of God is not a mere abstraction or general principle. It is the supreme concrete and individual idea, required as the principle of metaphysical deduction. (4) Finally, the primary elements from which thought should proceed are not the atomistic results of Cartesian reductive analysis, doubt, and introspection. We must begin with the primal nature and power of God. In the idea of God is found both the sovereign specific against error-and-doubt and the *primum* of methodic thinking about the real. Right order in philosophy consists in permitting the idea of the cause of all things to be itself the cause of our other ideas, so that the concatenation of our ideas will exactly reproduce the eternal order and law of things, as originally produced by God.

Yet even this elaborate treatment of error describes its conditions rather than renders intelligible *why* and *how* such conditions could arise in a universe comprised of but the one divine substance. The first two reasons for error, given above, amount to saying that error arises because we are finite, composite beings. They do not explain how we could have become so *forgetful* of our partial nature or so *reliant* upon, and vulnerable to, imagination and outside influences. Another question they raise is how there can arise, in a monism of substantial power, disruptive and deceiving lines of causal influence. Similarly, the last two reasons for error leave unanswered the question of why most people must find their way to the knowledge of God by starting with something more immediately within their experience and ability to comprehend. The *factual discrepancy* between the order of reasoning and the order of being, within a strictly determined universe, means that there is some unexpected gap between what is, and what should and (by right) must be, the order of our thinking. At least, the answer cannot be given in purely methodological terms.

Spinoza raises the hope that, whatever the difficulties of explaining the causes of error, at least they can be overcome by allying ourselves with the *eternally necessary laws* operative in the mind as well as in the external world. He bases this hope upon an analysis of the properties of the understanding, even risking a return to the third mode of perception, in which a thing's nature is inferred from its properties. He seeks to transcend a mere a posteriori inference by noting that, if we reflect sufficiently upon the mind's properties and thus come to know them and the mind *adequately,* then by the definition of adequate knowledge the mind will have manifested itself and provided the essential a priori grounds for grasping its own properties. This is typical of Spinoza's approach to the modes of perception. He is obliged, in human fashion, to work back to a nature from its properties. But, having reached the nature itself, he then takes a *de jure* view of the properties, as flowing from the nature, and maintains that this essential knowledge belongs to the fourth mode and overcomes its a posteriori origin. In point of fact, however, Spinoza reaches his highest mode of perception only by transforming the *way of discovery* into the *way of demonstrative exposition.* This methodological shift does not actually cancel out the inherent difference between the order of being and that of knowing, as far as *men* are concerned.

If we examine our own ideas from the standpoint of their objective or representative perfection, we see that those which express the *affirmative,* the *absolute,* the *eternal,* and the *infinite,* are more perfect than those which signify the negative, the relative, the temporal, and the finite. Hence the former set of traits furnishes Spinoza with a clue about the properties of the understanding and its essential nature. It is essentially fitted to grasp the idea of that being in which alone are realized the perfections by which knowledge is measured. If the mind be a thinking thing, which gives birth to a true idea, then the primary true idea, to which it is naturally ordained, is that of the affirmative, absolute, eternal, and infinite being of God. Method calls attention to the nature of the mind as the faculty of the divine, and asks philosophy to begin there. That is precisely where the *Ethics* does begin.

3. DIVINE SUBSTANCE AND ITS ATTRIBUTES

The *Ethics* is composed *ordine geometrico,* a phrase that can be interpreted in two ways. In its most obvious sense, it refers to the *literary mold* in which the matter is cast. Like Euclid, Spinoza begins his masterpiece by laying down certain definitions and axioms, and then proceeds to offer demonstration of a series of interdependent propositions, flanked by numerous corollaries, scholia, and lemmata. This machinery is intended to supply for the weakness of our mind, by fixing concepts clearly and distinctly, by spelling out the precise inferences, and by giving memory an easy path to retread. It also has the incidental advantage of presenting an impersonal philosophy impersonally and unsentimentally, so that the reader will be convinced that he is witnessing the fertile power of the idea of God working out its own articulations, through Spinoza's pen. A philosophy presented in the geometrical form also had, for Spinoza's century, an airtight appearance of absolute rigor and consistency. In actual practice, of course, Spinoza uses his frequent scholia and appendixes to break through the confines of the geometrical pattern. These asides contain a budget of unscheduled observations, polemical attacks, and psychological notes, which will not bear confinement.

The deeper meaning of the phrase *ordine geometrico* is that the *Ethics* has been thought out in Spinoza's mind in accord with the *geometrical spirit of philosophizing,* made familiar by Descartes. There is a passage from known premises to previously unknown conclusions, through demonstrative reasoning. Whereas Descartes had mainly employed the analytic method, as more appropriate to the discovery of first truths imbedded in our experience, Spinoza deemed the time to be ripe for using the *synthetic method* of starting at once from primary truths and demonstrating their consequences. The synthetic approach begins from that which is most intelligible in itself, God, and proceeds to the things of our experience. Hence the *Ethics* supposes that the methodological recall of man to meditation upon the idea of God within himself, has been successful. Thereupon, it begins at once with the first real being and advances synthetically to the things that proceed from God. What had been the proper theological order in the medieval *Summa* now becomes the only proper philosophical order in the modern system, constructed in the full mathematical spirit. Moreover, whereas Descartes banished final cause only from philosophy of nature, Spinoza removed finality and freedom from all philosophical investigations. He agreed with Hobbes that, in a thoroughly mathematical philosophy, they have no legitimate place, any more than does the Cartesian appeal to God as an *asylum ignorantiae* or inscrutable center of arbitrary power.

The first book of the *Ethics* begins with the following definitions, which determine the whole course of the argument.

I. By cause of itself, I understand that, whose essence involves existence; or that, whose nature cannot be conceived unless existing.

II. That thing is called finite-in-its-own-kind which can be limited by another thing of the same nature. . . .

III. By substance, I understand that which is in itself and is conceived through itself; in other words, that, the conception of which does not need the conception of another thing from which it must be formed.

IV. By attribute, I understand that which the intellect perceives of substance, as if constituting its essence.

V. By mode, I understand the affections of substance, or that which is in another thing, through which also it is conceived.

VI. By God, I understand Being absolutely infinite, that is to say, substance consisting of infinite attributes, each one of which expresses eternal and infinite essence. . . .

VII. That thing is called free which exists from the necessity of its own nature alone, and is determined to action by itself alone. That thing, on the other hand, is called necessary, or rather compelled, which by another is determined to existence and action in a fixed and prescribed way.

VIII. By eternity, I understand existence itself, so far as it is conceived necessarily to follow from the definition alone of the eternal thing.[7]

However arbitrary the assigned meanings may be, these propositions are in strict formal accord with the conditions, laid down in Spinoza's methodological treatise, for *definitions of uncreated and created things* (taking "creation" in the loose sense of any production from a first cause).[8] In the case of an *uncreated,* self-existent being or *causa sui,* four rules must be observed. (1) It must be defined solely through its own essence and not through another being as its cause — hence philosophy is not adequately defined by Descartes and others as a search after causes. (2) The definition must be such as to leave no room for doubt about the existence of the thing defined — it is to be specified as an eternal existent. (3) The definition must not be abstract but must express a particular affirmative essence. (4) Wherever possible, the definition should be generative of all the properties of the thing defined. A *created* thing, i.e., one that is not self-existent but dependent upon a cause, must be defined through its proximate cause. From the definition, one should be able to deduce all the properties of the thing, considered only in itself.

These canons of definition are followed scrupulously in the initial set of Spinoza's metaphysical definitions. Thus (1) it is clear that God as *causa sui* cannot be explained through anything else. He is

[7] *Ethics,* I, Definitions (Wild, 94–95).

[8] *On the Improvement of the Understanding* (Wild, 37–38). On the connection between the geometric method and Spinozistic metaphysics, cf. R. McKeon, "Causation and the Geometric Method in the Philosophy of Spinoza," *The Philosophical Review,* 39 (1930), 178–189, 275–296.

substance, which can only be conceived through itself. (2) As cause of Himself, God is also an essence which necessarily involves its own existence. He cannot be conceived except as self-existent, so that doubt cannot touch this connection. God is the eternal essence, whose existence must be regarded as flowing from its own essence. The latter retains its primacy in Spinozism, since existence is a consequence of essence. (3) It must not be supposed that these definitions are concerned with abstract, general categories and transcendental relations. Cause-of-itself, substance, freedom, and eternity are defined precisely as characterizing the particular affirmative essence of God. No passage is made from substance in general to the divine substance. It is already anticipated that substance, as so defined, refers to a unique, particular, yet infinitely powerful, existent. The affirmative essence of substance has, as its primary and most radical affirmation, its own eternal, particular existence. Whatever other things may exist, they cannot (by definition) exist as substantial entities. (4) The last requirement of the definition of an uncreated being cannot be satisfied by the human mind, under present conditions. Whereas the attributes of God are infinite in number, we can only define His nature in such a way that we perceive to follow from it the two attributes (thought and extension), whose modes constitute our own nature. This is one mark of our finiteness and dependence upon the given universe which Spinoza does not claim to erase by elevation to the divine standpoint. Finally, to place these propositions at the beginning of a philosophical inquiry, harmonizes with the spontaneous tendency of the human mind to know first of all the affirmative, infinite, eternal, and absolute. De jure, philosophy unfolds from the fountainhead of being; Spinoza's intellectual ascesis is undergone to insure that the de facto order of thought will conform with the de jure one.

By including definitions of the finite and the modal within a set of propositions devoted mainly to God, Spinoza is continuing his fundamental division of definitions into those for uncreated, and those for created, beings. The contrast is between that which is conceived through itself (uncreated being) and that which is conceived through its proximate cause (created beings). Spinoza is suggesting that, because only the particular substantial essence of God is conceived through itself, therefore other things are not substances but modes of the one divine substance. Spinoza identifies substantial existence in oneself with existence entirely from one's own power *of being,* and consequently he has no difficulty in concluding that no finite thing can satisfy the definition of substance. Already, a metaphysical dilemma is proposed implicitly in these definitions: a thing must be either *absolutely independent* in being or else *modally dependent* upon another as its cause. It is stipulated that to be caused by another is equivalent to being dependent upon that other, after the relation of mode to substance. Like Bruno, Spinoza regards "dependent substance" as a contradiction in terms. Under these conditions, there is place for caused, dependent, finite entities only as modes of the unique, uncaused substance of God. The verdict is sealed in the very definitions, before the case is tried.

Spinoza shows himself to be both the *heir and the critic of Descartes.* He exploits the latter's definition of substance, since even Descartes admitted that, in the strict sense, God alone exists in such a way as to need no other for His existence. As for Descartes' qualification that mind and body are at least relative substances, Spinoza replies that there is no middle ground between the absolute self-sufficiency of substance and modal dependence upon substance. Our ability to conceive of mind and body separately only indicates that they belong to different series of modes. Spinoza bolsters his monism of substance with the aid of three further hints in Descartes: the remark that the dependence of creatures upon God makes them abstract and, in a way, modes of God; the doctrine that, while there is a plurality of mental substances, there is but one material substance in the world of extension; the identification between God and the first of the meanings assigned to the term "nature." Although on all three counts Descartes offers a theistic explanation, Spinoza rejects the explanation in favor of one that disposes the mind toward his own pantheistic monism.

Spinoza consulted the current Protestant Scholastic manuals in regard to his definitions, but made significant alterations to fit his purpose. The addition of *conceived through itself* and *conceived through another* to the definitions, respectively, of substance and mode marks the decisive difference.[9] These added words indicate the

---

[9] The best Thomistic criticism of the Spinozistic definitions of substance and mode is made by S. Vanni Rovighi, "La teoria spinoziana della sostanza e la metafisica tomistica," in *Spinoza nel terzo centenario della sua nascita,* edited by the Faculty of Philosophy in the Catholic University of the Sacred Heart (Milan, Vita e Pensiero, 1934), 7–20 (also as a supplementary volume to *Rivista di filosofia neoscolastica,* 25 [1933]). The author shows that Spinoza and Aquinas part company over the

epistemological and methodological orientation of the new definitions. Substance and mode are designated *by our ways of knowing them,* even more than by their manner of being. This enables Spinoza to argue that, because knowledge of dependent entities involves a reference to a cause, their own being is that of a reference to, or mode of, their causal source. It also bolsters his contention that our knowledge of the primal being must itself be a primal principle, held independently of our knowledge of anything else. There is negative significance in the two facts that substance is not called the *subject* of the modes and that the latter are not referred to as *accidents.* The modes are not described as inhering in substance as a subject, lest something static, imperfect, and potential be imported into the divine substance. Spinoza agrees with the Scholastic arguments against applying accidents to God, because of the intrinsic imperfection of a subject requiring accidents. The modes are His *affections,* but they are not His accidents, and He is not their subject. It is easier for Spinoza to state what the relation is *not,* than to give an intelligible, positive account of how modes are "in" substance, without having substance as their subject. His problem is to ground the modes in the only available substance and yet to avoid destroying the infinite perfection of the latter. This is difficult to do, without covertly reinstating the equivalent of dependent but substantial created things.

Spinoza identifies a priori reasoning from cause to effect with reasoning from substance to its mode and makes this procedure the standard for philosophical inference. Because of the sameness between the order of things and the order of true ideas, there can be no strict a posteriori knowledge about God from the things that flow from Him. If our knowledge of the divine substance were dependent upon something else and yet pretended to be truly philosophical knowledge, it would compromise the independence of the divine substance. Hence Spinoza bases his *proofs of God's existence* ultimately on a clear and distinct *a priori idea* of His essence.[10] The a posteriori

---

question of whether the perfect, intuitive knowledge implied by these definitions is available to human minds, i.e., they disagree about whether or not these proposed definitions can function as principles within a *human* philosophy. The Cartesian methodic doubt and the Spinozistic theory of the degrees of perception and the nature of definition are jointly opposed to the Thomistic emphasis upon the existential limitations placed by the senses upon human intelligence.

[10] *Short Treatise on God, Man, and His Well-Being,* I, 1 (A. Wolf translation, as reprinted in *Spinoza Selections,* edited by J. Wild, 45–49); *Ethics,* I, 11 (Wild, 103–106). In the *Short Treatise,* the a posteriori argument seeks the formal reality which causes

proofs he does offer of God's existence are meant as concessions to the weakness of ordinary minds and, upon closer inspection, turn out to be dependent for their probative force upon the a priori idea of a necessarily existing and infinite essence, a substance having the power of self-existing. That a substance must be conceived through itself means, not only that *it must be asserted* to have its being in and from itself, but also that the *human knower must base his assertion* ultimately upon the idea of this substance and upon nothing else. Only the a priori proof rigorously satisfies this condition.

It follows also that a *plurality of substances* would either be totally irrelevant to each other and undeducible from each other, or else would share perfections with each other. Spinoza recognizes only one way in which substances could share perfections: univocally and by a mutually real relation (*commune cum se invicem*), and such sharing would automatically cancel their claim to be substances. Hence he concludes that there is but one substance, and it is infinite. What Spinoza proves is not the uniqueness of substance but the impossibility of conceiving many substances coherently, in a system which requires that the individual, existing substance be known a priori. The one Spinozistic substance must enter into all other things not merely as a cause present to its effects but also as a substance to its modes, a genus to its species, and a whole to its parts. The requirements of scientific deduction, after the manner of the highest degree of perception, dictate such a relationship and hence are incompatible with a multiplicity of created substances. A monism of substance is the only way in which the highest conceivable knowledge could also be regarded as the natural human way of knowing.

A distinction is made between the *properties* and attributes of God. The former are general characteristics, describing either the necessary existence of substance, by way of extrinsic denomination, or its essence considered as a source of actions. Properties are required in order that God may be what He is, but they do not reveal His essential nature in itself. Spinoza demonstrates that the divine sub-

---

the idea of God in the human mind; the a priori proofs examine the implications of the identity between the divine existence and the immutable, eternal essence of God. In the *Ethics,* the a posteriori proof states that, if finite beings exist, then surely the infinite being is not lacking in the power to exist; the a priori proof rests on the definition of substance as cause of itself and therefore as existing through itself, unhindered by any counterpower in the substantial order.

stance is infinite, unproduced, immutable, and enjoying identity between essence and existence. These properties establish the distinctive sort of existence belonging to the divine being. Other properties, based on His actions, concern the way in which God is a determining cause of things; they can best be discussed in the following section, on the modes produced by God.

Whereas the properties only define God by comparison with the finite, contingent, temporal universe of produced things, the *attributes* give direct access to what God is in His own nature. If they were not constitutive of the divine essence, we could gain no intimate knowledge about God. Later commentators have remained divided about whether Spinoza intends the attributes to have any reality apart from their function of enabling the intellect to grasp the divine substance.[11] The *subjective* interpretation states that the attributes express the divine substance only for intellect, either infinite or finite, and that their sole reality is that of being aids to intellectual perception of God's substantial nature. The more *objective* view is that the attributes are both auxiliaries to knowledge and real, objective constituents of the divine substance, from which the real world of modes takes its rise. Spinoza gives occasion to both interpretations, by stressing now their constitutive presence in substance and now their presence there precisely as the intellect's means of access to the substantial essence.

Spinoza's hesitation on this issue is connected with the problem of the *simplicity* of the divine substance. It is simple and indivisible in itself, since it is infinite and could not be divided, without leading to the contradiction of several infinite substances or several finite parts of one infinite substance. Yet because the divine essence is infinite, it must express itself in an infinite number of attributes, each of which is infinite in its kind. If the objective interpretation of the attributes is accepted, the plurality of real attributes destroys the simplicity and paves the way for some sort of divisibility in God.

---

[11] See, for instance, the subjective interpretation proposed by H. A. Wolfson, *The Philosophy of Spinoza*, I, 146–157, and the objective reading suggested by P. Siwek, S.J., *Spinoza et le panthéisme religieux*, 247–253. Since the discussion between Wolfson and Siwek turns about whether or not Spinoza's reference to the attributes as "expressing" the divine substance commits him to a subjective, purely logical view of the attributes, one may profitably read F. Kaufmann's essay, "Spinoza's System as Theory of Expression," *Philosophy and Phenomenological Research*, 1 (1940–1941), 83–97, which shows that the power of nature or substance is primarily an ontological expression, in the real order. This supports an objective approach to the attributes.

Spinoza admits that the attributes are independent of each other, at least to the extent that each is knowable by itself, without reference to the others, and that each gives rise to a distinct series of modes. If the objective reality of the several attributes is weakened, however, their function of leading to knowledge of the divine essence is correspondingly weakened. But at least the subjective reading makes it easier to reconcile manyness of attributes with simplicity of substance. The attributes would be really identical with the divine substance and each other, but distinguished rationally as an aid to the intellect's knowledge of God.

In any case, Spinoza states definitely that only two of the infinite number of divine attributes are known by us: *thought* and *extension*. His denial of secondary substances leaves him with no other recourse than to attribute to God these two most general characteristics, in which the Cartesian analysis of finite being terminated. If the world of experience discloses these ultimate traits, they must be traced back to God and acknowledged as His attributes. Since our minds operate only within the given universe, constituted by God under the attributes of thought and extension, our knowledge of the divine essence is limited to these two notes. There seems to be no intrinsic obstacle from the standpoint of eternity, however, against associating the modes of thought with the nonextensional modes that flow from the innumerable other divine attributes. But such knowledge is not within reach of human nature, constituted as it is precisely by the correlation between modes of thought and extension alone. Because of the definitive character of the Cartesian description of the world, Spinoza does not regard further attributive knowledge of God as being even conceivable for human philosophy.

The main difficulty concerns the attribution of *extension* to God.[12] Spinoza is well aware that this is repugnant to most religious and philosophical traditions. But he remarks that, just as his predecessors were mistaken in ascribing modes of intellect and will to God under the guise of attributes, so they were mistaken in failing to ascribe a genuine attribute, like extension, to Him. Like the medieval Jewish philosopher, Crescas, Spinoza is then compelled to reinterpret extension, so that it may become compatible with God's unlimited perfection. Characteristically, he settles the metaphysical issue by an appeal to his theory of knowledge rather than by a direct analysis

---

[12] *Ethics*, I, 14–15 (Wild, 107–113); *Letter XII* (A. Wolf translation, as reprinted in *Spinoza Selections*, edited by J. Wild, 412–413).

of the humanly available evidence. A distinction is drawn between extension as apprehended by *imagination* and as apprehended by *intellect*. The former power cannot grasp extension in its own nature but only in its modal expression, where it is perceived as being finite, composed of parts, and divisible. But imagination operates at the lowest level of perception and is the main source of error; its defect at this point is to confuse the finite manifestations of extension with its essential nature. By transcending the sphere of imagination, an unfettered intellectual view can be obtained of extension as something infinite, without parts, and indivisible in itself. It is this pure perfection of extension that constitutes an attribute of the divine essence.

A twofold price is paid for establishing this conclusion. First, the divine attribute is rendered completely *equivocal* in respect to the extended objects of our temporal experience. The only common bond between imagined and intellected extension, apart from the name, is the logical stipulation that the very widest properties of finite things must be grounded in corresponding divine attributes. What Spinoza proves to be present in God is not extension, in any settled and identifiable meaning with which we are acquainted, but some perfection sufficient to permit God to be the first cause of extended modes of being. To establish that extension is indivisible, for instance, he shows that *whatever* constitutes the divine substance must be indivisible. *If* extension were to belong to the divine being as an attribute, it would be free from imperfections like divisibility — this is the only conclusion reached. Such an inference does not demonstrate that God's nature is extended but only reiterates that whatever perfection is attributed to God, must be indivisibly present in Him. In the second place, Spinoza contrasts *imagined* matter or *unreal,* finite extension with extension as it *really* is, for the *intellect*. The purely finite aspects of extension are strangers to the domain of real things, as they actually are in the sight of eternity. Despite his best efforts to avoid it, Spinoza is thus obliged to erect a dichotomy between *illusion* and *reality,* in order to attribute extension to God. Although he does not deny the reality of the finite, modal world, he holds that it is unreal from any but the standpoint of his own eternal perspective. Since the traits of finitude, contingency, and temporal duration are implicated in the ordinary or "imaginative" view of extension, the shift to a purely intellectual and eternal treatment of these traits endangers their empirically grasped nature.

The dialectic of illusion and reality may formally posit eternal equivalents for them, but it is a question whether they themselves can survive the sea-change.

4. THE EMANATION OF THE MODAL WORLD

Regardless of whether the attributes are taken subjectively or objectively, Spinoza defends the thesis that, outside the intellect, there is nothing but substance and its modes or affections. The latter have their being somehow in God, and can neither be nor be conceived properly apart from Him. Hence a doctrine on the modal world must be the consequence of a doctrine on God as cause, and of modes as His effects and affections. It is important for Spinoza to establish the *fact* and *manner of divine causality* by means of a carefully chosen mathematical comparison.[13] God not only *is* a cause, as can be seen from the factual presence of effects, but *must* be a cause, just as an essence cannot but generate its own properties. It is this comparison between God and an essential definition that establishes the nature of divine causality. Just as an informed intellect sees that properties must flow from any defined essence, so it sees that from an infinite essence an infinite number of effects must flow. By the sheer fact of being infinite affirmative essence, God must give rise to effects. The existing things of the world are in exactly the same relation to God as are the properties of triangle to the notion of triangle: in both cases, the essential perfection of the nature cannot but entail consequences. For Spinozistic rationalism, there is a complete equivalence between the relation of *logical ground* and *consequent* and that of *real cause* and *effect*. This is made possible, because Spinoza conceives *causation* to be fundamentally an expansion or *explication of essence* as such. For the divine substance to be an affirmative essence, means that it is cause of itself and cause of modal effects.

This purely essentialist notion of divine causality has weighty consequences for the problem of God and the world. Essence and

---

[13] "From the supreme power of God, or from His infinite nature, infinite things in infinite ways, that is to say, all things, have necessarily flowed, or continually follow by the same necessity, in the same way, as it follows from the nature of a triangle, from eternity and to eternity, that its three angles are equal to two right angles." *Ethics*, I, 17, Scholium (Wild, 115). Cf. *ibid.*, I, 16–18 (Wild, 113–118), on the various aspects of divine causality. For an exposition of the Spinozistic doctrine on the procession of things from God as *causa sui*, and their causal return to God by intellectual love, see T. M. Forsyth, "Spinoza's Doctrine of God in Relation to His Conception of Causality," *Philosophy*, 23 (1948), 291–301.

existence are identical in God, not by reason of any distinctive perfection in the properly existential order but because the divine essence is infinitely active power. Consequently, God is *causa sui,* because His essence exists through its own active power and necessity. Essence, existence, and duration are distinct from each other in all finite, modal things, since their essence comes from another as a cause. Up to this point, Descartes would concur with this reasoning, but he would recoil from admitting the consequence that Spinoza next draws. God produces the world in the same way in which He is cause of Himself, namely, *by the necessity and power of His own nature.* He cannot *not* act in the production of modes, any more than He can cease to be His own essence or to affirm His own existence. All things flow from the divine nature with the rigid necessity of a mathematical demonstration. Even if the factor of knowledge be added, Spinoza draws a parallel between God's necessary knowledge of Himself and His necessary production of things.

Open issue is taken with the Thomistic doctrine that God creates the world not from the necessity of His nature but *through intellect and will.* Spinoza's reply reveals that, for him, the theory of the divine attributes is a storm center of the new outlook rather than a repetition of commonplaces. For him, intellect and will are not divine *attributes* at all, but are *modes* produced by the divine nature, under the attribute of thought. Hence they are not real principles in the first production of things. Since he also denies a real distinction between intellect and will from the human standpoint, Spinoza has none of the requisites for grasping the conception of a nonnecessitated creation by God. Spinoza does allow that, if intellect and will were taken as absolutely identical with the divine essence and its infinitely actual power, then they could be said to be present in God. But in that case, they would be predicated of God and creature just as equivocally as "dog" is predicated of the dog-star and of Fido. In proof, he cites the Platonic-Plotinian axiom that "an effect differs from its cause precisely in that which it has from its cause."[14] A divine intellect and will that would be identical with God's essence,

---

[14] *Ethics,* I, 17 (Wild, 117); the correct interpretation of this text is made by A. Koyré, "Le chien, constellation céleste, et le chien, animal aboyant," *Revue de Métaphysique et de Morale,* 55 (1950), 50–59. For a Thomistic appraisal of Spinoza's general doctrine on predication between God and finite things, cf. J. F. Anderson, *The Bond of Being* (St. Louis, Herder, 1949), Chap. V: "The 'Univocist' World of Spinoza" (70–76). Anderson's book sets forth the Thomistic doctrine on analogy.

would have only the name in common with our intellect and will, regarded either essentially or existentially. Lacking a doctrine of analogical predication, Spinoza is forced to move between a univocal and an equivocal view of God's causal activity. *Univocity* is present in the comparison between divine causality and the emanation of properties from a definition, since this favors a theory of divine determinism. *Equivocity* is invoked in the face of the Thomistic attempt to attribute intellect and will to God, and hence to establish that He does not produce the world from the necessity of His nature.

Although the world emanates from the necessity of God's nature, Spinoza does not therefore conclude that God lacks freedom. Instead, he revises the definition of *freedom,* so that it excludes coercion or external force but coincides with an internal necessity of action.[15] The divine power wells over into a spontaneous emanation, which is free because it is not compelled from without (there being no other substance, outside of God, to compel Him). God is not only free: He is the only free cause. This follows, since He is the only being that is not produced by another. The divine freedom is that of self-necessitation in existence; the being and operation of all other things are compelled or necessitated from without and hence are not free. God is also the *per se* and *first* cause, since He acts through His own primordial nature. His causality is only in the *efficient* order, efficient causality being equated here with the logical movement involved in a mathematical demonstration. God produces both the essence and the existence of finite things, and yet does so with all the necessity and purposelessness of a geometrical line of proof. In virtue of the attribute of thought, God is conscious of His own essence and its entailments in reality, but it is as though a mathematical essence were aware of its properties. Far from regarding this mathematicizing of divine causality as a derogation of God's perfection, Spinoza deems it the only proper way to conceive God's properties as first efficient cause.

God is the efficient cause but not the final cause of the modal world. The mathematical view of causation prescinds entirely from final cause, and even from any sort of efficient cause that is not reducible to the formal, logical entailment of properties from a definition. Spinoza interprets *finality* exclusively as an acting for

---

[15] Cf. M. T. Clark, "Plotinus, Spinoza, and Freedom," *The New Scholasticism,* 33 (1959), 273–290.

the sake of a good to be gained, and a perfection to be acquired, by the agent. Most theistic philosophers agree that it would be a derogation from divine perfection to regard God as *this sort* of final cause. But Spinoza fails to apply to final cause the technique of determining the meaning of the "pure perfection" involved, as he did in the attribution of extension to God. This is an indication that the conditions of mathematical explanation, rather than the analogical requirements of being, regulate the Spinozistic doctrine on divine causality.

Last, Spinoza teaches that God is an *immanent* rather than a transitive cause. By this proposition, he excludes the crude notion of a first cause placed spatially "outside" the world. He also directs it against the Cartesian view that, as an immaterial cause, God is substantially other than the world of material substance. The only kind of *transcendence* open to the first cause is that of the natural primacy belonging to absolute substance over relative modes or the primacy of a constitutive whole over its parts. God is a *remote* cause only in a relative way, insofar as some of His effects proceed more immediately than others from substance. Absolutely speaking, God as immanent principle is also the *proximate* cause of all His effects, and that is why the proper definition of any mode includes a reference to divine substance.

The divine immanence is reinforced by Spinoza's conception of "God or Nature," *Deus sive Natura.* Whereas Descartes had referred to God as nature and had nevertheless maintained the substantial distinction between Him and finite substances, Spinoza employed the phrase *Deus sive Natura* to express the substantial oneness of all reality, and the relation of substance and modes obtaining between God and the finite things of the world. Like Bruno, he revived the medieval terms *natura naturans* and *natura naturata* to advance this doctrine, but his position is more complex and technically articulated than that of Bruno.[16] *Natura naturans* includes the divine substance and attributes, considered as the dynamic source and free cause of all else; *natura naturata* embraces the entire world of infinite and finite modes. The universe of modes is determined by *natura naturans* and hence is subject to a necessitating compulsion, without any room

---

[16] *Short Treatise on God, Man, and His Well-Being,* I, 8–9 (Wild, 80–82); *Ethics,* I, 29, Scholium (Wild, 126). On the medieval background of the terms, cf. H. A. Lucks, *"Natura Naturans — Natura Naturata," The New Scholasticism,* 9 (1935), 1–24.

for freedom. God or the totality of nature includes both *natura naturans* and *natura naturata,* as seen in their proper order, connection and causal relations. Spinoza qualifies his pantheistic conception of nature to the extent that, although substance is constitutive of the essence of modes, still the modes do not belong to the essence of substance. Some distinction is maintained within the unity of nature between the first cause and its effects, but it is only that sort of distinction permitted by the uniqueness of the divine substance and the purely modal character of all other things. Within these limits, *Deus sive Natura* is a concise formula for Spinoza's pantheistic monism.

SPINOZA'S METAPHYSICAL FRAMEWORK

1. One substance (with a distinctive set of properties and an infinite number of attributes).	God		*Natura Naturans*
2. Two known attributes, infinite and eternal.	Thought	Extension	
3. General modes, infinite and eternal.			*Natura Naturata*
a) Immediate infinite modes.	Infinite Intellect	Motion-and-Rest	
b) Mediate infinite mode.	Pattern of the Entire Universe		
4. Particular finite modes.	Minds (ideas of bodies)	Bodies	

A complicated scheme of modes is elaborated in an attempt to explain the familiar world, without compromising the key doctrine of substance and modes. The two known attributes, thought and extension, are eternal and infinite in their kind and partake of the productive power of the divine essence. Hence each gives rise to an infinite series of modes, but does so according to a certain order. The broadest division of modes is into general and particular. *General modes* resemble the attributes in being themselves infinite and eternal. Among general modes, a further distinction is made between *immediate infinite modes* and a mediate infinite mode. The immediate infinite mode under the attribute of extension is *motion-*

and-rest in general; that under the attribute of thought is *infinite intellect* (from which will is not really distinct), having as its object the idea of God, in which all the properties and attributes of the divine essence are reflected. Spinoza mentions only one *mediate infinite mode,* calling it the *facies totius universae,* the face or pattern of the entire universe.[17] He does not indicate whether it belongs under only one attribute or both, but it is more likely that it comes under both attributes and proceeds from both immediate infinite modes. Perhaps by the "fashion or make of the entire universe" is meant the most universal pattern of the modal universe, considered not precisely as coming forth from *natura naturans* but as constituting a *natura naturata,* in which there is strict correspondence between modes of thought and modes of extension. This joint pattern remains the same in its general features and laws, even though it embraces an infinite number of particular, changing events and things.

From general or infinite modes flows the series of *particular* or *finite modes.* This is the domain of the particular things (minds and bodies) which we experience. Spinoza speaks of finite modes as *things,* without implying that they are *substances.* His main problem is to explain the origin and characteristics of finite reality. He agrees with the medieval emanationists that, from the infinite first cause, only an *infinite* effect can *immediately* proceed (although he adds that this effect can be a mode of extension as well as one of thought, since extension is also a divine attribute). This is consistent with his anti-creationist and nonexistential theory of God's efficient causality. The eternal and infinite attributes give rise to the immediate infinite modes, from which in turn the mediate infinite mode follows. It is from the mediate infinite mode that the finite modes proceed. Any given particular thing is determined by some previous particular mode of being, so that the finite modes proceed in an infinite series from the mediate infinite mode.

What Spinoza does not explain is how any sort of *finite* reality can proceed by necessary emanation from an *infinite* reality, regardless of whether the infinite reality is immediate or mediate, and regardless of whether there is an infinite number of finite modes. Although

---

[17]*Letter LXIV* (Wild, 463). The translation "fashion or make of the entire universe" was proposed by H. F. Hallett, in "On a Reputed Equivoque in the Philosophy of Spinoza," *The Review of Metaphysics,* 3 (1949–1950), 207, who suggested that this system of universal nature stands related to the finite individual mode as the macrocosm to the microcosm, as the complement to the self.

it is clear that any given particular thing follows from another, insofar as the prior thing is a finite, determinate mode, the transition from general to particular, infinite to finite, is never established. Even the *mediacy* of the mediate infinite mode is only a relative one, since the first cause remains a proximate cause, immanent to all its effects and modes. Spinoza has not escaped from the emanationist difficulty of rendering intelligible the advent of the many from the one, the finite from the infinite, within a conception of God as producing out of the necessity of his own nature.

Finite particular things are mutable, contingent, and temporal. These notes only render the emanation-problem more acute for Spinoza, due to the immutable, necessary, eternal nature of infinite substance and the everlastingness of the infinite modes. Yet, despite Hegel's charge that Spinoza's substance occupies a lion's den, where all the footprints of finite things point inward and none point outward again, Spinoza does strive to avoid an outright acosmism or denial of the reality of the universe of particular things. He distinguishes between two ways of viewing finite things: through *imagination* and through *reason,* thus using the same epistemological contrast that helped to explain error and extension. He never doubts the real existence of finite modes, but he underlines the inadequate and illusory character of the ordinary way of describing them.

Individual things are finite modes, having a determinate existence. Their *existence* can be approached from two perspectives: that of *eternity* or a necessary entailment from the divine attributes, and that of *duration* or indefinite and contingent continuation in being.[18] The eternal view of modal existence is that taken by reason; the durational view of modal existence is that taken by imagination. These two standpoints are open to us, since the essence of derived, finite things is not identical with its existence. Men ordinarily consider the essence of individual things in an isolated way, as being cut off from divine substance and the necessary causal order of nature. This is the work of imagination, which studies modal entities only in themselves and their factual, contingent connections. Imagination is not intrinsically erroneous, but it suffers from the twofold disability of being affected by the chain of external agents and of

---

[18] *Ethics,* II, Definitions 5, 7, and Propositions 8 (Corollary), 44–45 (Wild, 144, 151, 190–193); *ibid.,* V, 29 (Wild, 387–388). On contingency, as based upon a deficiency in our knowledge of the eternal order of causes, cf. *ibid.,* I, 33, Schol. 1, and IV, Definition 3 (Wild, 130, 287).

never rising beyond the domain of finite being as such. Hence it usually leads to error by encouraging the common-sense description of the *common order of nature,* in which things are not recognized as modes of the divine being or as necessarily determined by it, but are regarded as contingent, temporal substances. Because imagination can discover no intrinsic reason in the finite essence for its existence, people usually conclude that the individual thing is *contingent.* And because imagination cannot locate the proper cause in the order of nature, it is concluded that the individual thing is *merely possible* in itself or due to *chance* determinations. But contingency and corruptibility are only names for our lack of knowledge of the essence, taken in all its relations. Similarly, imagination treats the finite thing's continuation of existence in an abstract way, as duration. *Time* is a handy tool of imagination for measuring *abstract duration* by means of determinate units.

The contingent view of durational existence is due to the deficiency of our knowledge at the level of imagination. The only way to remedy this inadequate description of finite things in terms of contingency, chance, and duration, is to elevate the mind to the standpoint of reason. Only reason, brought to perfection in the intuition of God, can view the finite essence in intrinsic relation to God and the *eternal order of nature* (in contradistinction to the merely temporal, common order of nature, described by imagination), including the laws governing the infinite modes. From this adequate perspective, the finite essence is seen to be necessarily determined to existence through its first cause, even though it is not necessarily existent from any power in its own nature. Contingency is thus transmuted into the necessity proper to a particular entity existing within *natura naturata.* Actual existence is now known to be determined within the modal world and not to be due to chance or a mere external agency. Reason's function, at the highest level, is to know finite things as they are in themselves. Paradoxically, their true and real being *in themselves* is precisely their modal being *in another,* in the divine substance. Their continuance in existence is tracked back to God's necessary determination of their existence: hence it is no longer an indefinite, abstract, contingent duration but a determinate mode of eternal being. Temporal duration is thereby caught up in eternity or, rather, is replaced by eternity. For, to understand finite things according to their real and true essence, is to understand them from the standpoint of the eternity described in Spinoza's theory of substance, attributes, and modes. *Sub specie aeterni,* their existence is seen to flow from the causal necessity of God's nature and hence to be a shared eternity rather than a temporal duration.

It is for this reason that the question was posed, at the end of the previous section, whether the antithesis between imagination and reason, the abstract and the concrete, the erroneous and the true view of reality, can ultimately salvage the empirical content of our notion of finite things. It is not a question about the *fact* of their reality but about our *description* of that fact, on the basis of what is given through the senses. Spinoza teaches that the real and true being of finite things is not properly expressed in terms of contingency, duration, and temporality. This is a lower or interim viewpoint that becomes positively erroneous, unless it is overcome by his own interpretation of the emanation of the modal world. True, finite existence is necessitated *rather than* contingent, is a participated eternity *rather than* a temporal duration. This contrast is something more than a refinement of our experience of finite existents. It is a criticism and replacement of that experience to the extent that none of the original traits remain and an opposite meaning is installed in the philosophically formed mind. If the genuine reality of finite things is only their reality as modes affecting the divine substance, then Spinoza's view of existence maintains no continuity of meaning with the conviction that the finite existents are irreducibly contingent and durational entities. At least as irreducible characters of finite things, contingency and temporal duration are sacrificed to the exigencies of a metaphysical deduction. As traits due to the deficiency of imagination, they must give way before the systematic demands of Spinozistic pure reason or intellect. Spinoza is both the heir to Descartes' suspicion of sensuous cognition and the herald of Hegel's difficulty about explaining how any recognizable traits survive from "abstract" experience, once it has been "overcome" by the requirements of a pantheistic monism.

5. HUMAN NATURE

Spinoza's philosophical anthropology is not only in conformity with his epistemological and metaphysical principles but is also a strict inference from them. His doctrine in this field tells what human nature *ought to be* within the designated framework, rather than what it *discloses itself as being* in our actual experience. This a priori approach is indicated at once in the definitions of *mind* and *body*.[19] They are defined as modes that express in a determinate, finite way the essence of God considered, respectively, as a thinking thing and as an extended thing. Hence the main task of the philosophical study of man's mind and body is to show how they can be explained as finite, modal consequences of God's attributes of thought and extension, and of the infinite modes of intellect and motion-and-rest. The human composite is treated as a phase in the joint emanation of the finite modes from the divine nature. Our experience of human nature is rectified and reconstructed from this overruling standpoint.

Spinoza first proposes a *general theory of mind and body* and then makes a specific application to the human mind and body. The methodological postulate about the close agreement between the order and connection of ideas and that of things may now be stated in a more metaphysical way. God's active essence gives rise to an infinite series of finite things, that may be considered now under the attribute of thought and now under that of extension. Because of the oneness of the divine substance, it is *one and the same thing* that is being expressed *under the different modes* of extension and thought. That which is expressed in a corporeal way, as following from the divine nature under the attribute of extension, is given a mental expression under the attribute of thought. The content of the mode of thought is specified by its proportionate mode of extension.

Sometimes, Spinoza stresses the *sameness of the modal thing,* expressed under the two attributes, while at other times he stresses the *one-to-one correspondence* established between the co-ordinate series of the modes of thought and the modes of extension. Within the finite world, the extended modes constitute bodies, whereas the mental modes, regarded in their own formal nature, constitute minds. Every body has its proper idea or correlated mental expression, under the attribute of thought. Taken in its own formal being, the idea of a body is the same as the *mind* or *soul* of that body. All bodies are animated or besouled in this sense, but Spinoza differs from the panpsychism of many Renaissance Neo-Platonists and of Leibniz, in that the presence of a mind or soul need not entail some vague feel-

---

[19] *Ethics,* II, Definition 1 and Proposition 11 (Wild, 143, 155–156). For a sustained comparison between Spinoza's theory about man and the deliverances of human experience, consult H. Barker, "Notes on the Second Part of Spinoza's *Ethics,*" *Mind,* N. S., 47 (1938), 159–179, 281–302, 417–439.

ing or perception in every body. In its minimal and most widely exemplified meaning, a mind or soul is merely the ideal correlate of a body, the manner in which the bodily thing proceeds from God under the attribute of thought. There is *no causal interaction* between mind and body, however, since they are referred to different attributes of God.

Spinoza's doctrine on mind is worked out largely by reference to the nature of body, to which the mind or idea of the body is proportioned. He admits a hierarchy among minds, because of an evident gradation among bodies. The *grades of being* are not accounted for by graded actual and potential principles, however, since, for Spinoza, potency is due only to our inadequate knowledge of the actual fullness of the total system of beings. It is a true fact, however, that the infinite intellect conceives of an infinite number of finite, modal consequences of the divine essence, and that these are necessarily brought forth by the divine power. In the region of extended things, there is a continuous gradation from the simplest bodies or ultimate modal units up to material nature as a whole. *Individuality* is an extremely supple characteristic of things, being based upon the establishment of a proportion of motion and rest among the ultimate constituent parts. Spinoza gives an organic-functional account of the individual and its unity.[20] The dynamic harmony among several bodies, acting together as one agent in the production of effects, is sufficient to constitute them as one individual thing, since their joint action achieves some fixed proportion. Increasingly more comprehensive operational unities result in ever more comprehensive individual natures. Finally, Spinoza takes the whole of material nature as a single, inclusive individual, because all particular variations occur within the fixed pattern of motion-and-rest set by the laws of nature. This perspectival notion of corporeal individuality leads to a similar view of the individual nature of minds, since the ideas of bodies enter into similar relations of unity and subordination to a more inclusive whole.

There is something *distinctive* about both the human body and the human mind. The former is composed of many kinds of subordinate bodily individuals, each of which is composed in turn of the most simple bodies. The *human body* is thus a very complex sort of

---

[20] See H. Jonas, "Spinoza and the Theory of Organism," *Journal of the History of Philosophy,* 3 (1965), 43–57.

dynamic unity. It is sympathetically responsive to modifications from the various quarters of the material universe and, for its part, can act upon a broad field of things. These multiple contacts established between the human body and its environment are important for the human mind, since it can know other things only through their effects upon the human body. Both Spinoza and Leibniz agree that only through this medium are other material things brought to focus for the human mind. The human mind is of a higher nature than other types of minds or ideas of bodies, because it can become conscious of its own body. Alone among all the varieties of minds, this one is an *intellect* or *spiritual automaton*.[21] The human mind or soul is nothing other than the formal reality of the idea of the human body. As such, it is posited in being by the actual presence of the existing human body. It is axiomatic with Spinoza that we do have perceptions of our own body, by which conscious acts the human mind is rendered actual and distinctively intellectual.

Man's mind and body are not, as Descartes supposed, distinct finite substances. Rather, they are distinct modal aspects of one and the same thing, which is expressive of the one divine substance. The entire Cartesian discussion of the *per se* unity between two substances is undercut and dismissed by Spinoza's arguments that there is only one substance present in man; that it is the infinite substance of God and not a finite, human substance; and that the human composite is only a *modal unity,* under the divine attributes of thought and extension. Whereas Descartes' difficulty lay in the fact that these attributes are mutually exclusive and seem to require mutually exclusive substances in man, Spinoza makes them attributes of the same divine substance, issuing in one thing that can be regarded under two modally different series. There is, however, a strict correspondence and mutual implication between the modes of extension and of thought, and hence between body and mind. The mind is the idea of *this* body, whereas the body is expressed mentally by *this* idea, which is its mind and soul. Spinoza does not try to *solve* Descartes' problem of uniting two substances: he *substitutes* for it the more manageable problem of correlating an idea and its ideatum. In making this substitution, however, he has to rely upon his doctrine about the unicity of substance, in order to make it inevitable that mind and

---

[21] "Quasi aliquod automa spirituale." *On the Healing of the Understanding* (*Spinoza Opera,* edited by C. Gebhardt, II, 32).

body can be nothing more than mental and extended modes of one divine substance. This is the sense in which his theory of man is deductively constructed from his theory of method and of being.

Cognition is the fundamental activity of the human mind. This operation is not carried on by means of any faculty of knowledge. Spinoza rejected the *faculty theory* (as gathered from the Dutch Scholastic manuals), on the ground that it hypostasizes individual cognitive acts and thus creates metaphysical fictions.[22] In the Spinozistic view of the universe as *a plenum of mathematically determinate actual things,* it would be difficult to make room for *powers* that both perfect a thing and are ordained to further act. At most, he is willing to speak about the powers of the mind in the sense of class names for various kinds of individual activities. The mind is, by its very nature, a dynamic source of cognitive acts. Each one of these acts is determined by other such acts, in the infinite series of finite modes of thought, without the special intervention of any faculty for performing the operations. A consequence may now be drawn from the fact that man is not an ultimate, substantial supposit and that his mind — as a finite mode — is only a part of the divine intellect or infinite mode of thought. Spinoza says that when the *human mind has* an idea and knows an object, it is *God who has* that idea and knows the object. But God has this knowledge, not according to His infinite nature, but insofar as He causally forms the essence of the human mind (under the attribute of thought) and thus manifests Himself through the human mind. But it is a doleful fact that the "sensual man" has no awareness of God's implication in his cognitive activity or its ultimate attribution to God. Our consideration of this truth is achieved only by reflecting methodically upon the acts of thinking, in the light of Spinoza's own doctrine on substance and modes, which provides the higher viewpoint of eternity.

What the mind knows directly are the *ideas of the affections of its own body.* The bodily affections themselves do not enter the mind, but the mind is affected by ideas exactly representing the nature and state of the bodily affections. Spinoza thus provides a metaphysical anticipation of the nineteenth-century psychological hypothesis of *psychophysical parallelism.*[23] The reciprocal relation of mind and

---

[22] *Ethics,* II, 48, Scholium (Wild, 195–196).

[23] For an exhaustive critical study of this question, cf. P. Siwek, S.J., *L'âme et le corps d'après Spinoza* (Paris, Alcan, 1930).

body as a whole extends to that between the particular mental and physical acts. An event which is expressed formally or physically as a mode of extension, an affection of the body, receives its representative or psychic expression as a mode of thought, an affection of the mind. There is *no causal communication* between modes considered under different attributes, but there is a *strict correlation* between the individual acts of mind and those of the body. Yet Spinoza is not an occasionalist, like Malebranche, who denied all secondary causality. Spinoza allows a determined causation *within* the same modal series or among the modes which belong under the same attribute. Sometimes, he does refer to God as the sole efficient cause. This is intended to stress the unique origin and determination of all causal power, as well as God's causal presence in all modal activities, rather than to deny causal efficacy to modal agents, within the same series. God is the immanent cause of both the *esse* and the *fieri* of all modes, whereas finite modes of the same kind can contribute to the *fieri* or ordered becoming of things in *natura naturata,* in virtue of the original impulse received from *natura naturans.* Because there is no causal interaction between modes of body and modes of mind, the ideas are not derived from a bodily source. But since other bodies in the material universe leave their traces upon the states of our body, the ideas of our own bodily states tell us something about bodies other than our own. Mainly, however, the ideas of one's bodily affections inform the mind about these affections in themselves.

Yet it is a far cry from preoccupation with the affections of one's own body to loving contemplation of the divine essence. The distance between them measures the task Spinoza now faces, of elevating the mind from the lowest to the highest kind of knowledge. He feels that the work is made all the more difficult by reason of the *false starting points of philosophizing,* as proposed by the realists and Descartes. The former begin with the sensible world, the latter with the thinking self. Spinoza minimizes the knowledge of sensible objects that can be gained by beginning philosophical investigations with them. When the mind is dependent upon the ideas of affections of the body, it is operating at the lowest levels. Apart from what we can know in general about the most simple bodies, the common notions or traits of all bodies, and some immediate deductions therefrom, our ideas of the sensible world remain confused and limited in scope.

Taking a starting point in sensation, we can learn little about the specific constitution of external bodies or even our own body. Furthermore, there is no direct insight into the nature of the mind, taken merely as a thinking self. It is known only imperfectly by Cartesian introspection, since it is being viewed only as the correlate of the body and its affections. All is darkness, until it dawns upon a man that his mind is indeed a portion of an infinite intellect, that this intellect has for its necessary and proper object the idea of God, and that therefore this idea is the true gravamen of all human thinking. To make this light shine upon the mind is a major step toward wisdom and the happiness we all seek. Insofar as there are obstacles to its ready propagation in the human mind, the problem of man becomes a moral problem.

6. DETERMINISM AND THE AFFECTS

There are two features in the Spinozistic philosophy of man that seem to militate against any effective search for happiness: the denial of freedom and the emphasis on the grip of the passions upon us. The position on *freedom* is dictated by metaphysical considerations. Because of man's location within the modal world of *natura naturata,* he is, by definition, subject to a rigorous determinism in all his actions. The divine causality imposes compulsion or necessity-from-another upon all the modes, mental as well as bodily, thus preventing any modal entity from conforming with the definition of freedom. It does no good to distinguish mind from body: mind is not only modally determined in itself but is correlated, in all its acts, with the determined series of physical events. One finite mode of thought causes another in an infinite series of necessitated mental actions, each of which has its physical counterpart in the similarly compelled series of modes of extension. Even the last refuge of libertarian doctrine — free will — is scuttled by Spinoza. For if by *free will* is meant a *faculty,* it falls beneath the general criticism of faculties of the mind. And if it means an *act* of free choice, there is no special class of acts to sustain the general name. There is no real distinction between acts of knowing and willing. To will is nothing more than to affirm or deny that which is true or false in our ideas. This is a cognitive function and offers no ground of distinction for another class of powers or acts. Descartes had defended freedom by making judgment an act of will. Spinoza reduces the will to the cognitive function of judgment, making it subject to the same determinism governing all our cognitive operations.

Nevertheless, men do recognize themselves as beings of desire and striving. Hence Spinoza's next step is to study the appetitive aspect of our nature. His purpose is to acknowledge the power of the passions and then to suggest the means for becoming their master rather than their slave. This program he seeks to carry out, without reinstating the doctrine of free choice. His solution is *to convert ethics into a metaphysics of the degrees of knowledge,* a course that is prepared for by the suppression of any real distinction between the cognitive and appetitive orders. Hence Spinoza can echo Hobbes' boast of treating human actions and passions just as one would treat of lines, planes, and solids. The univocity of his philosophical method permits him to make this radical reduction of our affective and moral life to a geometrical determinism, which nevertheless leads eventually to happiness.

Cartesian ethics had hinged upon the passions of the soul and their control by free will and reason. Since he denied both free will and interaction between body and mind, Spinoza had to reject the Cartesian theory of the passions. For it, he substituted his own doctrine of the affects, which can be either passions or actions and which are not radically distinct from the virtues. *Affects* are defined as "the affections of the body, by which the power of acting of the body itself is increased, diminished, helped or hindered, together with the ideas of these affections."[24] They include, then, both the bodily affections and the ideas of these affections in the mind. In its broad meaning, an *affection* includes any modification that enters into the constitution of the human essence, whether under the attribute of thought or of extension, or under both attributes. The affections under consideration are precisely those that bear upon the power of acting, whether of the body or of the mind. An affection of the body helps to determine its modal nature; this affection entails a corresponding idea, which is, in turn, an affection of the mind. From the combination of a bodily affection and its idea is constituted an affect of human nature. An affect is essentially *dynamic* in nature, since it determines in some way the body's power of acting and the corresponding mental power of acting.

---

[24] *Ethics*, III, Definition 3 (Wild, 207); cf. *ibid.*, III, *ad fin.*: General Definition of the Affects (Wild, 281).

Spinoza does not allow any purely passive affective state, even in the case of the passions. The distinction between passion and action is not that between merely receiving and producing motion but rather between different ways and degrees of causing affections. The difference turns upon whether a man is an inadequate cause or an adequate cause in the production of affections of the body. In the former case, the affect is a *passion;* in the latter case, an *action.* The criterion of whether or not a man is the adequate cause of his affections is found in the condition of his knowledge, thus inserting a *cognitive* determinant and standard at the very core of *affective* life. An *inadequate cause* is one "whose effect cannot be understood by means of the cause alone," but which requires a reference to some external agent. This is due to the fact that the cause — the human mind, in this case — has only an inadequate or confused knowledge of its own nature and power, and hence regards itself as being only a partial cause. An *adequate cause,* on the other hand, is one "whose effect can be clearly and distinctly perceived by means of the cause," without an extrinsic reference.[25] Although there is causation of affections in both cases, Spinoza reserves the term "action" for what we do as an adequate cause, and "passion" for what we do as an inadequate or partial cause of the affection.

The human condition is a mixed one, a synthesis of actions and passions in various proportions. Man is never entirely the slave of passions and never entirely free from them, even though he begins perilously close to the former state and may strain eagerly toward the latter. Spinoza offers three instructive, metaphysical reasons for the *composite character of our emotional life.*[26] (1) Just as the human body is composed of many subordinate individual bodies, so the mind is composed of many subordinate ideas. Some of our ideas are confused, whereas others are clear and distinct. Hence some of the things we do proceed from adequate ideas and issue in actions, whereas others proceed from inadequate ideas and lead to passions. (2) Again, it is a metaphysical principle that every determination of being involves a negation. The divine substance is purely undetermined being, in that it is an infinite and affirmative nature, determining others and itself remaining undetermined. All the modes of *natura naturata* are determined by the first cause and hence have

---

25 The definitions of inadequate and adequate cause are combined in *Ethics,* III, Definition 1 (Wild, 206).

26 *Ibid.,* III, 1, 3, 61 (Wild, 207–208, 214, 259–260).

some negation, along with their modal reality. (This negation, entailed by determination of being, is Spinoza's substitute for the Thomistic composition of actual and potential principles in finite beings, and will become a mainspring in the Hegelian dialectic.) All finite, individual things may be regarded as determined partial causes, and to this extent man must have passions. But since we may also regard ourselves not merely in a confused way, as parts of the common order of nature, but also, clearly and distinctly, as one with the eternal order of nature, we are also capable of being the source of actions. (3) Finally, the melange of passion and action is similar to that of imagination and reason. We are subject to the passions insofar as we imagine, for to imagine is to know in a confused way and as being affected by our own body and some external cause. Reason, on the contrary, frees us from this extrinsic reference and hence permits our emotions to be evaluated as being actions that proceed from the mind's own nature.

Spinoza reduces Descartes' sixfold enumeration of the *basic passions* to three primitive ones: desire, pleasurable joy, and painful sadness.[27] They are already implicated in the definition of an affect. Increase or decrease of the body's power of acting supposes a standard by which to gauge the consequences of an affection. This standard is provided by the *conatus,* the drive, endeavor, or effort that is intrinsic to every body and mind, impelling it to persevere in its own being. Spinoza agrees with Hobbes in stating that the body's power of acting is increased or decreased in the degree that an affection furthers or hinders the drive toward self-preservation. But he leaves Hobbes behind with his further assertion that this endeavor is the permanent impress of God's power upon all modal entities, since He produces both the beginning and the continuance of their existence. No special act is needed for this *conatus:* it is one with the being's actual, existing essence or its natural appetite and love. The active essence of the body is to persevere in its own proper proportion of motion-and-rest, just as the mind's active essence is to persevere indefinitely

---

[27] *Ethics,* III, 11, Scholium (Wild, 218): *cupiditas, laetitia, tristitia.* I have translated the Cartesian-Spinozistic terms *laetitia* and *tristitia,* respectively, as "pleasurable joy" and "painful sadness." This somewhat redundant rendering brings out the pleasure-pain contrast and the co-ordination between mental and bodily states, in the passions. H. A. Wolfson, *The Philosophy of Spinoza,* II, 206–207, translates these terms primarily as "pleasure" (*hedone*) and "pain" (*lupe*), secondarily as "joy" and "sorrow." On the *conatus,* read *Ethics,* III, 6–11 (Wild, 215–219).

in the life of intellect, whether through confused or distinct ideas. There is an exact co-ordination between the inclination of the body toward its self-preservation and the so-called decree of the mind for its well-being.

Will, appetite, and desire are only various ways of designating the *conatus*. The only legitimate moral meaning of *will* is not as a special appetitive power but as the *conatus* itself, considered as related to the mind alone. When the same endeavor is related to both mind and body, it is termed *appetite*. Since the essence of any individual thing is precisely a modal correlation between mind and body, appetite expresses the effort of the individual's essence or composite nature to persevere in its being. Appetite is found in all modal things, but man alone is conscious of his appetite. *Desire* is nothing more than the conscious appetite present in man, who can become aware of the endeavor of his essence. Desire is the fundament and measure of all the other affects. The primary drive of the mind is to affirm the body's existence, since the mind is the affirmative idea of the body.

Along with desire, Spinoza lists pleasurable joy and painful sadness as the other primitive passions of man. They are dynamic developments of desire, and are required because our nature is subject to great changes. Insofar as our nature varies, so the desire varies. It differs from one individual to another, and undergoes increase or decrease within the same man, i.e., it expresses itself in him either as pleasurable joy or as painful sadness. *Pleasurable joy* is the passion whereby the mind increases its endeavor and passes from a lesser to a greater perfection. *Painful sadness* is the passion whereby the mind diminishes its endeavor and passes from a greater to a lesser perfection. All other passional affects are either compounded out of the three primitive ones or are derived from them, in respect to various objects by which we may be affected. Thus *love* and *hatred* are nothing other than pleasurable joy and painful sadness, respectively, along with an accompanying idea of an external cause.

Painful sadness cannot be an action, as well as a passion, since it always involves a lessening of the mind's power of acting. But there are *actions of desire and pleasurable joy,* as well as passions of the same. Man's endeavor or desire operates with either inadequate or adequate ideas, and hence desire can be either a passion or an action. Moreover, when the mind acquires adequate ideas, it takes pleasurable joy in conceiving them and contemplating, with their aid, its own true nature and power of acting. Hence, insofar as man thinks or employs the power of reason, instead of relying upon imagination, he has the active affects of desire and pleasurable joy. All other actions spring from some combination or relation of these basic components.

7. MAN'S LIBERATION AND BEATITUDE:
THE POWER OF REASON

The main ethical problem for Spinoza is to render possible the passage from passion to action. In order to clear the ground for his own solution, he first examines the view of the Stoics and Descartes that the passions are to be controlled by virtue and a knowledge of good and evil. This teaching is acceptable to him only on condition that it be thoroughly transformed, in conformity with his own leading principles. Spinoza's procedure consists, first, in giving a realistic account of man's actual condition and, then, in asking in what sense virtue and a knowledge of good and evil can improve the prevailing situation for man.

The first step is to emphasize the extent of our *bondage to the passions*. "A man is necessarily always subject to passions, and . . . he follows and obeys the common order of nature [as distinguished from the true, eternal order], accommodating himself to it as far as the nature of things requires."[28] This subjection to the passions is a necessary and permanent part of our human lot, since the individual man is a part of nature and must be conceived as being affected by the other parts. The effort or endeavor whereby a man perseveres in being is the power of God or nature, taken not infinitely but *finitely*, insofar as it is manifested in an actual, limited essence. Hence the *conatus* is limited in the individual, suffers changes, is subject to the passions, and is infinitely surpassed by the power of external causes. The individual man is a battleground for conflicting affects and causes, the stronger ones replacing or restraining the others. His limited endeavor is overwhelmed by the passions and alien influences, which exert their power upon him both from without and from within. He is impotent to control them or, at least, to retain his control for very long. Such is the somber picture Spinoza paints of the state of human bondage, which is to be the point of departure for the effort toward moral elevation and happiness. This is an analogue, in the order of

---

[28] *Ethics*, IV, 4, Corollary (Wild, 292).

the passions, to Hobbes' description of man in the state of nature. Of what use is a knowledge of good and evil to such a fragile and battered center of endeavor as man? Spinoza calls good and evil *entia imaginationis,* products of the mind insofar as it is subject to imagination and the rule of external causes.[29] They are completely relative notions, without any absolute standard. Their origin is traceable to the model of human perfection which we invariably set before ourselves. Anything aiding our approach to this paragon is called *good,* and anything hindering our approach is called *evil.* Good and evil, then, are nothing more than the useful and the harmful to us. Use and harm can be calculated by the standard of the individual's *conatus.* That is called useful or good which aids one's drive to persevere in being, whereas that is called harmful or evil which presents an obstacle to this drive. This also means that good and evil are the factors tending to increase or diminish our power of acting. Consequently, knowledge of good and evil is the consciousness of pleasurable joy and painful sadness: the idea of these states that necessarily follows from the affects themselves.

By itself alone, ordinary knowledge could not remove a passion. The latter is rooted in the influence of an external cause upon us, whereas the lower sort of knowledge does not rise above this "eccentric" viewpoint. At this level, the only remedy would be to call upon a stronger passion, one that is based upon a more powerful, but still external, cause. Only when *imaginative knowledge of good and evil is converted into a philosophical understanding of our affects of pleasurable joy and painful sadness,* does it acquire the intrinsic power to modify or remove the passions. Similarly, no fiat of a special power of will could overcome them. For if will has any meaning in an ethical context, it is as a name for the *conatus,* considered in relation to the mind alone. Since this endeavor is not an absolute and separate force but only the individual's actual nature, it partakes of his limits and plight as a partial, conditioned entity. No easy way to salvation is to be found in an appeal to will, taken as a special source of energy.

---

[29] For Spinoza's treatment of evil, see *Short Treatise on God, Man, and His Well-Being,* I, 10 (Wild, 82–83); *Ethics,* I, Appendix; III, 39, Scholium; IV, Preface (Wild, 140–143, 243, 285–286). In his article, "Spinoza's Doctrine of Privation," *Philosophy,* 8 (1933), 155–166, R. Demos discusses the antithesis between ordinary ethical motives and Spinoza's reduction of good and evil to a purely relative status, within a world governed by natural necessity.

The notion of *virtue* is also critically redefined by Spinoza in terms of philosophical knowledge. He begins with the etymological equivalence between "virtue" and "power." Human virtue is the same thing as the essence of man, regarded as having the power to perform deeds that can be understood through the laws of his nature alone. The *conatus* is the basic and sole foundation of virtue. What one's endeavor impels one to do, is also the supreme rule of virtue: "Every one is bound to seek his own profit."[30] To be virtuous is to follow our nature, which bids us desire what we deem to be good or profitable to us and avoid what is deemed evil or harmful to our endeavor. This explanation of virtue enables Spinoza to endow with his own distinctive meaning the old Stoic counsel: follow nature in our actions. We can *act* virtuously only when we have clear and distinct ideas, that enable us to be adequate causes and to follow the laws of our own nature. Hence the precept of *seeking one's own profit* means, basically, *seeking to heal and improve one's understanding.* The true significance of acting virtuously, of acting according to nature or according to reason, now becomes clear. No appeal is being made either to external forces or to an act of free will. We are asked, instead, to recognize that the necessary laws of our own inner nature are the laws of reason as well. The human endeavor is a prompting to increase the understanding's power by discovering a more definite criterion of the good and the useful than Stoic-Cartesian ethics can supply.

There is now a rapid convergence, in Spinoza's reasoning, between *goodness, virtue,* and *power.* Their synthesis is achieved in the *act of knowing God.* For this act is at once the highest good of the mind, its highest virtue, and its supreme source of inward power. Our true profit lies in the increase of our power of understanding, following upon its direction toward the infinitely actual being of God. Spinozistic methodology, metaphysics, and ethics concur in this conclusion. Since the useful and the good coincide, our knowledge of the good is most helpful when it springs from a contemplation of the divine essence. In this knowledge the supreme virtue or development of the mind's power of acting consists. The human *conatus,* strengthened by effective knowledge of the good and the discipline of virtue, is rendered most active, steadfast, and powerful when the mind shares in the vision of God. An analysis of this contemplative act will show

[30] *Ethics,* IV, 18, Scholium (Wild, 303); cf. *ibid.,* IV, Definition 8, and Proposition 22; V, 41 (Wild, 288, 305, 397).

how it comprises man's final happiness and the eternity of his mind.

The crux of Spinoza's ethical philosophy lies in the assertion that man *can* attain to the contemplation of God and that therefore he *can* pass from passion to action, from bondage to liberty and blessedness. He makes this assertion in a qualified way. Although in the present life we cannot completely transcend the passions, we can master them with at least the *major part* of our mind. The human mind may hope to obtain an unshakable foundation and a share of blessedness under present, temporal conditions. Spinoza re-examines the same three reasons previously adduced to show that the affective life of man is a mixed one, in order to demonstrate now that he can increase the scope of the active affects, through the power of reason.[31]

1. The fact that a man has *some* clear and distinct ideas is a pledge of his ability to develop still more such ideas, with the aid of philosophical method. Methodic intellectual progress is made by transforming our given confused ideas into adequate ones, after the pattern set by the *distinct ideas* already in our possession. The passage from confused to distinct ideas involves a *detachment* from reference to external causes and an *attachment* of the understanding to the eternal laws of its own nature. For Spinoza, this process of "inward conversion" is the foundation for a transformation of passions into actions, since what was previously done by the mind as an inadequate cause, is now performed by it as an adequate cause.

2. If it is true that every determination of finite being involves a negation, it is equally true that determinate finite things embody a positive expression of active divine power. The *self-affirmation* at the heart of our being is the *conatus,* which shares in the affirmative power of God's own self-affirmation. Like the Hobbesian individual in relation to the state, this endeavor can never be fully quenched or imprisoned by the passions. Under all circumstances, it retains its nisus of perseveration in being and acting. Although desire may display itself through confused ideas and the passional affects, it does not do so to its own satisfaction. Spinoza must now reinstate a kind of *intrinsic finality,* as a guarantee of the survival and orientation of the endeavor in man. Appetite or desire takes its own increase in perfection as the end, for the sake of which everything is done. The effort toward what supplies the maximum profit, viz., toward active

---

[31] *Ibid.,* V, 20, Scholium (Wild, 381–383).

understanding and adequate ideas, is a finite manifestation of the divine power itself. No matter how many external forces may over-awe and overwhelm the individual man, this internal impulse stubbornly continues to assert itself and seek progressive control over the passions and external deeds.

3. As crowning assurance, Spinoza recalls a major theme in his theory of knowledge: the doctrine of *the degrees of perception*.[32] This doctrine was never confined to the speculative domain: its secret ordination was always toward the ethical relief of man's estate. Its present application was skillfully prepared for through Spinoza's thoroughly intellectualized account of will, virtue, and the affects, especially the key remark that the prime difference between passive and active affects lies in one's state of knowledge. The four grades of perception enumerated in the treatise on method are reduced to three in the *Ethics:* opinion, reason, and intuitive knowledge. But under opinion, Spinoza includes the first two modes of perception listed in the previous classification, v.g., hearsay and what we gather through vague, uncriticized experience, memory, and imagination.

From an ethical standpoint, the defect of *opinionative* or *imaginative perception* lies in its partial view of man. It never rises above the common order of nature, the outlook dominated by contingency, chance, and determination by external causes. The passional affects are attitudes of mind and body proportioned to this fragmentary and even illusory conception of human nature and its operations. *Scientific reason,* the second grade of knowledge, subjects the opinions of sense and imagination to the mind's sifting process and hence begins to assert the proper activity of man. It reveals the common traits and necessary patterns present throughout the universe, thus proving that all modal entities are governed by the necessary, intrinsic laws of their own nature. This knowledge is true and adequate to the task of detaching the affects from the idea of an external cause. Reason, operating at this second level, can form clear and distinct ideas of the affects, taken in themselves, and hence can acquire greater power over them. The more we know their intrinsic nature and origin, the more we can control them and transform them from a passional to an active condition.

Scientific reason, however, still remains dependent upon external sources for its original data. With its aid, we might be able to frame

---

[32] *Ethics,* II, 40, Scholium 2 (Wild, 186–187; cf. above, note 2).

practical maxims for use in emergencies, but we could never achieve the maximal control over the passions that is open to us in this life. The latter is the gift of the third grade of knowledge, based wholly upon the mind itself and the intuitive exercise of reason. The *scientia intuitiva* grasps the divine attributes in themselves and proceeds to an a priori understanding of the essence of modal realities, including one's own affects. This accords with the requirements for the best way of defining uncreated and created things: to know God and the modal world by means of intuitive knowledge is to view reality *sub specie aeternitatis*. Insofar as our knowledge is of this sort, it contains the supremely clear and distinct ideas that make us the adequate causes of what we do. Since this is the condition for controlling the passions and developing the active affects, man is liberated by *scientia intuitiva* as much as he can be, within temporal existence, from servitude to the passions and the sway of fortune. Retrospectively, it can be seen that, unless such knowledge *were* within his grasp, Spinozistic man would be deprived, in this life, of the measure of stability and power upon which his *peace of mind* rests. This is the urgent practical motive behind Spinoza's earlier insistence that we have an adequate idea of God and can achieve an a priori and geometrically certain knowledge of Him.

This highest, intuitive knowledge gives birth to a *love directed toward God,* considered as an immutable and eternal object.[33] This love is not a passion but an active affect, since it springs from a perfect sort of knowledge of oneself in relation to the eternal order of nature. The mind is able to form an adequately clear and distinct idea of itself and its body, by viewing them intuitively and a priori in their eternal essence, as constituted by the eternal power and attributes of God. The mind rejoices in this perfect knowledge and refers the joy to God as its cause. Thus the definition of love is fulfilled at an eminent level, where the senses do not intervene and where the mind is serene in the face of the vicissitudes of temporal life. Hence the intuitive degree of knowledge is consummated in an intellectual love of God, *amor Dei intellectualis*. This love is just as eternal as the knowledge from which it springs. It furnishes the mind with an impregnable seat for controlling the passions, increasing the scope of the active affects, and thus achieving stable happiness in this life. Through our intellectual love of God, we become par-

---

[33] The doctrine on love of God is set forth in *Ethics,* V, 15–20 (Wild, 379–381).

takers in God's own love for Himself, insofar as He expresses Himself through the eternal essence of the human mind. But Spinoza's God loves men only in the sense that He loves Himself and makes *our* intellectual love for Him *a part of His* infinite love for His own nature, in all its aspects. There can be no distinctive love of God for us, since (on the definition of the active affects) this would involve an increase of perfection on God's part. Once more, the cleft of equivocal predication opens up between love as a human affect and God's love for Himself. Spinoza cannot accept St. John's sentence that God is caritative love, since he has no way of attributing such love to God without derogating from His infinite perfection.

Spinoza's entire methodology and metaphysics are ordered toward the outcropping of an eternal and intellectual love of God in time. This love is the most striking proof of the power of sovereign reason, operating according to its own laws, amid the passions, painful sadness, and misfortune of temporal existence. Fortified by his reflection upon the power of eternal substance, Spinoza brings the *Ethics* to a conclusion with this triumphant confession of faith: "Our salvation, or blessedness, or liberty consists in a constant and eternal love toward God, or in the love of God toward men."[34] Our intellectual love of God constitutes for us: salvation, blessedness, liberty, and eternity. Each of these notes deserves special analysis.

Spinoza's philosophy is for him a doctrine of *salvation*. It is a religious rationalism, bringing all the emotional power of the religious search to bear upon philosophical issues and, at the same time, transferring to philosophy the functions previously associated with religion. Our increase in knowledge, along with the corresponding moral ascesis or liberation from the passions, is a process of transforming our entire manner of being. Basically, it is a growth in understanding and the power of mind. Salvation comes from our moral advance, and the latter is acquired through a meditative, philosophical clarification of our ideas. Morality and philosophical reason thus appropriate the content of religion, insofar as it makes a truth-claim and seeks to save men. All that is left for *religion* — as distinct from the cultivation of reason and the active affects — is the practical work of encouraging us to seek personal perfection and social amity. Miracles,

---

[34] *Ibid.*, V, 35, Scholium (Wild, 392–393). R. McCall, "The Teleological Approach to Spinoza," *The New Scholasticism,* 17 (1943), 134–155, advises that an adequate evaluation of Spinoza must take account of his struggle to accommodate the idea of natural necessity to an ethicoreligious search after rebirth and social communion in God.

prophecy, revelation, and the supernatural are eliminated from an outlook that regards the universe as a rigidly determined and exhaustively expressive manifestation of God's power. Faith has nothing to do with the apprehension of *truth* but is confined to the inculcation of *piety* and *obedience*. Spinoza's *fides catholica* is a set of natural maxims about the existence and unity of God and our own duty of obedience.[35] It is recommended solely as a means of providing a minimal basis of practical agreement among all men. The Deists approved of this minimal code but made it the substance of their philosophy. For Spinoza, however, faith and philosophy are completely separate, the quest of truth being reserved for philosophy and natural reason.

At the outset of his treatise on method, Spinoza had stated that all men seek happiness or the possession of the highest good. He had also suggested that happiness would only be found in a knowledge of the union existing between mind and nature. Now, at the end of his investigation, he reaffirms this conviction in his statement that our *beatitude* comes from the love of God, insofar as it issues from the intuitive knowledge of God's attributes and their consequences in the modal world of *natura naturata*. Blessedness is not a reward for being virtuous but is, as the Stoics claimed, virtue itself. When we become aware that our endeavor is to persevere in our being as an eternal mode of God, power and virtue are perfected within us and comprise our beatitude. Blessedness is the peace of soul belonging to the wise man: it is indistinguishable from his hard-won wisdom.

Spinoza also revises the meaning of *liberty*, so that it can apply to man as well as God. Although he cannot accept the Stoic ideal of the free man in its original formulation, he does seek to reconcile it somehow with his own determinism. Insofar as man *acts*, in the pregnant sense of being an adequate cause, he is liberated from the passions and thus enjoys a negative freedom from external bondage. But he owes this liberation precisely to his unblinking recognition that, as a modal being, he is determined by God and hence is necessitated by another. The sole freedom available to us is just this lucid

---

[35] Cf. *A Theologico-Political Treatise,* Chap. XIV (Elwes translation, *The Chief Works of Benedict De Spinoza,* Dover reprint, I, 182–189). For orientation in this treatise, consult L. Strauss' essay, "How to Study Spinoza's *Theologico-Political Treatise,*" in *Persecution and the Art of Writing* (Glencoe, Ill., Free Press, 1952), 142–201.

consciousness of being inwardly determined by God and of doing what He determines us to do. Whereas God has the *spontaneous freedom* of the primitive power affirming its own substantial being and all other things, the enlightened mind may acquire the *acquiescent freedom* of being clearly aware of its inwardly necessitated mode of being. Since this is an adequate knowledge, the mind comes to view the necessary emanation of modes from God's eternal standpoint. This insight into the wellspring of all determined being is an act of love and our only true liberty.

Nevertheless, if freedom means no more than this, many aspects of Spinoza's argument become unintelligible. A number of covert admissions of another sort of freedom must be made, in order to explain the return of man to God. This is evident in the mind's turning away from imagination and its adherence to reason, as well as in its deliberate replacement of inadequate ideas by clear and distinct ones. Similarly, a positive measure of finite freedom is needed to detach our affects from the idea of an external cause and to concentrate attention upon our own nature. Spinoza gives a *retrospective* interpretation of these decisive conversions of soul, in accord with his metaphysical principles. But in their own nature and *original act,* they manifest a responsible and deliberate dominion that surpasses the conduct of even a spiritual automaton, however inwardly aware of its determination by an infinitely powerful cause.

Although Spinoza sometimes speaks in a popular way about the *immortality of the soul,* his characteristic doctrine concerns the *eternity of the mind.*[36] His position is not articulated with all desirable clarity, and commentators are divided about its precise import. The account in the *Ethics* is doubly complicated by the fact that Spinoza wants to adjust his solution to his total system and also take a critical stand toward the popular interest in personal survival. Significantly, he bases his argument for the eternity of the human mind

---

[36] *Short Treatise on God, Man, and His Well-Being,* II, Preface, Chap. 22, and Appendix 2 (Wild, 84–85 n., 86–93); *ibid.,* II, 23, 26 (A. Wolf's separate edition, 136–37, 147); *Ethics,* V, 22–23, 40, *Scholium* (Wild, 384–385, 397). In the *Short Treatise,* the soul is represented as being capable of looking either in the direction of the perishing body (in which respect, the soul itself disappears at death) or of turning by an act of love to the eternal, divine substance (in which respect, the soul undergoes a spiritual rebirth or regeneration in eternal life). In the *Ethics,* an attempt is made to demonstrate the mind's eternity, from the standpoint of the eternal essence of the body itself. For a personalist criticism, cf. R. A. Tsanoff, "Pantheism and Personal Immortality," *The Rice Institute Pamphlet,* 40 (1953), 1–23.

upon an analysis of the human body. The body can be regarded in two ways: either as a durationally existent, contingent arrangement of figure and motion or as the realization of an eternal, essential structure. Considered in the first way, the body has a limited duration and is perishable. Insofar as the human mind is the idea of this temporally existing, corporeal configuration, it is also perishable. Viewed in the second way or from the standpoint of eternity, however, the essence of the body is seen to flow with eternal necessity from God's essence. Correlatively, the idea expressive of the essence of the human body is an eternal mode of thought and appertains necessarily to the essence of the human mind. Hence there is an eternal aspect of the human mind which is not subject to temporal duration and dissolution. Spinoza concludes that "this something" (*hoc aliquid*) must have an eternal existence precisely as an eternal mode of thinking and an integral part of the infinite intellect or mode of God's attribute of thought.

In the Spinozistic system, there is no "personal survival," as this term is commonly understood. Spinoza eliminates the question of survival entirely, in the sense of a prolongation of the conditions of durational or temporal existence. For, his point is that our eternity (like our blessedness) belongs to us here and now, as soon as we cease to rely upon imagination and its standpoint of existence-as-duration. The mind is eternalized in the degree that it attains the *scientia intuitiva* and thus learns to view its own nature as an eternal expression of the divine attribute of thought, within the modal totality of the infinite intellect. Since the philosophically instructed mind can make the transition even now from *existence-as-duration* to *existence-as-eternity,* it is even now capable of gaining its eternity. In the process of eternalization, the contingent and temporal features of the mind are reduced to the status of deficiencies in the imaginative outlook. Hence after death, there will remain none of the empirical memories and durational experiences of our contingent life. Some individual, modal traits may share in the rebirth to eternity, but the integral personal self of our temporal experience is exchanged for a *hoc aliquid,* which is a subsumed part of the infinite intellect.

The doctrine on the eternity of the mind shows that Spinoza overcomes the Cartesian *horizontal* dualism of two co-ordinated subsubstances in man, only to fall victim to a *vertical* dualism of imagination and reason, durational and eternal existence. "Eternity cannot be defined by time or have any relationship to it. Nevertheless we feel and know by experience that we are eternal."[37] The nature of this quasi-mystical, experiential feeling does not become a direct subject of analysis for Spinoza. It cannot be identified with the lowest degree of perception but is rather a way of expressing the burning faith in the power and reality of eternal substance which permeates all his philosophy. The doctrine on the attributes and modes is an attempt to state geometrically how something other than this unique substance can exist. At the end of the systematic explanation, however, Spinoza admits that the approach of his a priori rationalism to the problem of the one and the many leaves us with no analogical mode of predication between the eternal one and the temporal many. Mind may eternalize itself and gain a new life in this system, but it does so at the cost of denying a relationship between time and eternity, considered as distinct and real ways of existing on the part of finite persons and the infinite person.

SUMMARY

How can the human mind gain the highest conceivable union with God? Spinoza begins his philosophical quest after happiness with this leading question. It supposes both that we are now deprived of this union and that it lies within our power to achieve it. The union with God is absent, insofar as we view ourselves and the world through the eyes of imagination and the common order of nature. Methodic, intellectual discipline is needed, therefore, in order to detach ourselves from inadequate cognitions (which stand for our temporal duration, contingency, and finite freedom) and attach ourselves to a superior kind of knowledge (which reveals the eternal and necessary power of God as constitutive of our own being). True philosophy must make the order and connection of ideas mirror exactly the order and connection of things. Hence Spinoza opens his metaphysics with the self-affirmation of the divine substance as cause of itself. His entire explanation of the attributes of God and the procession of the modal world is a bold essay at capturing in philosophical thought the creative power and causal order of the unique, divine substance itself. Human nature must be remade in conformity with this standpoint of eternity, which treats man as a finite union of mind and body, i.e., as a correspondence between two finite modes of the infinite attributes of thought and extension. This view of man is intended not only to eliminate the Cartesian dualism of substances but also to facilitate the moral return to God. The more the mind meditates upon the eternal order of necessary causes, the more is it enabled to transform its passions into active affects and thus increase its power and virtue. Following its proper *conatus*, the

---

[37] *Ethics*, V, 23, Scholium (Wild, 385).

mind feeds upon the intuitive vision of God and gives expression to an intellectual love of God. Thereby, it undergoes a rebirth to the eternity of its own essential nature as a part of the infinite intellect.

BIBLIOGRAPHICAL NOTE

1. *Sources and Translations.* The critical edition of Spinoza's *Opera* was prepared by C. Gebhardt, 4 Vols. (Heidelberg: Winter, 1925). The F. A. Hayes translation of Spinoza, *Earlier Philosophical Writings* (Indianapolis: Bobbs-Merrill, 1964), contains his exposition of *Descartes' Principles of Philosophy and his Metaphysical Thoughts.* A. Wolf's translation of Spinoza's *Short Treatise on God, Man, and His Well-Being* (London: Black, 1910) also includes Wolf's *Life of Spinoza.* The *Chief Works of Benedict De Spinoza,* translated by R. H. M. Elwes, 2 Vols. (London: Bell, 1883; paperback reprint, New York: Dover, 1955), contains: *Theologico-Political Treatise, A Political Treatise, On the Improvement of the Understanding, Ethics,* and *Selected Correspondence.* A relatively complete edition of *The Correspondence of Spinoza* (New York: Dial Press, 1928) is translated by A. Wolf. A mixture of translations is used in *Spinoza Selections* (New York: Scribner, 1930), ed. by J. Wild (using Elwes translation of *On the Improvement of the Understanding,* selections from Wolf translation of *Short Treatise* and *Correspondence,* and W. H. White translation of *Ethics*). A. G. Wernham gives the Latin text and a fresh translation of Spinoza, *The Political Works* (Oxford: Clarendon, 1958), containing the *Tractatus Theologico-Politicus* in part and the entire *Tractatus Politicus,* together with a helpful Introduction. Spinoza's *Hebrew Grammar* is translated by M. J. Bloom (New York: Philosophical Library, 1962).

2. *Studies.* Along with Wolf's *Life of Spinoza* (in his edition of *Short Treatise*) one may consult *The Oldest Biography of Spinoza,* ed. and translated by A. Wolf (London: Allen and Unwin, 1927), containing the French text and English translation of the *Life* probably written by J. M. Lucas in 1678 and first published in 1719. Important biographical and philosophical findings were made by S. von Dunin-Borkowski, *Spinoza,* second ed., 4 Vols. (Münster: Aschendorff, 1933–1936). His researches are summarized in the first part of P. Siwek's *Spinoza et le panthéisme religieux,* new ed. (Paris: Desclée, 1950), which is an excellent general account and Thomistic critique. Other quite reliable introductions are: R. McKeon, *The Philosophy of Spinoza* (New York: Longmans, Green, 1928); L. Roth, *Spinoza* (London: Benn, 1929); S. Hampshire, *Spinoza* (Baltimore: Penguin Books, 1952); H. F. Hallett, *Benedict De Spinoza: The Elements of His Philosophy* (Fair Lawn: Essential Books, 1957). H. Wolfson's *The Philosophy of Spinoza,* 2 Vols. (Cambridge: Harvard University Press, 1934; one-volume ed., 1948; also, Cleveland: World Publishing Co. Meridian Books, 1958) is invaluable for the medieval Jewish background, as well as for its careful analysis of Spinoza's argument. D. Bidney's *The Psychology and Ethics of Spinoza* (New Haven: Yale University Press,

1940) makes some acute dialectical observations but lacks historical control. Spinoza's methodology is examined by: H. H. Joachim, *Spinoza's Tractatus De Intellectus Emendatione, A Commentary* (Oxford: Clarendon, 1940); A. Darbon, *Études spinozistes* (Paris: Presses Universitaires, 1946); H. G. Hubbeling, *Spinoza's Methodology* (Assen: Van Gorcum, 1964). The levels of knowing are studied by C. de Deugd, *The Significance of Spinoza's First Kind of Knowledge* (Assen: Van Gorcum, 1966). G. H. R. Parkinson, *Spinoza's Theory of Knowledge* (Oxford: Clarendon, 1954), makes a radical critique through the epistemological crevice, whereas C. J. Sullivan weighs the split between the eternalistic and the naturalistic view of man, in *Critical and Historical Reflections on Spinoza's "Ethics"* (Berkeley and Los Angeles: University of California Press, 1958).

Commentaries on the *Ethics* are offered by: H. H. Joachim, *A Study of the Ethics of Spinoza* (Oxford: Clarendon, 1901), in terms of analytic idealism; A. Shanks, *An Introduction to Spinoza's Ethics* (London: Macmillan, 1938); R. L. Saw, *The Vindication of Metaphysics: A Study in the Philosophy of Spinoza* (London: Macmillan, 1951), a linguistic restatement and defense of the metaphysics on practical grounds. S. Zac, *L'Idée de la vie dans la philosophie de Spinoza* (Paris: Presses Universitaires, 1963), treats the unifying concept of life as a substitute for teleology in nature. J. Ratner, *Spinoza on God* (New York: Holt, 1930); W. Cramer, *Spinozas Philosophie des Absoluten* (Frankfurt: Klostermann, 1966); and A. Malet, *Le Traité theologico-politique de Spinoza et la pensée biblique* (Paris: Belles Lettres, 1966), study God and revelation.

Spinoza's medieval Jewish background can be understood with the aid of: J. Guttmann, *Philosophies of Judaism* (New York: Holt, Rinehart, 1964), Part Two; I. Husik, *A History of Medieval Jewish Philosophy* (Philadelphia: Jewish Publication Society, 1941; also New York: Harper Torchbook, 1958); L. Roth, *Spinoza, Descartes and Maimonides* (Oxford: Clarendon, 1924). The comparison with Descartes on the problem of God is deepened by P. Lachièze-Rey, *Les Origines cartésiennes du Dieu de Spinoza* (Paris: Alcan, 1932), while the Spinoza-Leibniz relationship is probed by G. Friedmann, *Leibniz et Spinoza*, new ed. (Paris: Gallimard, 1962). The Dutch setting, with its intermingling of Scholastic and Cartesian factors, is described by: E. J. Dijksterhuis and others, *Descartes et le cartésianisme hollandais* (Paris: Presses Universitaires, 1960), and by P. Dibon, *La Philosophie néerlandaise au siècle d'or*, Vol. I (Amsterdam: Elsevier, 1954). Spinoza's later influence in France and Russia, respectively, is traced out in P. Vernière's *Spinoza et la pensée française avant la révolution*, 2 Vols. (Paris: Presses Universitaires, 1954), and in G. Kline's *Spinoza in Soviet Philosophy* (London: Routledge and Kegan Paul, 1952). H. F. Hallett has written two metaphysical essays in the Spinozistic spirit: *Aeternitas, A Spinozistic Study* (Oxford: Clarendon, 1930), and *Creation, Emanation and Salvation: A Spinozistic Study* (The Hague: Nijhoff, 1962).

Chapter III. GOTTFRIED WILHELM LEIBNIZ

I. LIFE AND WRITINGS

BORN at Leipzig in 1646, Gottfried Wilhelm Leibniz had the advantages of comfortable circumstances and an intellectual environment. Although his father (who was a professor of moral philosophy at the University of Leipzig) died when his son was only six years old, the child had full access to the excellent family library. Teaching himself Latin, Leibniz read omnivorously in classical history, literature, and philosophy. He familiarized himself with Plato, Aristotle, and several of the later Scholastics. All his days, Leibniz remained basically a self-taught mind, even though he underwent a complete academic education. He entered the University of Leipzig in 1661 and prepared a remarkable *Metaphysical Disputation on the Principle of the Individual* (1663) for his bachelor's degree. This essay manifested his wide acquaintance with Suarez and other Scholastics, as well as his early preoccupation with a central problem in his later philosophy: the nature of the individual. After taking the master's degree at Leipzig, Leibniz continued his legal studies and presented himself for the doctorate in law. Since Leipzig refused to grant him this degree, because of his youth, he went to the University of Altdorf. There, he was not only awarded the doctor's degree for a brilliant dissertation, *On Perplexing Cases in Law* (1666), but was also invited to take a professorship. His refusal of this position indicated his desire to participate in practical matters and affairs of state rather than to devote himself professionally to the teaching of philosophy and jurisprudence. He did publish a *Dissertation on the Art of Combination* (1666), which set forth his project for a universal set of symbols, by the combination of which all philosophical problems could be solved with mathematical exactitude. This plan reflected his enthusiasm after spending a semester at Jena in mathematical studies. But he balanced this work with a treatise on jurisprudence, which won the attention of the influential Baron Johan von Boineburg, a councilor of the Elector of Mainz. With the Baron's aid, Leibniz secured a post with the Elector. He soon aided his employer's political cause with a demonstration *ordine geometrico* that the Elector's candidate, and no other, was fitted to be chosen King of Poland!

In 1672, Leibniz was sent on a diplomatic mission to Paris. His task was to distract Louis XIV from an attack on Holland and the Germanies by dangling before him the alternative of a glorious conquest of Egypt. The interview with the French king was never obtained but Leibniz profited in an intellectual way by his visit. He took a side trip to England, in order to establish scientific contacts. Back in Paris, he agreed with Malebranche and Arnauld that the Cartesian mathematical method was valuable, and yet added that Descartes' mechanistic physics stultified scientific research. Leibniz received expert guidance on mathematical problems from the great physicist, Christian Huyghens, and by 1676 he had worked out the calculus. Although he reached his conclusions quite independently of Newton, there was an unfortunate controversy, twenty years later, over the question of priority between Newton and Leibniz. While still in Paris, Leibniz transferred his services to the Duke of Brunswick-Lüneburg. On his way to the ducal court at Hanover, he paid a visit (1676) to Spinoza and copied some notes from the manuscript of the *Ethics*. Leibniz always respected Spinoza's metaphysical vision but sought to provide metaphysics with a more rigorous method of demonstration and to defend the freedom of God and the personal immortality of the human soul.

At Hanover, Leibniz served as librarian and historian of the House of Brunswick. He was indefatigable in tracing down genealogical lines, ransacking archives in several countries for the early history of the House, and defending its claims on historical and legal grounds. Yet he also found time to engage in correspondence with Bossuet and Arnauld concerning the reunion of Catholic and Protestant Churches, to invent a calculating machine for extracting root numbers, and to encourage the foundation of learned societies in the European capitols. He himself founded and was the first lifetime president of the Prussian Academy of Sciences at Berlin; he also founded the first learned journal in the Germanies: *Acta Eruditorum* (1682). His philosophical writings were somehow fitted into this busy schedule, although most of them were short notes, incidental papers, and outlines sent to correspondents. The *Discourse on Metaphysics* (1686) probably originated as part of the preface to a projected work aiming at the reunion of the churches. In the *New Essays concerning the Human Understanding* (completed in 1704 but laid aside at Locke's death; published, 1765, just in time to influence Kant), Leibniz made a careful analysis of Locke's empiricism and pointed to the active role of the understanding and its native ideas. In reply to Bayle's challenge that the goodness and power of God cannot be reconciled rationally, in view of evil, Leibniz composed his *Essays on Theodicy* (1710). He summarized his philosophy for a princely correspondent in *Principles of Nature and Grace* (1714) and especially in *The Monadology* (German translation published, 1720; French original published, 1840), which restated his fundamental views in terms of monads. Leibniz was engaged in a polemical correspondence with the English Newtonian, Samuel Clarke, concerning Newton's doctrine on space and time, when death put a halt to his work (1716). He had not been permitted to come to England in 1714 for the coronation of George I, of the House of Brunswick, because of his controversies with English scholars. His death went uncommemorated at home but a suitable eulogy was pronounced by Fontenelle before the French Academy.

2. A UNIVERSAL SCIENCE AND UNIVERSAL HARMONY

Leibniz' philosophical interests are so far-flung and his influence upon later developments so varied that it is difficult to hold his thought in proper focus. He has been hailed as a forerunner of symbolic logic, as a metaphysical genius, and as a religious apologist. These facets, and many more, are essential to the understanding of his mind. In order to obtain a principle of orderly interpretation of his work, we may pay heed to his own compendious statement that happiness depends upon knowledge of the nature of God and the soul, whereas this knowledge depends in turn upon the ability to demonstrate by means of a method of certainty. Leibniz was convinced of the solidarity between the *love of God,* the *promotion of human welfare,* and the *perfecting of reason.* These goals were the main ones that enlisted his energies, and he felt that if they could not all be promoted together, there would be a relapse of Western culture into barbarism. Philosophy has an ultimately religious and moral orientation in that it directs the mind to contemplation and love of God, along with a well-ordered relationship with one's fellow men. But there is no conflict between this exalted end and a conscientious regard for temporal problems, both practical and theoretical. The reconciliation of piety and reason is a basic premise of the efforts of Leibniz. Reason is able to offer strict demonstration of the basic metaphysical truths, but it can do so only with the help of a sound method. Mathematics provides the tools for over-hauling our logical techniques and assures a uniform rigor in all our inquiries. These are familiar themes in the seventeenth century, but they are given a vigorous and subtle development by Leibniz.

Beginning with his early writings and persisting to the end of his career, there is a dual leitmotiv that provides the organizing principle of his speculations: the foundation of a *universal science* (*scientia generalis*) and the elucidation and defense of the *universal harmony of being*. Leibniz' mathematical and logical studies are polarized around the former purpose, his metaphysical and ethico-religious studies around the latter. The relation between these two basic themes is one of mutual support and confirmation, rather than of conflict. The universal science is to provide the logical groundwork, without which all discussion about universal harmony would be mere loose dreaming, whereas the theory of universal harmony is to insure the relevance of consistent thinking for the real world. Together, these twin guideposts are to lead to a philosophy that is both rigorously constructed and fruitfully engaged in searching out the meaning of actual entities.

Even as a schoolboy, Leibniz was fascinated by Aristotle's teaching on the categories. For here was a classification that claimed to account for all our concepts and simple terms. Leibniz wanted to enlarge the boundaries of categorization, by working out the funda-mental classification of all judgments as well as concepts, so that all our thoughts could be derived from a few basic elements. Further-more, he sought to place the categorization of thoughts upon a sound, mathematical footing. Descartes had entertained a similar plan but — in Leibniz' estimation — had abandoned it, in the course of his actual attempts at physical and metaphysical analysis. Leibniz agreed with Descartes on two main points: that the human mind can elaborate a *common scientific method,* in abstraction from the content of the particular sciences, and that *analysis* and *synthesis* must be employed in constructing this common logic of the sciences. But he claimed originality on three further scores. (1) Analysis is to be brought to bear, not merely upon the ideas resident in the individual, introspective mind, but also upon the actual findings of the sciences. Hence Leibniz emphasized the need to make a *complete inventory* of our reliable knowledge, in order to provide the best materials for analysis. (2) Descartes had left in obscurity the type of order obtaining among the elements or simple natures, in which his analysis terminated. Leibniz agreed that it would be desirable to be able to arrange the analytic elements according to a natural order, but at least we can treat them as *components in a calculus or system of combination.* (3) The work of combining the elementary units of thought, in order to recompose the totality of our thoughts and discover new truths, is to be facilitated by assigning to every elementary object its *characteristic symbol* or number. From a combination or synthesis of these symbols, complex truths can be derived. "If we could find characters or signs appropriate for expressing all our thoughts as definitely and exactly as arithmetic expresses numbers or geometric analysis expresses lines, we could in all subjects *in so far as they are amenable to reasoning* accomplish what is done in Arithmetic and Geometry."[1] Leibniz was specially enthusiastic about the prospects for this universal language or *characteristica universalis.*

Once the content of human knowledge is gathered together in a Baconian sort of encyclopedia of truths, the operation of *analysis* or resolution can begin. Its aim is to reduce complex judgments and concepts to simpler ones, until at last the mind arrives at a "catalogue of simple thoughts . . . a kind of alphabet of human thoughts."[2] These analytically irreducible elements constitute a set of *primitive terms* and *universal principles,* which provide the groundwork of all scientific knowledge. These few primitive terms and principles are certain, and not merely hypothetical; they do not depend on any prior noetic conditions, but are known *per se.* Since they have been drawn from orderly bodies of knowledge, we can treat them as components in a system of combinations. This enables us to employ

---

[1] *Preface to the General Science* (*Leibniz Selections,* edited by P. Wiener, 15); cf. *Towards a Universal Characteristic* (Wiener, 17–25). The mathematical realism of this method is brought out in *Dialogue on the Connection between Things and Words* (Wiener, 6–11). Quotations from *Leibniz Selections* are made with the permission of Charles Scribner's Sons. For a comparison between Leibniz and Wittgenstein on the language — thought — fact relationship, see W. Kneale, "Leibniz and the Picture Theory of Language," *Revue Internationale de Philosophie,* 20 (1966), 204–215.

[2] *On Wisdom* (Wiener, 80); *Towards a Universal Characteristic* (Wiener, 20). The analytic discovery of basic terms and principles is outlined in two essays: *Precepts for advancing the Sciences and Arts* and *The Art of Discovery* (Wiener, 29–46, 50–58).

the methods of mathematical calculus, in working out the universal science or general logic of the sciences.

The *synthetic* or combinatory aspect of the new method is greatly aided by the substitution of universally accepted signs or characteristics for the basic categories of thought. Once the alphabet of thoughts is fixed in a set of symbols, Leibniz augured that the work of synthesis will become just as infallible as the combining of letters into words, and of words into phrases and sentences. At least in his early writings, he gave special preference to numerical symbols. Number is a sort of basic metaphysical form, because everything (including our concepts and judgments) can be subsumed under it. Later on, as his logical studies developed, he broadened his conception of the symbolic notations to be employed in the combinational calculus. But whatever the symbols, their use is advantageous. They fix the meaning of a term in a definite way, aid the memory, relieve the mind of excessive dependence upon its visualizing power, and reduce the incidence of controversies. Disputes can be settled by suggesting: "Gentlemen, let us calculate." Submission of issues to the impersonal and unequivocal test of symbolic calculation reveals errors and achieves unanimity.

Leibniz was interested, not only in constructing a universal logical method, but also in employing it for the discovery of philosophical truths. Hence he was concerned about the relation between the results of a combination of characteristics and the real world. He did not claim that the *isolated* symbols have any representative function or that they are natural signs of things. But he did hold that the symbolical notations are not arbitrary in their *relation of combination* with one another.[3] In their mutual connections, they are regulated by the order of our ideas and, ultimately, by the natural order of the things expressed in ideas. Because of this objective reference of the order among formal symbols, it is easy to explain, for instance, how it is possible in mathematics to reach the same conclusion through the use of different systems of notations. A common result can be obtained, because of a common relation of the several sets of signs

---

[3] *Dialogue on the Connection between Things and Words* (Wiener, 10–11). See F. Kaulbach, "Der Begriff des Charakters in der Philosophie von Leibniz," *Kant-Studien,* 57 (1966), 126–141.

to the order and connection of concepts and things. *Truth* is based upon the relationship that a system of characters bears toward things in their interconnectedness. Symbolical combinations express natural relations among our basic categorial concepts and among the things to which those concepts ultimately refer, in the real world. Hence Leibniz regarded his *scientia generalis* as a system of the fundamental concepts common to all the sciences, and not merely as a formal calculus of terms and propositions.

A distinction must be made, however, between the use of the common logical method in the more speculative fields and its use in the more practical fields of study. In *speculative* sciences, it is enough to have the primitive terms and principles, together with the new art of combination and discovery, in order to guide experimental work and arrive at remote conclusions. Even in matters which require some basis in experience, theory can anticipate practice, provided only that the experimental findings can be given some kind of rational explanation. The role of observation and experiment can never be completely eliminated from speculative studies, and it is given special prominence in the *practical* disciplines. In matters of personal and public policy, Leibniz bids us look with suspicion upon bare rational inference, unsupported by experimental findings. The same standard of certainty cannot be required in ethical and political problems as in mathematics or metaphysics, since we must make practical decisions on the basis of the more likely opinion. But the use of a scientific method can guide our determination of what is, in fact, the more likely opinion. Leibniz suggests that a theory of ethical and legal probability can be made just as reliable and objective as the statistical approach to games of chance and insurance risks, with the aid of a suitable symbolical language. Moral certitude can be obtained, not only from the testimony of human witnesses, but also from the logically calculated likelihood of events and consequences of practical decisions.

In attempting to realize this ideal of a universal science, Leibniz was soon confronted with three serious difficulties. (1) Like Bacon, he found that it lies beyond the power of an individual man to make an *adequate collection* of the materials of knowledge. Since Leibniz himself did not have the encyclopedia of knowledge at hand, he could not supply a sufficiently broad basis for the analytic phase of the logical method. His constant interest in the welfare of learned societies and journals indicated his hope that co-operative labor might eventually supply the materials for a comprehensive analysis. (2) But even granted the success of an encyclopedic project, analysis itself supposes the presence of a determinate set of elementary terms and real definitions, so that the analytic process can be terminated. Leibniz began by sharing the assumption of Bacon and Descartes that the number of simple terms is *finite*. His scientific studies and his metaphysical account of real substances soon convinced him, however, that their number is *infinite*. Since the number of primitive indefinable ideas and real definitions is infinite, the resolutive analysis can never be completed by our minds. It follows that the primitive terms reached by Leibniz' new art of discovery are not primary in an absolute way, but only in relation to the finite mind. (3) Finally, analysis can never completely *isolate* the basic terms and definitions. This is not due to any purely logical obstacle but to the interrelatedness of the beings in the universe to which our thoughts and categorial terms ultimately refer. Because an unconditionally primitive set of terms cannot be reached and given in isolation, the conditions are not present for a perfectly comprehensive process of synthesis or combination.

These considerations forced Leibniz to modify his claims for the universal logical method. But he never abandoned the ideal of a common logic of the sciences. From the inability of logical analysis to secure its own foundations with complete satisfaction, it does not follow that the search for a general logic of the sciences is futile. The only legitimate inference is that the human mind cannot make a purely *logical* founding of knowledge. Hence Leibniz set about integrating his methodological requirements with a general *metaphysical* outlook, so that the universal science might be as well founded as is humanly possible.

Leibniz sought this foundation in God and the principle of harmony. The only way we can have a priori assurance that the interconnected ideas (upon which our basic terms rest) are themselves in conformity with the interconnected universe of things is by reference to God. He is the *common creator* both of things and of our ideas of things. In creating the real order, He had regard for their conformity with the ideas to be communicated to our minds, whereas in furnishing our minds with the primitive set of ideas, He also had regard for their conformity with real things. Hence the process of logical analysis terminates properly in the primitive ideas, considered precisely as having their foundation in the divine intellect.[4] Even though the number of primitive indefinables be infinite, we can be sure that those which terminate our analytic resolution, do express the real relations obtaining among things. Furthermore, since God has *respect for the ideal of universal harmony* in his production of both the real things and their signs in our minds, we may achieve some systematic comprehensiveness and rigor, by regulating our finite set of terms and definitions according to the exigencies of this same ideal. In this way, at least a reliable approach can be made to the establishment of the universal method or common logic of all the sciences.

Leibniz did not have to cut the metaphysics of harmony hurriedly out of whole cloth. Already in his earliest writings, he evinced great sympathy toward the references of Platonic writers to the *principle of universal harmony*. He defined it tersely as "unity-in-variety," and added that "the greater the unity-in-variety, the greater is the harmony."[5] Harmony provided an answer to the *problem of the one and the many,* which Leibniz posed at all levels of his philosophy. The human individual is aware of his own abiding identity and also of the ceaseless succession of his perceptions: this is the psychological way of viewing the tension between the one and the many, being and becoming. The individual's perception reaches out to the bodies in the universe which are many and yet bound together, both by their inclusion in the same cosmos and by their common presence in the individual's consciousness. Moreover, if the universe is produced by God, the difficulty arises of reconciling the infinite simplicity of the first cause and the infinite multitude of its effects. In the moral order, we are asked to acquire the stability of virtue and a unified character, so that we will not become confused and disintegrated in the face of the bewildering number of situations and evils of life. Even the logical enterprise is an attempt to bring to the several sciences the unity of method and a common formal structure. Confronted with these various aspects of the problem of the one and the many, Leibniz felt that the notion of harmony alone could provide an adequate synthesis, capable of

---

[4] *What is an Idea* (Wiener, 282–283); cf. L. E. Loemker, "Leibniz's Conception of Philosophical Method," *Zeitschrift für philosophische Forschung,* 20 (1966), 507–524.

[5] *The Elements of True Piety (G. W. Leibniz, Textes inédits,* edited by G. Grua, I, 12); cf. *The Monadology,* 58–59 (Wiener, 544–545).

avoiding the extremes of Spinoza's monism and Gassendi's unbridled pluralism.

Harmony is impossible, if everything is reduced to the one or dispersed in the many. For it is nothing other than a *unity of order and relation among many factors*, a *diversity tempered by a certain identity*. Mathematics supplied a hint of the fertile power of harmony through the method of universals, employed successfully by Descartes and Pascal. They discovered certain harmonies or proportional similarities among figures hitherto regarded as quite unrelated, and in this way established a general idea for solving problems in several fields. The same technique could be used in physical questions, since the closer one studies nature, the more one sees it to be geometrical. But Leibniz did not accept a purely mathematical interpretation of nature, since he saw that mathematical principles cannot be *applied* to nature without first having recourse to a metaphysical explanation. He agreed with Galileo that the extension of mathematics to nature can be made with assurance only because *God* is "a perfect Geometer,"[6] the creator who produces things in accordance with the standards of harmony. Thus God supplies the fundamental link between harmony and the view that real, natural being is intelligible in a mathematical way. The project of a universal characteristic is fundamentally possible, because God has made all things according to number and harmony. The Leibnizian art of discovery receives its guarantee of objective validity for existential propositions, through its connection with the metaphysics of harmony.

Taken in the most general way, the idea of harmony is the *seminal source of the major doctrines* that control Leibniz' speculation. The close relation between harmony and intelligibility is a preparation for connecting harmony and essence. In seeking out the harmonies of the universe, philosophy is also bringing to light the essences or reasons of things. Confidence in the ultimate intelligibility of things and their availability to the a priori art of discovery supposes that every being has its *raison d'être,* or sufficient reason, grounded in its own essence. But there is nothing static about the Leibnizian conception of essence. Each essence is a center of striving after existence in its own right. In this respect, the role of harmony is to secure the existence of the greatest amount of essence that is possible.

6 *On a General Principle, Useful for the Explanation of Laws and Nature* (Wiener, 66). See A. T. Tymieniecka, "Leibniz' Metaphysics and His Theory on the Universal Science," *International Philosophical Quarterly,* 3 (1963), 370–391.

The principle of perfection or plenitude states that our universe contains the greatest possible amount of essential perfection. But this maximum is reached only because the claims to existence on the part of a certain number of essences have been reconciled in a harmonious system of compossible being. That the world is made in accordance with the ideal of harmony means, therefore, that it secures as great a variety of essential natures as is compatible with the greatest possible order. The endeavor of an essence for a foothold in the existential world is carried to fruition, only when a harmonious composition can be made between this endeavor and the possibilities of other striving essences. That is why, for Leibniz, *to exist* means *to be integrated harmoniously with other things* in a relation of mutual fitness and essential fullness or perfection. Existence signifies the effective entrance of an essence into the conditions of harmony governing our actual world.

Nevertheless, Leibniz does not want to erect harmony into an autonomous, impersonal, cosmic principle. It is basically an expression of God's own understanding and (in respect to the existing order) of His will. The essential intelligibility and the plenitude of the actual world are due to the fact that God creates things freely, in the light of His own wisdom or standard of harmony. Hence God is the radical seat of harmony, the *ultimate principle of reconciliation* of life's antagonisms. For this reason, Leibniz is confident about a final synthesis of the great dualisms that enliven his thought. Nature can be interpreted both mechanistically and teleologically; the order of phenomena is well founded in the order of being; mind and body are discrete and yet compose in a unity; the microcosm and the macrocosm are mutually proportioned; the kingdom of nature and the kingdom of grace enclose each other. These eirenic theses, so characteristic of Leibniz' approach to theoretical and practical problems alike, derive their logical force and coherence from his metaphysical conviction that the universe is conspiring toward a harmonious totality of being, under the dynamic governance of divine wisdom and will.

3. FIRST PRINCIPLES AND INDIVIDUAL SUBSTANCE

Of all the great seventeenth-century rationalists, Leibniz was the most concerned about establishing the foundations of knowledge in a formal way. He saw that the ideal of constructing a comprehensive and yet ontologically relevant system cannot be executed, until the basic principles have been secured beyond doubt. His studies in this fundamental area were marshaled around three universal *principles governing all essences and existences* (the principles of sufficient reason, contradiction, and contingency or perfection), and two *principles regulative of the actual universe* (the principles of the identity of indiscernibles and continuity). From these primary truths, most of the leading conceptions in his philosophy can be derived. And since the import of his principles is real as well as ideal, their examination also involves a study of *individual substance,* which supplies their point of insertion in the actual world.

LEIBNIZ' BASIC PRINCIPLES

1. Sufficient reason: the ground of all true propositions and of the intelligibility of things.
2. Contradiction and identity: the laws determining all true propositions which express necessary truths, through a finite, terminative analysis.
3. Contingency or perfection: the law determining all true propositions which express contingent truths, through an infinite, nonterminative analysis.
(NOTE: These first principles govern true propositions about all possible worlds and our actual world. The actual universe is a plenum of individual substances, the best possible world, conforming to the following principles.)
4. Identity of indiscernibles: a world of many qualitatively different individual substances, arranged in a graduated scale or hierarchy.
5. Continuity: there are no gaps or interruptions in this hierarchy of actual beings.

Every aspect of thought and reality is governed by the *principle of sufficient reason. Nihil est sine ratione:* nothing is without a sufficient reason — Leibniz hails this as the grandest axiom of his entire system. This principle states that the concept of the predicate is contained analytically in the concept of the subject of every true proposition. "The content of the subject must always include that of the predicate in such a way that if one understands perfectly the concept of the subject, he will know that the predicate appertains to it also."[7] At least in principle, every true proposition is analytic

---

[7] *Discourse on Metaphysics,* VIII (Wiener, 300); cf. the texts gathered under the heading: *The Principle of Sufficient Reason* (Wiener, 93–96). Cf. A. E. Manier, "Leibniz: First Principles and Systematic Philosophy," *The Modern Schoolman,* 43 (1965–1966), 39–54.

in its logical foundation, so that the predicate can be shown to be contained analytically in the concept of the subject. This is the foundation of our conviction in the radical intelligibility of the universe and of our solid hope that systematic explanation of things is possible, through a universal characteristic. Leibniz sometimes refers to it as the principle that a reason must be furnished (*principium rationis reddendae*), since a reason is supplied by manifesting the analytic connection between the concepts of predicate and subject.

Although the principle of sufficient reason regulates all true propositions, it does not furnish specific directions for determining which propositions are, in fact, true. Leibniz noticed that, in its actual operation, human reason employs two different ways of establishing the truth or analytic character of propositions, depending upon what is being expressed in the propositions.[8] Some propositions express *necessary truths* or *truths of essence,* the contradictory opposite of which is absolutely impossible. In determining that propositions belong to this class of truths, the mind can employ a finite sort of analysis. Every *finite analysis* is *terminative.* Demonstration of the truth is made through a limited number of steps, reducing complex propositions to simpler ones and eventually terminating in some primitive, irreducible principles and ideas. The connection among the primitive ideas, to which the complex proposition has been reduced, is immediately seen either to involve a contradiction or to be self-coherent. Hence the process of finite or terminative analysis is regulated by the *principle of contradiction,* with which Leibniz regularly associates what he calls the *principle of identity.* Every finitely or terminatively analytic proposition is known to be true, according to the principle of contradiction. For any proposition seen to involve a contradiction is known to be false, and whatever is opposed to the false is true. The primary principles themselves are identical propositions, in which the analytic inclusion of the predicate in the concept of the subject is immediately evident.

But another process of analytic reduction is needed, in the case of propositions expressive of *contingent truths* or *truths of fact and existence.* For here, the contradictory opposite of the proposition is not absolutely impossible, in the sense of involving a logical con-

---

[8] *Discourse on Metaphysics,* XIII (Wiener, 305–309); *The Monadology,* 31–38 (Wiener, 539–540). For a discussion of the views of Couturat, Russell, and other logicians on Leibniz' first principles, together with a careful exposition of the theory of principles, read chs. 2–4 of Nicholas Rescher, *The Philosophy of Leibniz,* pp. 22–57.

tradiction. The truth of such propositions can never be established by a finite analysis, relying solely upon the principle of contradiction, since they concern the sphere of contingent, existential facts, where the number of states or details is infinite. Two questions faced Leibniz, in regard to propositions containing truths of fact: (1) how are such propositions shown to be true; (2) can they express a contingent truth and still agree with the analytic requirements laid down by the principle of sufficient reason for all true propositions? He found an answer to both questions in the *principle of contingency or perfection,* which he also called the *principle of existence* and the *principle of the best.* This principle governs the mind, when it is forced to make an *infinite* or *nonterminative analysis* of a proposition containing matters of fact or existence. Some truths can be ascertained in this latter domain, by adverting to the law that God creates things according to His standard of choosing the maximum amount of perfection or the best possible world. Although the finite mind cannot reduce existential propositions to the point where their relation of compatibility or incompatibility with the principle of contradiction is evident, it can at least make an indirect demonstration of the analytic inclusion of the predicate in the concept of the subject. For, it can show that the contradictory opposite of such a proposition would, indeed, involve a violation of God's standard of promoting the most perfection or what is best. In a positive way, the truth of a proposition about contingent matters is established by determining that the perfection of the world or the maximum quantity of essence is promoted more by the inclusion of this particular predicate in its subject than by any other one.

Such an analytic process is infinite or nonterminative, from the human standpoint. Although the divine mind can see the direct inclusion of the predicate of an existential proposition in the concept of its subject, we can only see their *convergence.* We approach analytic insight as a mathematical limit, by appealing to the principle of contingency or perfection, as regulative of God's choice of the actual facts and existential conditions prevailing in the world. Thus we can know indirectly *that* the analytic inclusion of predicate in subject does obtain, even though the connection itself escapes our direct gaze. This is sufficient to satisfy the principle of sufficient reason and hence to establish the *truth* of the proposition in question. At the same time, the *contingency* of the existential fact is respected, since the nonterminative analysis does point to infinity. It is important to notice that what Leibniz really establishes here is the contingency of *our knowledge,* rather than the contingency of the *existential order.* This distinction will play a considerable role in evaluating his defense of the divine freedom in creation.

As the next section will show, the principle of contingency or perfection is operative in the sphere of pure essences themselves, insofar as they strive with each other for the opportunity to enter the world of actual existents. Hence Leibniz is sure that there is a rational ground accounting for the existence of all actual things, and this ground is the cause. "Nothing exists but that some reason can be given (at least by an omniscient mind) why it should be rather than not be, and why it should be thus rather than otherwise. . . . Nothing happens without a cause."[9] Hence, although the finite mind is not omniscient and not intuitively aware of analytic inclusions concerning matters of fact, it can explain contingent events with the aid of the *principle of causality.* Causal explanation or furnishing of reasons is made with the aid of both the mechanical, *efficient* cause and the *final* cause. Physics employs the efficient cause to give a mechanistic account of the universe: this approach is accurate but is not a definitive explanation. Hence metaphysics makes distinctive use of the final cause, especially by inquiring about what tends toward achieving the maximum perfection in the actual universe. Philosophical demonstration of essential truths can attain *metaphysical necessity,* since the opposite of the true proposition in the essential order entails a contradiction. But the philosophical investigation of existential affairs can attain at least a *moral necessity.* A proposition is morally necessary, when its opposite would violate the principle of perfection or contingency, especially as specified in terms of final cause. Because of its extension into the existing order, in function of efficient and final cause, the principle of contingency or perfection gives sufficient rational determinateness to existential propositions to assure metaphysics a wide field of scientific research, over and above the truths it ascertains about purely essential relations.

The entire Leibnizian discussion of the first three principles rests upon an analysis of the characteristics of *true* propositions and of our ways of establishing their *truth.* The truth-value of propositions rests ultimately upon the actual existence of real beings, in which the analytic connections are realized. When Leibniz speaks about the

---

[9] *The Elements of True Piety* (Grua, I, 13); untitled fragment (Wiener, 94).

concept of the subject, he means primarily an essence or intelligible form that is eventually embodied as a real, subsistent thing. Propositions concerning the inherence of predicates in the concept of a logical subject are true, in final analysis, because this concept is grounded in a real subject of inherence or a *substance*, containing the qualities or events expressed in these predicates. It is because the truth of propositions is founded ultimately upon real beings, that Leibniz is confident about using a logical argument in favor of the reality of substance.[10] He defines substance as the ultimate term of predication in which the various predicates inhere, and which is not itself predicated of anything else. The logical relation of *in-esse* between the predicates and their ultimate or absolute subject is true, only because it is a reflection of the real relation of *in-esse* between attributes or modes and a substantial subject, existing in the real world. The subsequent rationalistic textbooks in Germany used this subject-predicate argument, without making clear its connection with the theory of truth. Hence it became a favorite target for later empirical critics, who could only discover a grammatical argument, divorced from metaphysical considerations.

Leibniz himself, however, furnished an a posteriori, existential proof for the reality of individual substances. In addition to the three basic principles of sufficient reason, contradiction and contingency or perfection, there are also two irreducible, primitive truths of a wholly existential sort. These latter are given through experience: the *fact of thinking* and the *fact of thinking a variety of thoughts*. The former truth implies the existence of at least my own individual, substantial, thinking self, which is the real source of my cognitive operations. So far, Leibniz agreed with Descartes. But he added that the fact of my having a variety of thoughts is just as distinct, irreducible, and indubitable as the fact of thinking. Now the only sufficient reason of this variety is that I, an individual substance, am not alone in existence but am one member of a universe of many individual, existent substances. My perceptions are representative of what *is*, i.e., of a universe composed of many perceiving substances. Leibniz did not deem himself obliged to argue his way out of solipsism, since he regarded the existence of other individual sub-

---

[10] *Discourse on Metaphysics*, VIII (Wiener, 299–300); *Further Discussion of Vis Viva* (Wiener, 181). For the a posteriori proof, cf. *New Essays concerning Human Understanding*, IV, ii, 1 (Langley translation, 404–405).

stances as being given in a truth, just as primitive as that upon which the assurance of my own substantial existence rests. For Leibniz' empirical successors, this proof presented the challenge of explaining the facts of mental life sufficiently, without supposing the inherence of thoughts in a real subject.

Within the Leibnizian universe, only the *individual substance* is fully real and qualifies as a complete being. It is the ground and reason of all the predicates attributable truly to the thing. The individual substance is no mere static subject of inhesion but a *center of force,* an active source from which the various operations and modifications dynamically emerge. By definition, a *"substance* is a being capable of action."[11] Hence from the concept or essence of the individual substance can be gained, at least in principle, an a priori knowledge not only of the substance itself but also of all the operations and relations that belong to it in its temporal course. Although the human mind cannot complete this analysis of the predicates dynamically enfolded in the individual substance's concept, it can conduct its investigations with the assurance of a rational origination and radication of all contingent, temporal happenings. For the individual substance is precisely the *regulative law* and *active tendency* governing the development of the orderly series of perceptions or phenomena, by which a thing lives its effective existence in the actual universe. In Leibniz' system, the view of individual substance as the *nature,* or active law of its series of perceptual operations, is much more important than the role of substance as the *subject* of inherence. His emphasis upon substance as a regulative law or active tendency prepared the way for Kant's phenomenalistic interpretation of the category of substance, as signifying a permanent ratio or pattern among phenomenal events themselves. The Kantian position on substance as a category represented a compromise between Leibniz' ontological meaning of individual substance and the empiricist criticism.

By integrating his three first principles with the reality of individual substances, Leibniz hoped to counter the assertion of Hobbes that all our definitions and demonstrations are purely nominal. Since his first principles explain the reality of existing substances, Leibniz claimed for them a *real,* and not merely a nominal, significance. Hence

---

11 *The Principles of Nature and of Grace,* 1 (Wiener, 522).

he was confident about their extension to the entire actual universe. Their application to the existing universe is facilitated by the two principles of the identity of indiscernibles and continuity.[12]

The *principle of the identity of indiscernibles* states that no two substances in the actual world are completely similar. Substances cannot differ merely in respect to their spatial location and configuration, as atomistic philosophy contends. Spatial and configurational differences are relatively superficial: they are consequences of more deep-seated differences, which reach down to the very substances or seats of activity themselves. Things do not differ merely in number or because they are quantitatively two, but in virtue of some more profound qualitative and operational differences. This qualitative basis of differences among individual substances is required by the principle of contingency or perfection. For if two substances were completely similar, there would be no sufficient reason why God should choose them both for inclusion in the best possible world. Since the addition of the second would not contribute significantly toward the maximal possible perfection of the universe, God would have no adequate ground for bringing it into existence. Things or states that are completely indiscernible from each other are really identical and not distinguished in the real order. Leibniz admitted, however, that the differences among existing things often remain hidden from our mind and especially from our imagination, so that they seem to be distinguished only by position and shape. His principle of the identity of indiscernibles provided research workers with the rule that they may expect to find that the differences among objects of investigation are basically of a qualitative nature, stemming from differences in structure and function. He pointed to the microscopic findings of a Leeuwenhoek as evidence of radical structural differences even among drops of water or snow.

Underlying all other types of differences among individual substances are those based upon *perception,* which is the native activity of substances. Leibniz sought to balance two affirmations: that all finite substances are basically *homogeneous,* and that they are *qualitatively differentiated* one from another. Their likeness is founded upon their sharing in a common kind of activity: perception. Their qualitative differences spring from their different capacities for perceptual

---

[12] *Letters to Samuel Clarke,* IV, 5–6, and V, 26 (Wiener, 228–229, 245); *New Essays concerning Human Understanding,* Preface (Langley, 50); *Letters to De Volder* (Wiener, 157–158); *On the Principle of Continuity* (Wiener, 184–188).

a universe of change and contingency. Hence a question arises about *the passage from essential necessity to existential contingency.* First, Leibniz attempts a solution based solely upon essences and first principles themselves, and then he shows the need to base this reasoning upon a reference to God as the ultimate ground of existential and essential being.

We may start from the given fact of contingent existence. A sufficient reason must then be sought in the essences themselves, why they exist rather than do not exist, since they are under no absolute necessity of existing. This reason can only be that actual being is better than possible being. If there were no such reason, nothing could ever become an actual existent, for lack of a sufficient ground for making the existential determination. Essences are not indifferent to existence but have an intrinsic inclination toward it. Every essence has a *conatus for existence.*[15] Yet although all essences agree in possessing such a drive toward existence, each one expresses its drive according to its own distinctive *degree of perfection* or *quantity of essence.*

It is a further fact that not all possibles are actualized, not all essential exigencies for existence are carried out. There is, as it were, a *strife among the essences* for the privilege of coming into existence. Certain essences, possible in themselves, are yet incompatible with each other: if one essence or series of essences exists, another essence or series is prevented from having simultaneous existence. Since there may be an infinite number of combinations of essences and their series, the only basis for a decision between competing essences and combinations lies in the principle of contingency, perfection, or the best, which states that, in the actual world, the quantity of essence or perfection must be as great as possible. The wider the range of any system of compatible essences, the stronger is its claim to be given actual existence. That combination of possibilities must ultimately prevail which assures the entrance into existence of the greatest amount of essence or the richest system of compatible natures.

Leibniz is compelled on logical grounds to posit this *principle of plenitude* and its optimistic consequence that *our world is the best possible one.* He is not moved by any silly sentimentality, after the manner of Voltaire's *Candide,* but by the unavoidable consequences of his premises. The only reason why *our* world exists and exists in *this* particular way (rather than another world or another course of

---

[15] *The Exigency to Exist in Essences: The Principle of Plenitude* (Wiener, 91–93).

things) is the relative perfection of our system. It affords more opportunity than any other arrangement for the realization of a harmonious totality of graded, continuous essences. This position is dictated neither by an empirical weighing of evidence nor by apologetic aims, although Leibniz is confident of its agreement with both. He admits the presence of imperfections and even dire disorders in the several parts of the universe, but he has the a priori weight of his principles to assure him that things as a whole attain to the greatest possible perfection and essential plenitude, achieved at a minimum expenditure or with perfect economy of means.

Leibniz recoiled from the suggestion that this "divine mathematics or metaphysical mechanics" might explain the production of the world in a quite autonomous and impersonal way, without recourse to God's creative act.[16] Yet he represented essences as full-bodied things, jostling with each other and securing their own hold on existence, in virtue of an internal dialectic of relative fullness and harmony of meaning. Given two mutually incompatible essences, that one can gain a real hold on existence which is compatible with a wider range of other essences, systematically correlated. "Moreover, it is my principle that whatever can exist, and is compatible with others, does exist."[17] There is nothing more distinctive about the existential act than being the outcome and resolution of a conflict among essential structures, concerning their systematic compatibilities. Instead of making a radical criticism of this view of essence and existence, however, Leibniz tried to combine it with a theory of free, divine creation. The result was a compromise, that held together only in virtue of alternating concessions on the part of the doctrine on God and that on essence and existence.

Leibniz was now placed in a delicate position between Descartes and Spinoza. He sided with Spinoza in removing *essences* and eternal verities from the free decrees of the divine will: God cannot

---

[16] *On the Ultimate Origin of Things* (Wiener, 348). In the third section of his Aquinas Lecture on *Saint Thomas and the Greeks* (Milwaukee, Marquette University Press, 1939), 50–57, A. C. Pegis observes that there can be no such thing as a best possible world, if the world is genuinely created by God, through freedom of choice and not through necessity of nature; cf. P. Siwek, S.J., "Optimism in Philosophy," *The New Scholasticism*, 22 (1948), 417–439. St. Thomas explains (*Summa Theologiae*, I, 25–26) that the actual universe could not be made in a better way, i.e., made from greater wisdom, order, and goodness. But God could make a better universe, i.e., He could make other things or give further perfections to the things already made.

[17] Untitled fragment (*Opuscules et fragments inédits de Leibniz*, edited by L. Couturat, 530); cf. *On the Analysis of Notions and Truths* (op. cit., 360).

make and unmake the eternal possibilities of things, at will. Yet he did not care to follow Spinoza in affirming that the world emanates from God by absolute necessity. Although essences do not depend upon God's will, all *existential* perfections do proceed from the will, as well as the understanding, of God. There are two characteristics of the divine creative act: it proceeds from *choice* (in accord with God's adherence to His own decree to choose the best), and it has only a hypothetical or *moral necessity* (the actual product is a contingent existent, whose contradictory opposite is not impossible but would be a violation of the resolve to choose the best universe). An act that proceeds from choice and moral necessity fulfills the Leibnizian definition of a free act.[18] *Creation is a free act* not because it proceeds from God's indifference to the outcome, as Descartes held, but because it issues from His regard for considerations of His own wisdom and goodness. The more a will is determined by these motives, the more sovereignly free it is. Spinoza had also maintained a sort of divine freedom, but one that is identical with an absolute necessity of the divine nature to produce its effects. Leibniz proposes his notion of a hypothetical or moral necessity as a median position between the Spinozistic and Cartesian versions of divine freedom in creation.

In saving the divine freedom, however, this explanation makes it an *active acquiescence* in the results of the *calculus of essences*.[19] Once the maximum of compossible perfection is presented to the divine understanding, God cannot fail to will to create the prevailing combination, expressive of what is best. Leibniz qualifies this consequence as much as he can, without giving in to the Cartesian notion of divine liberty. He repeats Plato's remark that reason is an inclining or persuasive force, rather than an absolutely necessitating one, in respect to the creative decision. Regarded absolutely or in an isolated way, the divine power could either refrain from creating or could create things otherwise than in the best possible combination. But God's power must, in fact, be considered along with the divine

---

[18] See *Theodicy*, I, 37, and II, 132 (translated by E. M. Huggard, 144, 203); *Letters to Clarke*, V, 4–10, 76 (Wiener, 238–240, 264); *On the Ultimate Origin of Things* (Wiener, 346). In this last opuscule, Leibniz refers to moral necessity as an inclining, rather than a necessitating, reason; for the comparison with Plato, cf. P. Schrecker, "Leibniz and the *Timaeus*," *The Review of Metaphysics*, 4 (1950–1951), 495–505.

[19] For a criticism of the sufficient-reasons-in-themselves, which determine the choice of Leibniz' Deity, cf. A.-D. Sertillanges, O.P., *Le problème du mal*, Tome I: *L'histoire* (Paris, Aubier, 1949), 234–237.

understanding (the region of the possibles and eternal truths) and the divine will (which freely chooses to create the best possible world). Under these conditions, God's power is *morally bound,* by hypothetical necessity, to create only that system which emerges from the ideal conflict among essences, in His understanding, as being the most perfect possible series of things. Otherwise, a sufficient reason for producing this particular combination of things would be lacking — in which case, the divine creative act would have no intelligible ground. Existence may now be taken to mean entrance into the universal harmony, precisely in virtue of *God's ratification* both of the entire system and of any particular component's consequent right for inclusion in actual existence. If an essence is compossible with the prevailing system, its existence is assured and God's creative act in its regard will not be withheld.

Leibniz adds that the essences are the *objects* but not the *products* of the divine understanding. His final problem is to retain this bulwark against Descartes and yet to establish as close a dependence of essence, as well as of existence, upon God as is compatible with this view. Although existence can never be conceived properly without reference to God, there is a way of viewing essences without such reference. They are *possible in their own right,* insofar as they have an intrinsic, intelligible nature of their own. But when essences are considered in isolation from God, they are *irreal* and *ineffective,* as far as their bond with a possible existing order is concerned. Only through their relation with God's understanding are they "realized," to the point of having real essential being or an exigency for existence. The acquiescence of the divine will and power are required, however, to settle which system of competing exigencies-for-existence will actually be brought forth. God, in whom alone essence and existence are identical, is the cause not only of the actual existence of finite essences but also of their *real striving* toward existence. Consequently, all other essences are contingent in respect to their existential *conatus,* as well as their actual existence. So far forth, these essences are implicated from eternity in God's understanding and, conversely, the divine essence cannot be conceived perfectly except as being inclusive of all other essences, as objects of its understanding. Hence Leibniz concludes that God is the source of all essences, as well as of all existences.

Leibniz cannot achieve a closer synthesis of the several strands of his solution. His difficulty is the fundamental metaphysical one of trying to avoid both arbitrary chaos and a necessitarian world, without benefit of a thoroughgoing doctrine on the relation between the *divine exemplar ideas* and the *divine essence*. He is prevented from settling this relationship, because he is the heir of the Cartesian and Spinozistic tendencies to conceive of the divine essence primarily in terms of self-affirming power, rather than as the subsistent act of existing. Leibniz is reluctant to ground the essential possibilities of things entirely and unequivocally in the divine essence, lest the intelligible structures become compromised by the bottomless force of the divine power. Hence he reserves an inviolable zone for the essences, considered just in themselves and their intrinsic meaning. They constitute a shadowy kingdom of their own, as a safeguard against any incursions by an arbitrary divine power. They have an "irreal being" of pure, essential meaning, anterior to their endeavor toward existence. But this attempt to consider essences in themselves and apart from an intrinsic reference to the act of existing, leads to serious difficulties. For the inherent relations of compossibility among essences constitutes a *prior* law and an *autonomous* standard, to which God must submit, thus endangering His freedom and creative primacy. The kind of "irreal being" belonging to the essences is not explained, since the distinction between logical constructions and real principles is wiped out, when essences are given a structure that has no intrinsic reference to existence. Essential relations and the principle of sufficient reason enjoy an independent, obscure being of their own and succeed in imposing themselves upon the divine geometer.

The situation is not improved when a real tendency toward existence is invoked, by bringing the possibilities into relation with the divine understanding. For the *conatus* toward finite existence, which God now gives to the essences, is an overflow from the self-affirming power of His own essence. Leibniz does not successfully answer Spinoza's argument that God affirms the *conatus* and existence of other things with the same necessity wherewith He affirms His own existence. The Leibnizian answer is that God is not under any absolute necessity to choose the world He actually does choose, but does so only in conformity with His own freely accepted standard of the best. Everything depends upon whether it can be established that God's adherence to the principle of perfection, contingency, or the best is a free one. What Leibniz actually proves is not the freedom of the divine choice of this standard but the inability of our minds to see the connection between God's power, goodness, and adherence to the best. He shows that, in dealing with this question, we must employ an infinite analysis rather than a finite one. This establishes the contingent character of *our proposition* about the creative act but not the freedom of the *creative act* itself. The fact that our analysis is unterminated and directed toward infinity rescues our knowledge from Spinozistic determinism, but it does not save God's creation from determinism. Whether existence be conceived as the outcome of the strife among the essences or as the result of the ratification of this strife by God, it remains only a consequence in the line of essence itself. God's choice of this world as actual, is a recognition of the finite terminus for the maximum assertion of essential quanta of power. Our world is guaranteed as the best possible one, but it also ceases to be the handiwork of creative freedom.

5. A WORLD OF MONADS

The various strands of Leibniz' speculation are woven together in his monadology. In this doctrine, he comes closest to realizing the systematic ideal toward which his logical and metaphysical findings were directed.

1. *The Existence and Nature of Monads.* Leibniz begins his treatise, *The Monadology,* with these two keynoting propositions:

> 1. The *monad* of which we shall here speak is merely a simple substance, which enters into composites; *simple,* that is to say, without parts.
> 2. And there must be simple substances, since there are composites; for the composite is only a collection or *aggregatum* of simple subtances.[20]

The second proposition suggests that the theory of monads has a basis in facts of our experience. Given the existence of composite things, Leibniz infers the existence of their irreducible, composing elements. These elementary components cannot be found on the side of matter, however, since matter is indefinitely divisible and hence cannot account for the substantial unity of experienced composites. The principle of substantial unity must be sought in some formal, "metaphysical atoms" or *immaterial* monads. Through the composition of several simple, monadic substances, the complex things of our experience are formed. Because each individual monad is simple, it is also *indivisible* and *free from parts of extension.* Its simple character prevents the individual, monadic substance from being subject to

---

[20] *The Monadology,* 1–2 (Wiener, 533).

object of perception, since they all express the universe in its infinite variety. But they differ profoundly among themselves in respect to the *act of perceiving,* i.e., in their subjective ability to achieve distinct perceptions of the things in the universe. A scale of perfection exists among the various types of perceptions. At the lowest level, there is bare perception or expression of the universe, unaccompanied by any glimmering of consciousness. This is the field occupied by the in-sensible or *unconscious* perceptions. A new plane is reached, when perception is accompanied by memory and thus gives rise to *con-sciousness* and automatically connected experience. Finally, the summit of the grades of perception is occupied by *reflective knowledge* or *apperception,* in which there is awareness of the very act of per-ceiving and of the substantial self, from which the act proceeds. Like Spinoza, Leibniz is interested in the problem of the degrees of perception mainly for metaphysical, rather than strictly psychological, reasons. For, the degrees of perception provide him with a standard for arranging simple monads in the hierarchy of being and, at the same time, enable him to give a systematic explanation of the actual objects of perception: the composite things peopling our universe.

What we perceive directly are not simple substances but composite things or aggregates of simple substances. Although there is no composition *within* the substance of the individual monad, there can be (and, in the case of finite monads, there must be) composition *among* several simple monads to constitute a *composite thing.* The sufficient reason for this aggregation is to be sought in the fact that a given finite monad requires the proximate co-operation of several associated monads, so that it may bring its perceptions to a condition of maximum clarity and distinctness. Hence the composite thing is an operational unity between the particular monad, attempting to clarify its perceptual states, and those other monads that contribute proximately and directly to this process of clarification. The self-clarifying monad in question is called the *entelechy;* the associated monads are called the *body* of this entelechy. Thus in any composite thing, that monad whose own states are being perfected as a con-sequence of the composition is the entelechy-monad, whereas those monads contributing proximately to the improvement of this other monad's perceptions are body-monads. Thus a special relation of domination and subordination is set up, resembling the relation between the queen bee and the workers in the beehive. The entelechy-monad assumes a dominating role, and the body-monads are sub-

alteration by external, finite agents and from undergoing the process of generation and corruption. Monads can only come into existence through creation by God; thereafter, they are subject only to an increase and diminution of their native power and effective combina-tion with each other. Monads "have no windows through which anything can enter or depart."[21] Each is a world by itself, a "little divinity" sealed off from any direct interaction with the other finite monads, inhabiting the teeming pond of the universe. Direct, causal contact is maintained only between the individual monad and God, upon whom every monad depends for its being.

Although they are simple and unextended, the primary substances have some intrinsic modifications and multiplicity, in addition to their substantial nature. Without some further modifications or affections, the monads could not be differentiated from each other and hence could not exist as distinct entities. At this point, Leibniz brings his previous doctrine on individual substance to bear upon his general theory of monads. Each individual substance or monad is a primitive, unified center of force, which is the source and regulative law of all its activities. There is a composition of powers plus activities, even though there is no composition within the substance. These activities are of an immaterial nature, considered in themselves, since the monads are unextended, unitary beings. Flowing from the simple substance are two main kinds of activities: *perceptions* and *desires.* The monad is essentially a thing capable of perception, in the widest sense of giving rise to a living representation or expression of the universe. Desire or appetition is nothing other than the tend-ency of the monad to make a transition from one perception to another, for the sake of securing the maximum clarity and distinctness among its perceptual states. These activities introduce the factors of *transiency* and *multiplicity* into the life of the monad. The multiplicity does not militate against the unextended nature of the monadic individual, since it is a manyness of perceptual and appetitive acts and relations, rather than of extended parts. The transient and multiple character of these immaterial activities is an indication of the *finitude* of the individual monads. The drive of their desire or natural appetite is toward ever more adequate perceptions of the universe and hence toward constant increase of perfection.

Since all monads exercise the operations of perception and appetition

[21] *Ibid.,* 7 (Wiener, 534); cf. *Discourse on Metaphysics,* XXVI (Wiener, 327–328).

—in which *life* itself consists—ours is a world of living things. Leibniz makes no fantastic claim that all monads enjoy conscious life, but he does clash with Locke over whether *unconscious perception* is a contradiction in terms. Although some perceptions are able to cross the threshold of consciousness, there is an entire lower order of perceptual activity which remains below this conscious level. In order to show the reasonableness of his theory of unconscious perceptions, Leibniz gives a metaphysical interpretation of *perception*.[22] He defines it, in the most general way, as any expression of, or structured correspondence to, the universe. Now the individual, monadic substance is created by God in such fashion that its being and activity are adapted and proportioned to the structure of the rest of the universe. There is a one-to-one correspondence between the traits of the microcosm and those of the macrocosm, such that the activities of the former are expressive of the structure of the latter. Hence the activities of every monad are expressions in conformity with the universe, and fulfill the general definition of perception or representation. There is no need to confine the meaning of perception to a conscious expression of objects.

Leibniz makes a distinct advance over Paracelsus and Bruno, when he provides a metaphysical foundation for the venerable *microcosm-macrocosm* doctrine. He regards it as a logical consequence of his teaching that an individual essence can acquire existence, only by proving its harmony or *compossibility* with the rest of the given universe. This relation of compossibility means that the essential structure of this particular essence is intrinsically related and proportioned to the other essences. The compatibility is a *dynamic adaptation,* that reaches down to every activity stemming from the essence, considered as an individual substance. Hence it is the very nature of a monad *to be representative* of the entire universe. Perception is only the operational development of this intrinsic correspondence between the individual monad and other beings, with which it is harmonized to constitute our universe. In creating the individual substance, God ordains its operations to be expressions of

---

[22] *Letters to De Volder* (Wiener, 161); *New System of Nature and of the Communication of Substances,* 14–15 (Wiener, 114–116); *The Monadology,* 14, 60–62 (Wiener, 535, 545–546). J. Jalabert, "La psychologie de Leibniz," *Revue Philosophique de la France et de l'Étranger,* 136 (1946), 453–472, shows that the profoundly tendential and dynamic quality of Leibniz' psychology stems from this view of perception, as an expression of inner spontaneity and conformity with the world.

the universe. These perceptual expressions can transpire either consciously or at the level of consciousness.

Leibniz supports his metaphysical doctrine with an empirical th of *unconscious* or *minute perceptions,* backed up by the deman his principle of continuity.[23] Since a monad cannot exist withou activities, the latter must be constantly present, even apart from scious states. From internal experience, it is evident that there gradation among our perceptions, some being relatively obscure others attaining considerable clarity. The clear and distinct percep are those which have been brought successfully to conscious awar But the principle of continuity is warrant that there are no su gaps in our perceptual life: perceptual activity is not cut off abi at the point where the clarity of consciousness ceases, but con down into the depths of the unconscious. There is an uninterr series of perceptual activities reaching from states of reflection to those that are unconscious, yet genuinely expressive of the un The continuity of psychic life amid sleep, dreams, and other ruptions of consciousness, indicates that conscious perception upon a vast substrate of unconscious perceptual activities. Th a constant increment of "minute perceptions," operating benea surface of consciousness. A person living beside a waterfall i stantly perceiving the sound of the water, but habit deade conscious attention, during most of the time. Similarly, a walking along the seashore pays no conscious attention to indi waves. But sometimes, he does advert to the roar of the surf, at point where a combination of smaller sounds is strong enou engage his notice. Our conscious knowledge is made possible th the unnoticed contributions of innumerable unconscious, minut ceptions. Thus Leibniz laid the philosophical cornerstone fo modern psychological conviction that a great part of our ment transpires in the dark pool of the unconscious. He also stresse great importance of the *petites perceptions* in shaping our att moral decisions, and general outlook.

2. *The Hierarchy of Monads.* All monads agree in the g

---

[23] The classical development of this teaching is in *New Essays concerning Understanding,* Preface, and II, i, 10–15 (Langley, 47–52, 111–117). The bombardment of the mind by unconscious perceptions belies the *tabula rasa* th the mind, assures the individual mind's objective connection with the rest universe, and provides the unnoticed determining factors inclining our will to c one definite direction. For the Cartesian background of this issue, cf. G. Le *problème de l'inconscient et le cartésianisme* (Paris, Presses Universitaires, 195

ordinated teleologically to the needs of the entelechy. Leibniz' functional view of the composite thing resembles Spinoza's functional theory of the individual.

Although he borrows the term "entelechy" from Aristotle, in order to signify the organizing principle, setting the end or measure of perfection for the entire composite, Leibniz does not accept the Aristotelian theory of act and potency. Instead, he regards the composite as an *operational union between a principal act and subordinate acts*. Since each of the subordinate acts or bodily monads remains a simple substance, Leibniz discovers no obstacle against regarding it, in turn, as an entelechy in respect to a new set of inferiors. Every bodily monad retains a nisus toward perfecting its own perceptual activities, as well as those of another. Hence it can also operate as an entelechy-monad, by subordinating and organizing some other monads around its own purpose. This functional relationship of entelechy-to-body goes on to infinity, reaching far below the range of our distinct, conscious perception of the divisions among composite things.

LEIBNIZ' HIERARCHY OF MONADS

1. God as infinite, prime monad and principle of pre-established harmony among created monads.

2. Finite, created monads.

a) Entelechy or dominant monad.	b) Body or subordinate monads.	c) Living composite of entelechy and body, regulated by pre-established harmony.
1) Bare entelechy.	1) Lower body.	1) Inferior living matter, having only unconscious perceptions.
2) Soul.	2) Animal body.	2) Animal, having conscious perceptions.
3) Spirit or mind (rational soul).	3) Human body.	3) Man, the higher animal, having reflective consciousness and knowledge of eternal truths.

The variety and specific gradation of composites are due to the presence of entelechies of different degrees of perfection. The hierarchy among entelechies is determined according to the increasing perfection of the power of perception. Entelechies or dominating monads belong to three main classes: bare entelechies or perceptive principles, souls, and minds. The higher orders include the perfections found at a lower level. "As therefore mind is rational soul, so soul is sentient life, and life is perceptive principle."[24] The *bare entelechies* or *mere perceptive principles* have some perceptual and appetitive activities, and hence they are true principles of life. But their perceptions resemble a dreamless sleep or a permanent swoon, since they remain forever in a confused and unconscious state. Consciousness appears at the higher level occupied by *souls.* In the soul-monads, perception is accompanied by memory, attention, and feeling. Souls can have some sort of connected experience but are incapable of reflecting upon their operations. Reflection or apperception is characteristic of the highest class of dominant monads: the *minds* or *rational souls* or *spirits.* They can reflect upon their conscious acts, become aware of their own selfhood, and thus achieve freedom and moral character. Minds are also able to apprehend simple innate ideas, eternal truths, and first principles of philosophy. Hence rational knowledge can rise from empirical truths of fact to essential truths of reason. Leibniz states the contrast between bare entelechies and souls, on the one hand, and minds, on the other, in a decisive way: the former are images of the universe alone, whereas the latter are images both of the universe and of God, the creator of the universe.

The grades of composite things are constituted by the union between bodily monads and entelechies of these three sorts. *Lower living things* are composed of a bare entelechy and its bodily aggregate of monads. *Animals* are constituted through the union of a soul with an appropriate bodily group of monads. *Men* or rational animals are composite things, made up of a mind or rational soul and the body proportioned to the highest level of perceptual activity. No finite entelechy, of whatever sort, can exist without its proper set of bodily monads. To be a finite monad means to require the proximate aid of other simple substances in the work of perfecting one's perceptions, and hence to require a body. Only the infinite monad, God, is entirely free from union with a body.

[24] *On the Active Force of Body, on the Soul of Brutes,* 3 (Wiener, 505). Cf. *Discourse on Metaphysics,* XXXIV–XXXV (Wiener, 339–342); *The Principles of Nature and of Grace,* 4–5 (Wiener, 524–26); *The Monadology,* 18–30, 63–70 (Wiener, 536–539, 546–547). In Leibniz' explanation of the monadic hierarchy, the tensions latent in his previous compromise between the homogeneity and differentiation among individual substances are made explicit. In order to defend his view of the basic homogeneity of all monadic substances from the charge of agreement with Spinozistic monism, he is obliged to emphasize the sharp differences between rational and nonrational monads, thus opening the door once more to a Cartesian dualism. Cf. G. Lewis, "La critique leibnizienne du dualisme cartésien," *Revue Philosophique de la France et de l'Étranger,* 136 (1946), 473–485.

3. *A Monadological Description of the Physical World.* With the aid of his theory of monads, Leibniz tried to describe the familiar world. This was a difficult task, since he had to show how the universe of material, extended things can be constructed out of immaterial, unextended substances. The only route open for him was to reinterpret body, extension, space, and time in purely perceptual terms. This did not explain the material world, but rather gave a description of what this world *would be like,* were it composed of simple substances, having only perceptual and appetitive activities.

Within such a context, the *body* and bodily organs can only mean a subordinate group of monads, providing functional aids to the clarification of one's perceptions.[25] Leibniz' main concern was to show that there is a sufficient reason why every entelechic monad must have a body, as so defined. This reason can be seen from a comparison between finite monads and God. God alone is without a body, since He alone has an infinite understanding of the world and needs the aid of nothing else. Hence his knowledge of the universe is infinite or confined to no special viewpoint. But every finite understanding does operate within a special viewpoint, and this is supplied by the monad's body. Although the monad's knowledge is not *derived* from the body, it is *proportioned* to the states of the bodily monads. Thus the body is a principle of individuation for the finite monad, providing it with a *distinctive perspective* in time and action. The entelechy-monad knows the entire universe, but it knows the world through knowing its own body. The rays from the rest of the monadic cosmos are concentrated in a distinctive focus, and that focus is called the body. The body is the *point of insertion* of the individual substance in the harmonious system of the existing world. Were the body eliminated, the bodiless monads would become "like deserters from the general order" of things.[26] In Leibniz' system, the body is the proximate means for securing the connectedness among individual monads and thus for guaranteeing the harmony in the existent universe.

Leibniz' treatment of *extension* is complicated by a double polemical aim. He wants to explain extension in such a way that he can fit

---

[25] The body is described as "the organized mass in which the point of view of the soul lies." *New System of Nature and of the Communication of Substances,* 14 (Wiener, 115). Cf. *Discourse on Metaphysics,* XXXIII (Wiener, 338–339), and *The Monadology,* 60–62 (Wiener, 545–546).

[26] *Considerations on the Principles of Life, and on Plastic Natures* (Wiener, 199).

it into his system and, at the same time, provide a refutation of the Cartesian and Spinozistic views of material substance.[27] He draws a distinction between *extension* (which he sometimes calls "prime matter") and *the extended thing* (sometimes called "second matter"). Extension is an abstraction made by our mind, whereas the extended thing is what really exists and serves as a basis for the abstraction. The extended thing is the physical mass, constituted by a plurality of monads, coexisting and actively continuous with each other. The co-existing and continuous mass of monads constitutes a functional unity, and this *common field of activity* is the extended thing. The human mind can gain a confused and indistinct perception of the mass, by making an indefinite repetition. At this level, it abstracts from the substantial differences among the coexisting substances and regards them as one indiscernible whole of extension. In this way the notion of homogeneous extension is acquired.

Leibniz employed this theory of *dynamism* to defend his philosophy against both Descartes and Spinoza. Against the former, he noted that, if extension does not exist but is a mental abstraction, it cannot serve as the special *real attribute* defining material substance. Furthermore, if the real ground of extension in "the extended thing" is reducible to the plurality, coexistence, and continuity of several simple and unextended substances, then an extended thing is not a *substance* at all. It is only an operational effect flowing from the conjoint activity of several real substances. The Cartesian *res extensa* must therefore be reduced to the Leibnizian *res agens:* the simple substance, considered as a primitive center of force. This does not provide any solace, however, for Spinoza. For the real foundation of the extended thing or mass is a *plurality of finite substances,* rather than the one divine substance. A bodily mass is an aggregate of substances. Because of the confused perceptions in the aggregated substances, as well as in the perceiving mind, we may regard the extended world as an indefinitely repeatable region of homogeneity. But more careful analysis shows, with the aid of the principle of the identity of indiscernibles, that the manyness of extended things is due ultimately to the manyness of finite substances. Leibniz refuses to define substance in such a way that it can apply only to God. He points out that the powers and operations of things really do belong to them and are exercised by them, precisely because they are finite centers of

---

[27] *Letters to De Volder* (Wiener, 163–175); *Refutation of Spinoza* (Wiener, 485–497).

force or finite substances. The minimal definition of a substance as "a being capable of action," permits the perfection of substance to be applied to finite things, as well as to the infinite being.

This doctrine is more successful as a polemical device than as a positive analysis of extension. Its net effect is to explain away extension. This is done, not so much by making extension a consequence of active forces, as by ascribing its origin to the confused condition of perception. Matter and extension are possible only through the conjunction of two sets of confused perceptions: on the part of the extended thing or mass of bodily monads, and on the part of the perceiver, who abstracts the notion of extension. The indefinite repetition could not be made *by* the perceiver, and *in respect to* the mass, if it were not for this dual confusion, which encourages an imaginative view of a homogeneous, extended world. Leibniz claims to "demonstrate that the ideas of size, figure, and motion [the so-called primary qualities] are not so distinctive as is imagined, and that they stand for something imaginary relative to our perceptions, as do, although to a greater extent, the ideas of color, heat, and the other similar qualities in regard to which we may doubt whether they are actually to be found in the nature of the things outside of us."[28] Although he gives to extension a real foundation in the extended thing, he removes primary qualities just as completely as secondary ones from the extended thing. Extension is "a well-founded phenomenon," but it has a foundation in existent substances, only insofar as they are subject to conditions of imagination or confused perception — conditions which their native tendency seeks to overcome.

A similar result follows from Leibniz' account of space and time.[29] Things are said to be near at hand or far distant, of recent or remote occurrence, depending upon whether our perception of them is clear or not, and whether a lesser or a greater number of mental steps is required to grasp their mutual order. *Space* is the order of *coexisting*

[28] *Discourse on Metaphysics*, XII (Wiener, 304–305). Leibniz' obscure views on the nature of matter are examined by J. A. Irving, "Leibniz' Theory of Matter," *Philosophy of Science*, 3 (1936), 208–214, and by S. Russo, "The Concept of Matter in Leibniz," *The Philosophical Review*, 42 (1938), 275–292. See E. Manier, "Matter and Individuation in Leibniz," in *The Concept of Matter*, Vol. 2, ed. E. McMullin.

[29] *Metaphysical Foundations of Mathematics* (Wiener, 201–212); *Letters to Clarke*, III, 4–6; IV, 41; V, 47 (Wiener, 223–224, 235, 251–254). For an analysis of the Leibniz-Clarke correspondence, read E. Cassirer, "Newton and Leibniz," *The Philosophical Review*, 52 (1943), 366–391. Read F. S. C. Northrop, "Leibniz's Theory of Space," *Journal of the History of Ideas*, 7 (1946), 385–498. Also, K. E. Ballard, "Leibniz's Theory of Space and Time," *Journal of the History of Ideas*, 21 (1960), 49–65.

things, and *time* the order of *successive* things. Space and time are real but they are also relative and phenomenal. Newton was wrong in treating them as substantial entities, since they depend upon our perception and ability to grasp a universal order of coexistence and succession. Space and time are *well-founded phenomena,* however, since there are real coexisting things and real successive actions, upon the perception of which the universalized notions of space and time rest. Since we cannot acquire God's perfect knowledge of the order of coexistence and succession among monads, our spatial and temporal notions are always deficient. Nevertheless, they help us to organize our knowledge of the world and to place our practical plans on a sound footing.

Leibniz is justifiably critical of the Newtonian conception of absolute space and time, since he shows the considerable part played by the *mind* in the elaboration of our notions of space and time. His suggestion that these notions are really founded upon the coexistence and change of existing things, is also sound. But his efforts to give a detailed account of the real foundation meet with systematic frustration. For, in explaining the relations of coexistence and succession, as they obtain among several simple and unextended substances, he must bear in mind both his doctrine on the isolation of the individual monads and his explanation of the extended thing as a secondary feature. Since the monads constituting the real foundation are related to each other only in an "ideal" or nonphysical way, through the mutual reference of *their perceptions,* he does not secure a foundation for space and time beyond the order of perceptions. Hence it is customary for Leibniz to shift attention from the monadic foundation in the world to the conditions of perception found in the perceiver himself. He observes that the mind's own acts of perceiving display the traits of psychological quantity, togetherness and succession. This involves a substitution, once more, of the *conditions of perceiving* for the *objects of perception.* The latter collapse into the former, thus rendering doubtful the establishment of the foundation for the phenomena of space and time.

6. GOD AND PRE-ESTABLISHED HARMONY

To cope with some special problems concerning the relation between minds and bodies, Leibniz had to bring to the fore the role of God in his monadology. He formulated several proofs of God's existence, recasting some of his predecessors' arguments in function of his own system.[30] In its usual Cartesian form, the *ontological argument* has only a moral force, since it assumes the possibility of the idea or essence of God, considered as the all-perfect being. Leibniz set out to remedy this defect. To do so, he returned to the given fact that some things exist. Since they do exist, their essences enjoy a real possibility, not merely a logical one. These essences are real and not merely logical or imaginary, because they are founded in God, who is the region of all ideas, essences, and eternal truths. If God were not unconditionally and *really possible in Himself,* the essences of existing things would not have real claim upon existence and would not be really embodied in existents. Finite essences are really possible, only by reference to the self-founded, real possibility of the divine essence.

This proof of the real possibility of God's essence is, simultaneously, a proof of His existence and infinite perfection. For God's essence is intrinsically possible, precisely as being the foundation of the claim of real finite essences to their perfection or degree of essence, which is the principle of existence. Hence their reality must be grounded in a metaphysically necessary essence or subject, which draws its actual existence from itself alone. If God is really and unconditionally possible, in this sense, then He must exist. For, His possibility is that of the all-powerful source of the reality of essences or their *conatus* toward existence. Other things are really possible and eventually existent, only in virtue of their harmonious relation with the *actually existing, divine essence.* That this essence is infinitely perfect, follows from the consideration that it draws its whole reality from within itself and through its own power. Since there is nothing within His own existing essence (or outside it) to thwart the absolute affirmation of His absolute quantity of essence or perfection, God exists as the *infinitely perfect being.* Thus Leibniz renovates the ontological argument, by drawing upon his own theory of the conditions under which alone essences can enter into the zone of existence.

It is imperative for him to prove the possibility of God, since otherwise the essence of God would not be established. Because Leibniz accords to essence a sort of pre-existential reality of its own, the divine

---

[30] *New Essays concerning Human Understanding,* IV, x (Langley, 499–511); *On the Ultimate Origin of Things* (Wiener, 345–350); *The Principles of Nature and of Grace,* 7–8 (Wiener, 527–528); *The Monadology,* 36–38, 43–45 (Wiener, 540–542); *New System of Nature and of the Communication of Substances,* 16 (Wiener, 116); *The-odicy,* I, 7 (Huggard, 127–128). See *Critical Remarks concerning the General Part of Descartes' Principles,* in the Schrecker tr. of Leibniz, *Monadology and Other Philosophical Essays,* 27–30.

essence must first be demonstrated as possible. Then, existence can be established as a necessary consequence of this essence. Whereas the meaning of existence in other things consists in the relations of compatibility of their essences within the prevailing system, the meaning of the necessary being's existence is drawn entirely from its own unbounded essence or affirmation of power. Criticism of Leibniz' argument has focused upon the view that existence is contained within essence, regarded as an underlying principle or "power." Kant objects that an unconditioned essence can never be given more than the standing of a *possible concept* in our minds, so that we cannot know it as a *real subject*. Thomistic realists agree with Kant in denying that existence is a predicate or result, flowing from essence. They also point out that the precise problem is not that of determining the meaning of existence but of demonstrating the truth of the proposition *God exists*. The task of an existential proof is to ascertain not *what God's essence affirms* but *what we can affirm demonstratively about His existence*. Otherwise, one becomes involved in equivocation concerning the different meanings of "power" and what we can validly assert about it.

The monadology also affords Leibniz an opportunity to give a distinctive turn to the usual *a posteriori arguments*. On the basis of the dual axiom that existence can be explained only by existence and the contingent only by the necessary, he traces back all contingent existents to God, viewed as the necessary existent and cause of the existing universe. The *contingency of finite monads* is seen from their subjection to continuous change of perception and appetition. They lack a sufficient reason within themselves for their existence. And since the condition of transient perceptions is a universal one, the entire world of existing monads demands a sufficient reason in a being existing outside itself. Hence God exists and gives being to all finite monads.

That the transcendent cause of the monadic universe is an intelligent being — *intelligentia supramundana* — is the conclusion of what Leibniz calls his new proof from the *harmony among all monads*. The marvelous mutual correspondence between individual monads, as well as between groups of monads (such as mind and body or several interrelated bodies), is not the outcome of any direct, causal influence from one to the other. Each monad is a sealed-off empire of its own, and yet it is an empire *within* the larger empire of the harmonious universe of monads. The delicate adaptation and ordering of things obtain in the actual world, only because all the monads stand under the effective guidance of a single intelligent cause, itself existing above the world and yet working powerfully and meaningfully within it. Only a being at once transcendent and intelligent can provide the sufficient reason for the harmony of the existent world. This is Leibniz' version of the argument from order and design.

Leibniz sometimes refers to God as the *prime monad,* since He possesses, in an eminent way, some of the characteristics of monads. He is an active substance, although one that admits neither of a reactive-passive aspect nor of any reference to another as its cause. Corresponding to the substantial subject, perceptual and appetitive powers in finite monads are, respectively, the divine power, knowledge, and will. They are one in the simplicity of the divine substance, which escapes all internal change, accidental composition, and determination by correspondence with other things. God is unique, absolutely perfect, and self-sufficient. He is limited by no particular, perspectival views of the universe but embraces them all in His infinite vision of all aspects of all things. In Him, the meaning of mind, spirit, and person finds its highest fulfillment.

Imagery redolent of Neo-Platonic and Spinozistic emanationism is often used by Leibniz to describe the *genesis of things* from God, whose name is *ens existificans.* Created or derived monads proceed from the underived monad "by continual fulgurations [outflashings] of the Divinity, from moment to moment."[31] These words connote the unquenchable welling-over of the divine power, in its drive to realize the maximum of perfection in the universe. Recognizing that this sort of description compromises the transcendence and freedom of a creator-God, Leibniz seeks some compensating safeguards. Created things derive their *perfections* from God, but their *imperfections* and limitations come from their own natures. Hence they are both dependent upon God and really distinct from Him. The distance is that between infinite and finite substances. Leibniz' *principle of limitation* is not a distinct constituent of finite essences but the relative systematic requirement that *mutual concessions* and *accommodations* must be made by a plurality of essences, in order to constitute one, harmonious world. The fact that every derived monad possesses a body is an index of its submission to the condition of finitude and co-existence in a system of essences. The principle of

---

[31] *The Monadology,* 47 (Wiener, 542). For a comparison with Plotinus, see W. E. May, "The God of Leibniz," *The New Scholasticism,* 36 (1962), 506–528.

limitation retains the same sort of *tenuous independence* of God as do the essential meanings, considered in themselves, since it is nothing more than the requirement of mutual compatibility and adjustment among these meanings.

Once he has established the freedom of the creative act, in the sense of its moral but not absolute necessity, Leibniz allows the requirements of the best possible world to hold sway over God's creative action. God is constantly viewing the various aspects or perspectives of the world He has chosen. *Each aspect viewed by God* is eventually given existence as *a monad* or *collection of monads.*[32] God thoroughly comprehends each monadic essence, both as an individual entity and as an integral component of the world, both in its intrinsic possibility and its *com*possibility with the rest. And the monad is brought into existence by God, just as it is comprehended by His divine understanding: it is actualized as a complete thing, adapted to the conditions of coexistence with other monads in the best possible world. This is the metaphysical foundation for the doctrine of pre-established harmony.

The reason why Leibniz was compelled to advance the doctrine of *pre-established harmony* can be appreciated by recalling his conception of the individual substance. By definition, a complete, individual substance is a being whose nature affords a concept so complete that from it can be deduced all the predicates of which it may ever be the subject, throughout the course of its temporal career. Whatever happens to the monadic substance is a strict consequence of its own nature, considered as the regulative tendency to give rise to such happenings or representations. One implication of this teaching is that there can be *no direct, physical influence* of one finite substance upon another. Each individual monad is a world apart, cut off from causal influxes from other finite monads, and incapable of producing any causal influx in them. Given these monadic, sealed fortresses, how can the evident harmony and apparent interaction among the components in the universe be explained? This is the question that led Leibniz to formulate his theory of pre-established harmony.

The harmony among things must be *pre*-established, since it cannot be the achievement of genuine causal relationships among the empirically existing substances. There are two stages in the anterior harmonization of things, and Leibniz does not always respect the

---

[32] *Ibid.,* 57, 60 (Wiener, 544, 545); *The Principles of Nature and of Grace,* 12–13 (Wiener, 529–530).

distinction between them.[33] The *immediate* ground of harmony is found in God. For although the finite monads are isolated horizontally from each other (as far as causal communication is concerned), they are all vertically open to the causal influence of God, upon whom they depend for actual existence. It is the *regulative influence of God* that prevents the monadic world from disintegrating into chaos. Although one simple substance does not act upon another, God regulates them all in such fashion that what happens within one substance is co-ordinated with what happens in all the others. In creating each individual substance, God bears in mind the requirements of the whole universe, and in creating the universe He bears in mind the needs of each individual. In this way, there is perfect harmony and mutual adaptation among the activities of all monads. Monads can influence each other, *indirectly* and *ideally,* through God. Leibniz explains the apparent system of actions and passions among things, in terms of God's "regarding" or intellectual consideration of the needs of each and all. Without entering into causal transactions with each other, things may be said to be related by bonds of action and passion, since the activities of each individual promote, and in turn are promoted by, the welfare of the entire cosmos.

But there is a *more ultimate* ground of the anterior harmonization of things. There must be a sufficient reason why God chooses to create precisely this universe, instead of the other possible combinations. This sufficient reason is found in the superior fitness of our universe, its ability to contain a greater amount of essence, and hence of perfection, than any other combination of essences. Now any particular essence has a right to inclusion in our universe, only if it can establish such connections with the entire system as will achieve a greater unity-in-variety or harmony. The connectedness of the component essences in our universe means that there is a *relationship of mutual adaptation* among them, viewed merely in their own essential structures. Considered in their "irreal being," anterior to their reception of a *conatus* toward existence, the essences contain relations of mutual inclusion and adaptation, in order to form a systematic whole. God's "regarding" of the needs of each and all, which is the proximate basis for the harmonious actions and

---

[33] *The Monadology,* 49–61 (Wiener, 542–545); on action and passion, see also: *Discourse on Metaphysics,* XXXIII (Wiener, 338), and *Refutation of Spinoza* (Wiener, 494–495).

passions of things, is a recognition and ratification of the *inherent, essential connectedness* among the component members of that system which contains the greatest amount of essence or harmony. The ultimate reason for the harmony of our universe lies in the relations of mutual fitness and proportion, among the essences comprising the system. Once again, the divine geometer must submit to the independent relations holding good among the essences, as well as to the principle of sufficient reason.

The most striking instance of such harmony is the relationship between *mind* and *body*. Leibniz agrees with Malebranche and Spinoza in ruling out any *causal interaction* between them, but he adduces his own reason. Mind and body are not modes under utterly different attributes, as Spinoza taught; mind is a substance in its own right, and body is an operational unity of several subordinate monads. Malebranche was also in error, when he held that finite substances have no real, causal efficacy. Leibniz admits that the individual monad controls its own perceptions in a causal way. His denial of causal interaction between mind and body is simply an application of the general doctrine, denying causal influence between *any* finite substances or collections of substances. Nevertheless, there is a marvelous correspondence between the activities of mind and those of body. They are perfectly harmonized through a system of noncausal actions and passions, having a one-to-one correspondence. Leibniz compares mind and body to *two clocks,* which have been perfectly synchronized by God, at the outset. Although the two series of activities merely run parallel, within any causal interchange, everything happens "as if each influenced the other."[34]

This "as if" is as far as Leibniz can go, since neither at the finite level of existence nor at the level of purely essential meanings is there any mutual causal influence. He divorces action and passion from the causal relationship and, indeed, from any framework of act and potency, so that they become only *ways of regarding the order*

---

[34] *The Monadology,* 81 (Wiener, 550). For the example of the synchronized clocks, compare *Second Explanation of the System of the Communication of Substances* (Wiener, 118–119); *Considerations on the Principles of Life, and of Plastic Natures* (Wiener, 192). Here, as well as in *New System of Nature and of the Communication of Substances* (Wiener, 113–116), Leibniz denies that pre-established harmony is a *deus ex machina* or extrinsic tinkering with the machinery of the universe. But his real task is to show that his description of the causal necessities governing the creation of the cosmic machinery itself, is not a mere contrivance for saving the unity of the universe, in the face of his analytic doctrine on individual substances.

among essential structures, belonging to the same system of harmonious perfection. Although Leibniz thinks that this "as if" explanation of mind and body covers the appearances and saves the divine veracity, it raises a special problem concerning the widespread belief that there *is* some causal relationship between mind and body. This question left Hume wondering whether the *causal belief* may not always be reducible to an "as if" situation, which has a purely psychological explanation, without foundation in really interacting principles.

Leibniz accepted, integrally, the mechanistic explanation of the physical world in terms of *efficient causes*. For, the harmonious correspondences within the physical plenum constitute a visible image of the correspondences among essential structures. In neither case is there any causal operation of one being upon another, although there is a detailed adaptation of activities, in function of the preestablished harmony. Leibniz also sought to rehabilitate *final cause* as a way of supplementing the mechanistic description of nature. Souls and minds act according to the laws of final cause, rather than of efficient cause. Since their activities suppose the presence of consciousness, we must take account of the influence of conscious desires, chosen ends, and the known relation between ends and means. These considerations belong in the domain of final cause. Preestablished harmony operates to achieve a correspondence between the realms of mechanism and teleology, so that, within the context of the world of *nature* and efficient causes, a moral world of *grace* and final causes can grow. The latter world is the joint product of the activities of spirits or minds. They are images expressive not only of the universe but also of the eternal God Himself. Hence spirits can enter into reflective relationships of knowledge and love, both with God and, through and in Him, with each other. The social communion of spiritual monads in God constitutes the *City of God,* which is a teleological order that comes to birth within the framework of a world of natural, efficient motions.

7. HUMAN KNOWLEDGE

The theory of monads obliges Leibniz to take a definite position concerning certain epistemological issues. In the debate between Descartes and Locke over the *origin of ideas,* he sides with the former. Since monads are basically independent of each other, there can be no abstraction of knowledge, in the sense of an abstractive derivation of ideas from the outside world. Their only possible source is from the monad itself and, ultimately, from the creator of the monadic nature. The simplicity of the finite monad is a dynamic, fecund one, spontaneously giving birth to all the ideas and actions constituting its temporal experience. This conclusion is confirmed by the logical doctrine on the complete individual substance. Since the notion of the individual contains within itself all the predicates belonging to the thing, the real substance must be equipped, from the outset, with the active tendency to bring forth the ideal content of its various states of consciousness. By "innate idea," Leibniz means not only the *meaning-content* but also the intellectual *power and impulse to express* this content and thus to know the object of perception.[35] Innate ideas, in this plenary sense, are in the mind by the very fact that the mind is a dynamic inclination to bring forth the essential content of thought, in an orderly and appropriate way.

Leibniz repeats the Scholastic axiom that there is nothing in the intellect which was not first in the sense — but he adds the significant qualification that the intellect itself does not have a sensory origin.[36] Under the term *intellect,* he includes not only the power of understanding but also the primary ideas (such as substance, being, possibility, cause, perception, and identity) and the first principles, based upon these primary ideas. Hence the intellect is not, as Locke maintains, an unmarked tablet that must wait upon sense experience for its first traces. It is already *preformed with dispositions* and aptitudes, both active and passive. Ideas and principles are inbornly present in the understanding, in at least a virtual way. Whereas Locke limits the presence of ideas to those that are actually being experienced or that are memories of past experiences, Leibniz widens the meaning of the mental presence of ideas to include the active

---

[35] "Our soul has the power of representing to itself any form or nature whenever the occasion comes for thinking about it, and I think that this activity of our soul is, so far as it expresses some nature, form or essence, properly the idea of the thing. This is in us, and is always in us, whether we are thinking of it or no." *Discourse on Metaphysics,* XXVI (Wiener, 327); cf. *What is an Idea?* (Wiener, 281–283). Against Malebranche, Leibniz insists that the idea is *in the soul* and not in God; but against Locke, he insists that the idea is in the soul *at all times* and not merely during conscious perception. Cf. L. E. Loemker, "Leibniz's Doctrine of Ideas," *The Philosophical Review,* 55 (1946), 229–248.

[36] "*Nihil est in intellectu, quod non fuerit in sensu,* excipe: *nisi ipse intellectus.*" *New Essays concerning Human Understanding,* II, i, 2 (Langley, 111). The first book of Leibniz' *New Essays,* like the first book of Locke's own *Essay,* is entirely devoted to the problem of innatism and is the major source for this aspect of Leibniz' doctrine.

capacity to bring them forth from the mind, through the native vigor of its immaterial dynamism. The acquisition of knowledge means the passage of ideas and principles from a *virtual* to an *actual* state of being known.

Since "intellect" is such an important exception to the sense origin of knowledge, Leibniz must specify the way in which *any* knowledge is due to the senses. Here, the distinction between truths of reason and truths of fact can be given a new significance. Necessary *truths of reason* are known by the mind, operating in an independent and purely intellectual way. It can summon forth the ideas and principles constituting these truths, without invoking outside aid and in sole reliance upon its own natural light. *Truths of fact,* however, do require sense experience in order to be distinctly apprehended. Sensation is a necessary, but not a sufficient, condition for grasping truths of fact. It provides the *occasion* for this knowledge but does not serve as its strict *cause.* The ideas comprising a truth of fact are drawn from the mind, on the occasion of a sense experience. The function of the latter is only to arouse the mind's attention concerning some particular connection of ideas, and thus to urge the mind to bring its own ideas to a state of distinct awareness.[37] It is not the *truth* or *meaning-content* itself but only our mental *act of thinking about* the truth which requires a sensory occasion. The actual, empirical perceiving of the meaning-content may be excited through some external expression of a connection which arouses the understanding to advert to a similar (but, until now, unattended) connection among its own ideas. But although our thoughts about truths of fact require sense experience, the truths themselves are of innate origin. They fulfill the definition of an innate truth, namely, one whose entire causal source lies in the understanding.

Three questions immediately come to mind, with respect to this innatist view of knowledge. Why does Leibniz want to reduce the scope of sensation so drastically; what meaning can be given to sensation in a monadic context; what guarantees the objectivity of knowledge, since sensation plays no genuinely causal role?

1. In discussing the hierarchy among monads, Leibniz has already stated that minds or rational souls are distinguished by their ability to apprehend necessary truths of essence or eternal verities. This

---

[37] *Discourse on Metaphysics,* XXVII (Wiener, 329). On the anti-Lockean distinction between the content of truth and the actual considering of that content by the mind, cf. *Specimen of Thoughts upon the First Book of the Essay on Human Understanding* (Langley, 21).

is the mark of the distinctively spiritual level of monadic life, where the human self is found. Hence Leibniz does not want to compromise, in any way, the characteristically human ability to have distinct knowledge of truths of reason, upon which the sciences themselves depend. Since he is fortified by no realistic conviction that our minds can reach things directly and can make abstraction of their necessary and essential structures, he has no confidence in an experiential origin of knowledge, in which the senses make a real contribution. His historical referent, in this instance, is Locke. Since Locke's empirical explanation for the universal and necessary aspects of knowledge fails to satisfy him, Leibniz despairs entirely of finding a source in sense experience for them. Hence his historical position, as well as his general metaphysics of substance, forces him to depreciate the senses and to rule out any abstractive origin of first principles and necessary truths.

2. But in reducing sensation to the position of a mere occasion of knowledge, Leibniz nevertheless does not eliminate it entirely, especially with respect to existential truths of contingent fact. Indeed, it is one of his basic theses that the *finite mind must have a certain area of confused perception* and hence a certain measure of knowledge affected by sensation.[38] Since the substantial being of every mind is structurally proportioned to the rest of the universe, the proper object of perception is the universe in its infinite variety. But the finite nature of our mind prevents it from reducing this object to a perfect unity of rational order. Our limited attention is directed now toward one sector of the universe and now toward another, bringing some particular objects of perception to clear and distinct knowledge, but leaving a wide area of peripheral objects in the condition of confused perception or sensation. Sensation and intellection do not differ in kind but they do differ in degree of clarity and distinctness. With respect to purely intellectual knowledge, the mind is relatively active and autonomous, whereas in sensation it is passive and dependent upon occasions furnished by other monads, especially bodily monads. Although knowledge of contingent truths is not derived from the outside world, the indispensable function of the latter is to direct the attention of the mind upon hitherto unseen mental relations. Sensation, then, signifies the mind's condition of

---

[38] *Discourse on Metaphysics,* XXXIII (Wiener, 338–339). The need for senses, observation, and hypothesis is stressed by A. H. Johnson, "Leibniz's Method and the Basis of His Metaphysics," *Philosophy,* 35 (1960), 51–61, against B. Russell's purely logical derivation.

passion and confused perception, which compels it to have regard for the determinate state of the body and the rest of the universe. This is a large concession to empiricism and the given character of our knowledge of matters of fact. Yet Leibniz never concedes any authentic reception of the content of knowledge from the world. Both his metaphysical analysis of action and passion, and his assumption that a cognitive operation is not truly intellectual if it has any potential and receptive phase, stand in the way of recognizing the full extent of the dependence of the human intellect upon the actual world revealed by sense.

3. Leibniz is supremely confident that his innatism and reduction of sense experience to the status of an occasion will not lead to *subjectivism*. The ground of his confidence is not an empirical study of cognition but an a priori, metaphysical certainty.

> God has from the first created the soul or any other real unity in such a way that everything arises in it from its own internal nature through a perfect *spontaneity* relatively to itself, and yet with a perfect *conformity* to external things. . . . And this nature of the soul being representative of the universe in a very exact though more or less distinctive manner, the series of representations produced in the soul will correspond naturally to the series of changes in the Universe itself.[39]

This teaching on the natural conformity of our representations with the world is merely an epistemological consequence of the pre-established harmony among substances. For the cognitive operations share in the substance's correspondence-to-the-universe, which is the condition under which alone any essence is realized, both in its substance and its activities. Our ideas arise spontaneously or innately from within ourselves, but the requirements of universal harmony guarantee that they are in natural conformity with the being of the objects perceived. Hence every monad is a reliable, *living mirror* of the world.[40] Leibniz' answer to the Lockean query about how we can ever be sure that our ideas — which both thinkers admit to be the immediate objects of perception — conform with real things, is that the question can never be settled at the finite and empirical level. We must turn to the harmonizing Deity and to the even more fundamental metaphysics of essential systems of perfection, for complete assurance that the spontaneity and real conformity of our ideas are the graven laws of mental life.

---

[39] *New System of Nature and of the Communication of Substances*, 14, 15 (Wiener, 114–115).
[40] *Letters to Clarke*, V, 87 (Wiener, 267); *The Monadology*, 56 (Wiener, 544).

Berkeley will accept this way of settling the epistemological problem, but it will prove unsatisfactory to both Hume and Kant. Hume's difficulty is that the use of God as a guarantor of the conformity of our ideas with things is invalid, since the arguments for God's existence already suppose the objective conformity of our ideas. Furthermore, the distinction between necessary truths of reason and contingent truths of fact runs deeper than Leibniz suspects. Empirically viewed, the mind requires the senses to provide literal data — *given contents* — and not merely occasions for intellectual reminiscence or introspection. The fact that necessary truths concern the essential order, whereas contingent truths concern matters of existence, is also indicative of a wider cleavage than Leibniz is willing to admit. Once Hume realizes the *distinctiveness of the existential order* and its resistance to reduction to the status of a mere culmination of an essential dialectic, he can point out that the existence of God is not established through an analysis of essential requirements and that the metaphysics of harmonizing essences may not be relevant for questions about existential matter of fact. Consequently, he can reject the two pillars underlying Leibniz' confidence in the natural conformity between his ideas and the actual world. The stage will then be prepared for Kant's tremendous effort to synthesize the Leibnizian world of necessary, universal truths of essence and the Humean world of contingent, existential facts, without making appeal to God and a metaphysic of essences.

Finally, Leibniz bases his theory of the *personal self* upon his doctrine of perception. The natural desire or tendency of every monad is to introduce the greatest amount of clarity and distinctness into its perceptions. This movement toward maximum perfection accounts for the upward-tending, continuous effort of perceptual states, from unconsciousness to animal consciousness and finally to human self-awareness. The apex is reached in *reflection* or spiritual apperception, which deliberately relates our ideas to first principles and the divine source of all ideas. Complete clarity and distinctness of thought can never be reached during our temporal existence. Nevertheless, we may approximate unceasingly to this ideal, by reflecting upon our own nature and seeing it to be an image of God as well as of the world. Personal perfection is attained in proportion to one's reflective approach to God.

Leibniz distinguishes between the *physical,* real identity of every monad with itself and the *moral identity* or selfsameness of spiritual monads or minds. His view of personality is similar to Locke's but has a definitely religious coloration. The *person* is a moral identity or reflective affirmation of the selfhood of a rational soul or mind. It consists in a *conscienciosité* or heightened self-awareness, which is the immanent goal of mental life. This goal must be harmonized with the transcendent one of making approach to God. Their reconciliation is found in the consideration that a human spirit becomes fully aware of its own nature, and hence attains the full stature of personal self-possession, only in the act of recognizing itself as a son of God. This clarity about one's personal being is man's true *immortality*.[41] In this sense, Spinoza is right in saying that we have our immortality in this life. But, for Leibniz, immortality entails personal survival. No individual monad ever goes out of existence, and even the composite only increases or diminishes its range of perceptibility. But it is the distinguishing mark of the continuance-in-existence of spiritual monads that they persist as moral identities — individual, substantial subjects which are also personal selves — retaining all their happenings and moral responsibility for their temporal choices and orientation. His personalist metaphysics of spiritual monads kept Leibniz from accepting the Spinozistic solution to the problem of immortality.

8. FREEDOM, EVIL, AND OPTIMISM

Human freedom raises some special difficulties, when it is brought into relation with the doctrine of pre-established harmony. Leibniz gives a secular version of the theological dispute about divine predestination and man's freedom. The notion of the individual substance contains all that will happen to it, thus enabling God to have an a priori, analytically certain knowledge of the individual's entire life and actions. The entire content of the individual's temporal career unrolls from the constitution of its essence, from the moment of its entrance into the existent world. How can freedom be reconciled with God's foreknowledge and causation, as well as with the essential

---

[41] Since every simple, finite monad is imperishable and forever attached to a body, death (in the strict sense of substantial corruption) cannot transpire. Monads come into existence by divine creation and can go out of existence only through annihilation by God. Nevertheless, Leibniz distinguishes between the mere *incessibility* of nonrational monads and the *immortality* of rational persons. Cf. *The Monadology*, 73–77 (Wiener, 548–549); *On the Active Force of Body, on the Soul and on the Soul of Brutes* (Wiener, 505–508); *New Essays concerning Human Understanding*, II, xxvii, 9 (Langley, 245–247).

determination of all predicates belonging to the individual?

In searching for light on the relationship between divine fore-knowledge and human freedom, Leibniz read widely in the current theological controversy about the assistance of divine grace. He tried to reconcile God's mediate knowledge with His predeterminism.[42] The *foreknowledge* of God has nothing to do with determining the truth of contingent futurities (events which will freely happen or which would happen, under certain circumstances). These truths are already determinate, and foreknowledge adds nothing to their truth or specific content. Yet they are foreseen by God, precisely as being what they are: truths about free contingencies. Hence the divine mediate knowledge (*scientia media*) preserves the freedom of our actions. Nevertheless, God's *foreordinances* or decrees do con-tribute toward the determination of contingent futurities and hence toward the foundation of God's certain knowledge of these truths. In the case of what *would* happen under certain circumstances, the free contingencies are not arbitrarily specified but depend on the harmonious combinations possible within a given collection of essences. God can assign as a determinate reason for possible happenings, that which would promote the best within a given system of essences. As for what *will* actually occur in our free acts, God does pre-determine the will, insofar as He decrees the existence of the best possible world and its essential requirements, but He does not pre-determine it with absolute or metaphysical necessity. For the achieve-ment of the best possible world, God decrees that men will always do that which appears best to them, and will do it in a rational or free way. This decree inclines their will certainly and efficaciously, through a moral necessity, and yet it does not *coerce* the will. Hence Leibniz holds both that the divine foreknowledge is infallibly true (since it is based upon certain, determinate truths) and that our choices remain free. The worth of this argument depends upon the relation between essential combinations and divine decrees, as well as upon the implied doctrine about human choice.

On the human side, freedom is the *spontaneity of an intelligent being*.[43] It is grounded neither in indifferent equilibrium nor in

---

[42] *Theodicy*, I, 36–48 (Huggard, 143–150); *Letters to Clarke*, V, 5–8 (Wiener, 238–239).

[43] *Theodicy*, I, 51–52, and III, 288–311 (Huggard, 151, 303–314); *Letters to Clarke*, V, 11–17 (Wiener, 240–242); *New Essays concerning Human Understanding*, II, xxi (Langley, 179–221).

abstention of judgment. For, indifference is not a sufficient reason for a free action, whereas abstention is itself a prior act that has a prior reason. Our wills are laden with the spontaneous dispositions of our rational nature, including the influence of the unconscious, "minute perceptions." Moreover, intelligent agents can grasp the nature of the good and, within our universe, will *always choose what appears to be the best*. This provides the only sufficient reason for their action. A free act is always rationally motivated and is the more perfectly free, the more it is determined by what seems best, i.e., by the strongest motive. Leibniz argues here in much the same way as in his explanation of divine creative freedom. Human choice is not a blind impulse but proceeds from a reflective deliberation upon our motives and desires. Although whatever seems best will be the prevailing motive, this reason inclines or persuades the will efficaciously rather than coerces it. We act not under an absolute necessity but under a *moral necessity,* which is the condition of freedom. Nevertheless, we always do that which seems to be best and which therefore provides the strongest motive or reason of choice.

Leibniz' theory of human freedom encounters the same difficulties as his doctrine on divine creation, since in both cases he regards the sufficient reason of an action as imposing itself independently upon the agent. The difference between absolute and hypothetical necessity becomes nugatory in a theory that identifies freedom with rational spontaneity. Although intellectual apprehension of the grounds of choice prevents it from being a *blind* impulse, the choice is nevertheless *determined* by the total spontaneous striving of one's nature and not by the agent's uncoerced judgment. Leibniz shows that human choice is internally motivated but not that it is freely made. He confuses a merely passive and motiveless indifference with the intellect's dominating power to judge a particular good in the light of the good in general, and thus to control its own final practical judgment.[44] If a man is bound to follow the most strongly inclining apparent good, it is difficult (as Locke observed) to see how his

---

[44] In his *Traité du libre arbitre* (Liège, Sciences et Lettres, 1951), 105–110, Y. Simon remarks that the real question in free choice is not about which is the greater or lesser good, but about the condition under which a particular good becomes unconditionally desirable here-and-now for a rational appetite, so that it will actually choose this concrete good. Whether the multitude of insensible perceptions and sentiments inclines us to regard an object as a greater or a lesser good, there is still need for a last practical judgment, declaring this object to be a good absolutely desirable, to the point of being here-and-now chosen in a concrete way.

choice could ever be determined freely by himself. Leibniz recognizes that an objection can be drawn from the fact that men often choose deliberately a *lesser good* or even a *known evil*. His reply does not salvage his position. He states that no action is possible unless it be determined by the strongest motive, which alone gives a sufficient reason for this particular choice. The strength of the motive is determined not merely by rational appraisal of the proposed action but also by all the habits, dispositions, and passions that make up our character. This notion of freedom is little different from Spinoza's outright necessitation by another, the "other," in Leibniz' case, being the total bent of one's nature and character. Whatever one does, would then bear the stamp of spontaneity and hence of freedom, leaving no distinction between the acts merely done by man and the distinctively free or human acts that are morally significant. For both Spinoza and Leibniz, the human mind is best characterized as a spiritual automaton, whose law of spontaneous, rational necessity is its only freedom.

The presence of evils in the best possible world compels Leibniz to compose a *theodicy* or justification of God's ways in the world. He borrows from the Scholastic discussions of the problem of evil, but reformulates the issues in accord with his own philosophy. On God's side, a fundamental distinction must be drawn between the antecedent and the consequent divine will. In his *antecedent* or *previous will,* God simply wills the production of every good, considered as such and separately, and the prevention of every evil, also considered as such and by itself. The antecedent will is directed toward essences, each taken individually and without reference to the conditions of existence. But for the production of any actual world, the several goods and evils must be considered together, in order to determine the essential, systematic relations of compatibility and incompatibility, which constitute the conditions of existence. God's "consequent will, final and decisive, results from the conflict of all the antecedent wills, of those which tend toward good, even as of those which repel evil; and from the concurrence of all these particular wills comes the total will."[45] Whereas God's antecedent will tends toward *the good,*

---

[45] *Theodicy,* I, 22 (Huggard, 137). Leibniz' argument in the *Theodicy* is labyrinthine and repetitious, reminding one of the discussions engaged in by the more subtle minds among the ranks of Milton's fallen angels:

"Others apart sat on a Hill retir'd,
In thoughts more elevate, and reason'd high

His *consequent* or *decretory will* (from which the act of creation emerges) decrees the actual existence of *the best possible world*. Through His consequent will, God wills physical evil, not absolutely but as a means to greater good or as a penalty for sin. But even His consequent will never wills moral evil. The conditions of the best possible world require Him to *exclude* some goods that are incompatible with the prevailing system of essences, and to *permit* moral evil, but His infinite goodness prevents God from ever *willing* moral evil, even as a means to a good. The mixture of goods and evils is a concomitant result of the consequent will to make the best possible world exist.

Leibniz' explanation of the divine consequent will is solidary with his stand on the divine freedom and the relation between God and the world of pure essences. This consequent will is a rational acquiescence to the mechanical, vector resolution of the countertendencies among various essences, striving objectively among themselves. At the pre-existential level, even evil has an essence of some sort and exerts its weight upon the possible combinations of essences. The transition from the antecedent will of the good to the consequent will of the best possible world is left obscure by Leibniz. It is here that he regards God as adopting the standard of perfection or the contingent existence of the best possible combination of essences. Once this standard is taken as the rule of creative production, God freely chooses the maximum system of essential perfection, one which must contain a mixture of goods and evils, in accord with the relations among essences. Leibniz' theodicy amounts to a moral justification of the ways of essences among themselves and as the ultimate determinants of the structure of our world.

Evil as such is a privation, and its cause is a deficient one.[46] This thesis is advanced by Leibniz, once evil is considered in respect to the actual world. It does not lead him, however, to underplay the strength and bitterness of evil or the imminence of a barbaric submergence of all civilized values. Hence he does not claim any more

---

Of Providence, Foreknowledge, Will and Fate,
Fixt Fate, free will, foreknowledge absolute,
And found no end, in wandring mazes lost."
Paradise Lost, II, 557–561.

[46] *Theodicy*, I, 10–12, 21–25; II, 119 (Huggard, 129–130, 136–138, 189–190); *Summary of the Controversy* (Huggard, 383); *On the Ultimate Origin of Things* (Wiener, 351–355).

than that ours is the best *possible* (or "least defective") world. An imaginative selection can certainly be made of all the most desirable features of existence, omitting the undesirable ones. But this is an idle exercise, since it ignores the question of compatibility among the various elements selected for inclusion in an absolutely perfect universe. Leibniz only contends that, among the compossible combinations, ours is the best. Taken as a whole, it could not be improved. There cannot but be defects and deformities in the particular parts, considered in isolation. Evil is of three sorts: metaphysical, physical, and moral. These varieties correspond to the three kinds of privation or lack to which we are subject: finitude or lack of unlimited essential perfection (*metaphysical* evil); suffering or lack of bodily well-being and integrity (*physical* evil); sin or lack of adequate judgment and rectitude of choice (*moral* evil). The possibility of any sort of lack or evil stems from our finite nature, so that metaphysical evil is the ultimate reason for the other kinds. It is an evil in a very loose and general sense, however, since there could not be any sort of harmonious universe composed of many entities, without the composing members being finite. With regard to the special evils, physical and moral, Leibniz asks us to consider them within the larger context of the world order.

There would seem to be no opportunity for moral evil in a universe in which man's actions are directed to what is best. In dealing with this problem, Leibniz scrutinizes the fact of human finitude, in order to find a reason why men are prone to sin. From the very fact that they are limited beings, men cannot avoid having some of their ideas, and hence some of their motives of action, in a relatively confused state. Because their knowledge is not perfectly clear and distinct in all respects, men can be mistaken and hence can sin. They can, in effect, *act upon confused perceptions and mistaken judgments*. This explanation of moral evil has the drawback, however, of reducing good conduct to distinct knowledge, sin to ignorance and error. It fails to recognize a man's definite moral responsibility for the state of what *seems* best to him and for acting in the absence of adequate knowledge. Malice has no meaning in this perspective, and vice is reduced to the hindrance placed upon the power of acting, by reason of imperfect perceptions. Moral evil is thereby transformed into the disorderly consequences of acting upon certain of one's unclarified motives. Here, as well as in Leibniz' analysis of freedom, attention is deflected from the will-act of *election itself* to some of the *conditions* surrounding it and *effects* flowing from it. The logic of sufficient reason hides freedom and sin from view, in the very process of explaining their possibility in perceptual terms.

In discussing the actual presence of physical and moral evils, Leibniz follows the lead of pagan and Christian apologists in making a comparison with our evaluation of a great painting or symphony. If we confine ourselves to one section of the picture, it may appear to be only a confused mass of colors and jagged figures, grotesquely incomplete and jumbled together. But if we view this fragment as integrated with the rest of the painting, its harmonious function in the total pattern becomes clear. Again, a composer mingles discords with harmonies in order to achieve a satisfactory, total effect. The sweet is pointed up by the bitter, the secure by the dangerous. Without labor, no crown of satisfaction; without temptation, no triumph of loyalty; without sin, no repentance and conversion of heart. These laws of finite being warn us to suspend judgment about the physical and moral universe, until we can comprehend the total harmony of being in the light of eternity. God, the supreme artist, uses physical evils to place the goodness of things in sharper relief. God, the omnipotent provider, can draw good out of even the evil of sin, and can reconcile individual interests with cosmic harmony. Leibniz reminds us that the Holy Week liturgy refers to Adam's sin as *felix culpa,* in respect to the Redemption it brought. Our world is not only a vale of tears but also (as Keats phrased it) a vale of soul-making. We should come to love the place where the maximum of moral, as well as physical, perfection is realized, within the limits of finiteness.

The main reason why Leibniz bids men love the world, wherein they suffer, is that the dominion of God is bound to work not only to the universal good but also to the particular good of men. This optimism is not a pious wish but the consequence of the logic of the best universe. The achievement of the maximum reality of essence means the realization of the most perfection. Now the physical perfection of man is itself in the moral order, since it involves the actualizing of a spiritual nature. Hence the perfecting of the universe requires a *distinctive perfecting of man in his moral and spiritual being*. Good and bad actions are given their proper reward with mechanical efficiency, since the mechanism of nature promotes the ends of spiritual beings. The ultimate reconciling of the physical and moral realms of being is the work of divine omnipotence. The same God is both the architect of the world's mechanism and the monarch of the kingdom of spiritual beings.

Whereas God brings all monads to their proper measure of perfection, He confers a distinctive *personal happiness* upon minds or spiritual monads. Their reflective and loving participation in eternal life is the same as their eternal happiness. This participation supposes the immortality of the rational soul, not only in its substantial nature but also in its entire personality, including memory and acquired knowledge. This is the moral-religious face of the teaching on personal immortality. Minds are called to a special union of knowledge and love with God, considered as Lord and Father. This common vocation of all men should find outward expression in the religious organization of the earth, through a single, universal, or Catholic faith. Leibniz' work for the reunion of the Christian Churches was intended as a first step in this direction.[47] And men can win citizenship in the City of God only by performing the free and reflective act of giving glory to God, from whom the harmony of being comes and to whom it returns through the office of men.

SUMMARY

A logical and a metaphysical vision of the universe are combined in Leibniz' philosophy. If all things have their characteristic numbers and if the elementary concepts are both finite and ordered, then there can be a universal science, based on the interconnection among the logical characteristics. Such calculation need not be confined to mathematical objects but may extend to all fields, including moral judgments. Even after he saw that the number of primitive elements is infinite, Leibniz did not abandon his logical ideal of a priori demonstration. Instead, he synthesized it more closely with his metaphysics of the harmony of the universe: the underlying unity amid the variety of individuals and aspects of experience. His analysis of the basic first principles and the nature of individual substance supplied the foundation for a universe in which the greatest number of compossible essences is realized. Leibniz' metaphysical center of gravity was the intelligible essence, which jostles with its neighbor for the privilege of entering into the existing order and thus of contributing to the perfection of this best possible universe. The great problem was how to reconcile this logico-metaphysical position, required as the basis of scientific certainty, with the traditionally accepted divine attributes

---

[47] Cf. J. H. Crehan, S.J., "Leibniz and the Polemics of Reunion," *Thought*, 10 (1935–1936), 16–29. For a historical study of the ideal of the City of God, see E. Gilson, *Les métamorphoses de la cité de Dieu* (Louvain, E. Nauwelaerts, 1953; 228–247, on Leibniz).

of freedom and omnipotence. Leibniz made the essences of things existentially dependent upon the divine will, while at the same time he reserved for them a certain quasi-independence in respect to their content of meaning. Hence the divine creative will operates as a ratification of the outcome of the strife among the essences, granted God's free decree of choosing the best. The actual outcome is a world of monadic substances, each of which microcosmically mirrors the entire universe from its own finite, bodily viewpoint. Leibniz called upon God and the order among essences to pre-establish the harmony among monads, in view of achieving the best possible world. Although there is no direct causal interaction among finite monads, they conspire together to constitute a harmonious and unified system of activities. Spiritual monads can rise above animal consciousness to a knowledge of first principles and the infinite being of God. Persons or spiritual monads enjoy a special, intimate communion in the City of God.

BIBLIOGRAPHICAL NOTE

1. *Sources and Translations*. Great masses of unpublished Leibniz manuscripts remain at the Hanover library. The Berlin Academy of Sciences began a complete, critical edition of his writings, but the project still drags on at a slow pace. This edition of the *Sämtliche Schriften und Briefe* (1923 ff.) is to contain forty volumes, divided into the following seven series: (1) general, political, and historical correspondence, 11 Vols.; (2) philosophical correspondence, 6 Vols.; (3) mathematical, scientific, and technical correspondence, 5 Vols.; (4) political writings, 4 Vols.; (5) historical writings, 4 Vols.; (6) philosophical writings (also theological and juristic writings), 6 Vols.; (7) mathematical, scientific and technical writings, 4 Vols. To date, nine volumes in the political and historical fields have appeared, together with the following: (1) the first volume in the second series, *Philosophischer Briefwechsel* (Darmstadt: Reichl, 1926); (2) the first volume in the sixth series, *Philosophische Schriften* (Darmstadt: Reichl, 1930), containing the early works of Leibniz from the Leipzig-Altdorf period (1663–1666) and the Frankfort-Mainz period (1667–1672); (3) the sixth vol. in the sixth series, containing *Nouveaux essais sur l'entendement* and related material (Berlin: Akademie-Verlag, 1962). For practical purposes, one must still rely upon the two collections made by C. I. Gerhardt: *Die mathematischen Schriften von G. W. Leibniz*, 7 Vols. (Berlin: Asher, 1849–1863; reprint, Hildesheim: Olms, 1962), and *Die philosophischen Schriften von G. W. Leibniz*, 7 Vols. (Berlin: Weidmann, 1875–1890; reprint, Hildesheim: Olms, 1960–1961). French scholarship has made available some reliable texts of both Leibniz's manuscript remains and his main published works: L. Couturat, *Opuscules et fragments inédits de Leibniz* (Paris: Alcan, 1903; reprint, Hildesheim: Olms, 1961); G. Grua, *G. W. Leibniz, Textes inédits*, 2 Vols. (Paris: Presses Universitaires, 1948); H. Lestienne ed. of *Discours de métaphysique*, second ed. (Paris: Vrin, 1952); A. Robinet ed. of *Principes de la nature et de la grace*

and *Monadologie* (Paris: Presses Universitaires, 1954); J. Jalabert ed. of *Essais de théodicée* and *Monadologie* (Paris: Aubier, 1962); G. Lewis ed. of *Lettres de Leibniz à Arnauld* (Paris: Presses Universitaires, 1952); A. Robinet ed. of *Malebranche et Leibniz: Relations personelles* (Paris: Vrin, 1955). A critical text of the short but important 1692 *Essay de Dynamique* is established by P. Costabel, *Leibniz et la dynamique* (Paris: Hermann, 1960), who provides a complete commentary. Microfilms of the Leibniz papers in Hanover are now available at the University of Pennsylvania Library.

Logical Papers, ed. by G. H. R. Parkinson (Oxford: Clarendon Press, 1966), shows the influence of mathematics and logic on philosophy. There is a translation by J. M. Child of *The Early Mathematical Manuscripts of Leibniz* (Chicago: Open Court, 1920, and paperback, 1960). There are three excellent general selections from his writings: P. Weiner, *Leibniz Selections* (New York: Scribner, 1951); L. E. Loemker, *Leibniz: Philosophical Papers and Letters*, 2 Vols. (Chicago: University of Chicago Press, 1956); *Monadology and Other Philosophical Essays* (Indianapolis: Bobbs-Merrill, 1956), translated by Paul and A. M. Schrecker. Translations of individual works include: P. G. Lucas and L. Grint translation of *Discourse on Metaphysics* (New York: Barnes and Noble, 1953); G. R. Montgomery translation of *Discourse on Metaphysics, Correspondence with Arnauld, and Monadology* (Chicago: Open Court, 1902); H. W. Carr translated and edited *The Monadology* (Los Angeles: University of Southern California Press, 1930), with commentary; E. M. Huggard translation of *Theodicy* (New Haven: Yale University Press, 1952), with Introduction by A. Farrer; A. G. Langley translation of *New Essays concerning Human Understanding*, third ed. (Lasalle: Open Court, 1949). H. G. Alexander has edited an important exchange, *The Leibniz-Clarke Correspondence* (New York: Philosophical Library, 1956).

2. *Studies*. The biographical material in G. E. Guhrauer's German work was condensed in English by J. M. Mackie, *Life of Godfrey William von Leibnitz* (Boston: Gould, Kendall, 1845). A recent circumstantial account of his early years is given by P. Wiedeburg, *Der junge Leibniz*, 2 Vols. (Wiesbaden: Steiner, 1962). Among introductory studies are: B. Russell, *A Critical Exposition of the Philosophy of Leibniz*, second ed. (London: Allen and Unwin, 1949); H. W. B. Joseph, *Lectures on the Philosophy of Leibniz* (Oxford: Clarendon, 1949); H. W. Carr, *Leibniz* (London: Benn, 1929; reprint, New York: Dover, 1960); R. L. Saw, *Leibniz* (Baltimore: Penguin Books, 1954); G. Stammler, *Leibniz* (Munich: Reinhardt, 1930); K. Huber, *Leibniz* (Munich: Oldenbourg, 1951); K. Hildebrandt, *Leibniz und das Reich der Gnade* (The Hague: Nijhoff, 1953). Russell and Joseph take an analytical approach, rather than a historical one; Carr relates the metaphysics to his own idealism, and Saw relates it to analytic interests; the metaphysical and social aspects are stressed by Stammler, Huber, and Hildebrandt. Students will profit from Nicholas Rescher's acute study, *The Philosophy of Leibniz* (Englewood Cliffs, Prentice-Hall, 1967).

Genetic problems are raised by W. Kabitz, *Die Philosophie des jungen*

Leibniz (Heidelberg: Winter, 1909); logical issues are to the fore in L. Couturat, *La Logique de Leibniz* (Paris: Alcan, 1901; reprint, Hildesheim: Olms, 1961); and the scientific concerns are stressed by E. Cassirer, *Leibniz' System in seinen wissenschaftlichen Grundlagen,* second ed. (Hildesheim: Olms, 1962). Recent research centers around the logic-metaphysics relationship and the metaphysical structuring of the entire philosophy: G. Martin, *Leibniz: Logic and Metaphysics* (New York: Barnes and Noble, 1964); G. H. Parkinson, *Logic and Reality in Leibniz's Metaphysics* (New York: Oxford University Press, 1965); A. M. Tymieniecka, *Leibniz' Cosmological Synthesis* (New York: Humanities Press, 1965); P. Burgelin, *Commentaire du Discours de Métaphysique de Leibniz* (Paris: Presses Universitaires, 1960); A. Wildermuth, *Wahrheit und Schöpfung: Ein Grundriss der Metaphysik des Gottfried Wilhelm Leibniz* (Winterthur: Keller, 1960); W. Janke, *Leibniz: Die Emendation der Metaphysik* (Frankfort: Klostermann, 1963), on the active conception of substance and subjectivity. On special metaphysical issues, consult: M. Guéroult, *Dynamique et métaphysique leibniziennes* (Paris: Les Belles Lettres, 1934); J. Iwanicki, *Leibniz et les demonstrations mathématiques de l'existence de Dieu* (Paris: Vrin, 1934); J. Jalabert, *La Théorie leibnizienne de la substance* (Paris: Presses Universitaires, 1947); J. Jalabert, *Le Dieu de Leibniz* (Paris: Presses Universitaires, 1960). The theoretical foundations of theodicy, ethics, and social philosophy are analyzed in G. Grua's two books: *Jurisprudence universelle et théodicée selon Leibniz* (Paris: Presses Universitaires, 1953), and *La Justice humaine selon Leibniz* (Paris: Presses Universitaires, 1956).

Leibniz's German university background is clarified with the information supplied by M. Wundt, *Die deutsche Schulmetaphysik des 17. Jahrhunderts* (Tübingen: Mohr, 1939). His cultural, social, and religious impact is measured by: R. W. Meyer, *Leibnitz and the Seventeenth-Century Revolution* (Chicago: Regnery, 1952); J. Baruzi, *Leibniz et l'organisation religieuse de la terre* (Paris: Alcan, 1907); P. Hazard, *The European Mind (1680–1715)* (London: Hollis and Carter, 1953); W. H. Barber, *Leibniz in France* (Oxford: Clarendon, 1955). Leibniz's crucial philosophical relationships with Descartes and Spinoza are explored by: Y. Belaval, *Leibniz critique de Descartes* (Paris: Gallimard, 1960); G. Friedmann, *Leibniz et Spinoza,* new ed. (Paris: Gallimard, 1962). Since his efforts in theodicy were aroused by the criticism of Bayle, one may consult Pierre Bayle's *Historical and Critical Dictionary: Selections* (Indianapolis: Bobbs-Merrill, 1965), translated and edited by R. H. Popkin, as well as the intellectual biography by E. Labrousse: *Pierre Bayle,* 2 Vols. (The Hague: Nijhoff, 1963–1964).

INDEX

Affects and affections, 98 f. *See* Passions

Analysis, 10 f, 74, 118 ff; terminative and nonterminative, 128 f

Anselm, St., 34

Aristotle and Aristotelian, 1, 4; categories, 118; entelechy, 145

Attributes, 41 ff, 75, 79 ff, 87 f

Augustine, St., and Augustinism, 5, 23 *n;* theory of active sensation, 53

Automaton, spiritual, 94

Bacon, Francis, 6, 8, 14, 70, 119; finite terms and data, 121 f

Belief, natural, 45. *See* Faith, religious

Berkeley, George, 45, 162

Bernard, St., 30

Body as extended substance, 40 ff; as modality, 87 ff; as monadic, 144 ff. *See* Extension

Bruno, Giordano, 27, 77; microcosm, 142; nature, 86

Calderón, 22

Categories, 118

Causa sui, 34 f, 74 ff

Causality, 25, 28; adequate and inadequate, 99 f, 105; divine, 32 ff; ideal influence, 129, 154 f; mind-body, 96; modal emanation, 83 ff; of nature and grace, 157

Circle, Cartesian, 24, 26 f

City of God, 170

Cogito theory, 23 ff, 32; criticized, 69, 96 f

Conatus, 100 f, 102 f, 105; for existence, 135, 138 f, 151, 155

Contingency of existence, 135 f, 140; of knowledge, 89 ff, 129; of monads, 152; of self, 29

Creation, 37 f, 75, 84, 137; as outflashing, 153 f

Crescas, 62, 81

Criterion of clarity and distinctness, 12 f, 31; God as, 68 f; and memory, 26 f

Darwinism, 134

Deduction, 11, 15 f 69

Deism, 109

Demon hypothesis (Cartesian *spiritus malignus*), 22 f

Descartes, aim of philosophy, 2 ff; Cogito theme, 23 ff; compared with Leibniz, 1, 14, 36, 38, 50 f, 53; compared with Spinoza, 10, 14, 16 f, 38, 50; critique of senses, 39 f; divine attributes, 35 ff; external world, 44 ff; innatism, 27 f, 52 ff; life and writings, 1 f; mechanistic view of life, 51 f; methodic doubt, 17 ff; methodology, 6 ff; mind-body dualism, 44, 46 ff; moral theory, 54 ff; proofs of God, 27 ff; the self and the man, 48 ff; substance-attributes-modes, 41 ff

Distinctions, 43 f

Doubt, methodic, 16 ff; criticism of, 71

Du Vair, Guillaume, 54

Dynamism in bodies, 147 ff; in essences, 135 ff. *See* Conatus

Entelechy, 144 f

Emanationism, pantheistic, 87 ff; theistic, 153 ff

Emandatio of the mind, 65 ff

Emotional life as composite, 99 f. *See* Passions

Error, 29 ff, 71 ff

Essence, active, 124 f; and attribute, 42 f; divine, 31 f, 35, 83 f, 151 f; drive to exist, 134 ff; formal and representative, 67; irreal being, 138 f; truths of, 127; unity of, 48

Eternal truths, 36 f, 71, 83, 136 ff, 151

Eternity, 89 ff, 110 ff

Ethics. *See* Moral Philosophy

Evolutionary mentality, 133 f

Existence, divine, 31, 35, 84; and doubt, 18 f, 25; emergence from essence, 134 ff, 151 f; and eternity, 89 ff; and harmony, 124; and methodic order, 10, 14 f; and substance, 41 f, 50 f; truths of, 127 ff

Experience, 39, 46 ff, 121, 160; of eternity, 112